# DOCTOR

# NOT GUILTY

MUHAMAD ALY RIFAI, MD

# Forward from Dr. Fred Moss

In the pages that follow, you'll find the voice of a healer caught in a system built not for healing, but for accusation. You'll find the story of a man—Dr. Muhamad Aly Rifai—who did what all true doctors are sworn to do: care, protect, serve. And you'll find, in stark relief, the jagged edges of a legal and bureaucratic machine that has forgotten the human being at the center of medicine.

I have spent my life in mental health—over four decades listening to stories, guiding souls back to themselves, and championing the radical notion that connection, conversation, and human understanding are the true sources of healing. I've come to see that the greatest threat to healing is not sickness itself, but the systems we've built to control, regulate, and commodify the act of care.

Dr. Rifai's book is more than a memoir. It is an indictment of those systems—of the structures that turn the compassionate choices of doctors into criminal offenses; that mistake complexity for deception; that treat healers as suspects rather than servants of humanity.

Reading his words, I felt the echo of my own convictions: that our industry is deeply broken; that we cannot legislate or litigate our way to wellness; that healing must be reclaimed from the halls of bureaucracy and returned to the sacred realm of human-to-human service.

For those of us committed to changing the narrative of mental health—and health care more broadly—this book is not just a cautionary tale. It is a guide. A clarion call. A testament to the power of courage, truth, and the refusal to surrender.

In *Doctor Not Guilty*, you will find the scars left by an unjust system. But you will also find resilience, integrity, and the irrepressible light of someone who refused to be silenced. That light, like all true healing, can become a torch we carry together as we build a new paradigm—one rooted in humanity, in connection, in trust.

May these pages inspire you, enrage you, and above all, remind you that real healing begins when we dare to speak the truth—even when the world tries to punish us for it.

**— Fred Moss, MD**
The "UnDoctor" Author of *The Creative Eight and Find Your True Voice*

# CONTENTS

─────

# Prologue

I knew fear.

In 1981, when I was in third grade, I witnessed a horror that has never left me. Riding the school bus home, we came to a sudden halt behind another bus, one carrying high school students. Soldiers stopped it, ordered every student off, and lined them against a wall. We children sat frozen in paralysed silence as the soldiers opened fire. The horrifying images etched themselves permanently into my memory—the lifeless bodies collapsing to the ground, the dreadful silence that followed, and the chilling realisation that we could have been next.

Only a month later, as our bus travelled that same haunted route, a spray of bullets suddenly tore through its side. I remember the deafening scream of metal being torn apart, the violent holes punched inches from where I sat. I remember not screaming, not moving, feeling only the unbearable ringing in my ears and the thundering pulse of my heartbeat. These experiences didn't merely scar me—they moulded the very essence of who I became.

That trauma is in me, below the surface, waiting to pounce and paralyse me.

Years later, the call came without warning, shattering. My phone vibrated violently, wrenching me awake after another exhausting day. That same gut-wrenching dread returned, my heart hammering. "This is it," I thought. I'd seen the news—doctors paraded in cuffs, offices turned into crime scenes, reputations obliterated overnight. They had come for me.

But the voice on the other end wasn't what I expected.

"We need your help," said the officer urgently. "There's a suicidal man barricaded in his home."

In that surreal moment—still trembling from fear, my medical licence hanging by a thread, my name smeared across headlines—I was needed. The same authorities who branded me guilty now pleaded for my expertise to save a life. I answered without hesitation. Because doctors show up, even when their worlds collapse.

Yet, even as I confronted that crisis, fear lingered in the shadows.

One week later, compelled by a force deeper than mere curiosity, I drove myself to Otisville Federal Prison. My hands trembled on the wheel, my breaths shallow and sharp. I needed to see the reality of what might soon become my life. As I stepped onto those grim grounds, the oppressive walls loomed menacingly above, watchtowers scrutinised coldly, and razor wire clawed viciously at the sky. Inside, the expressions of prisoners haunted me—some hardened by years, others hollowed by despair, many simply bewildered, just as I was.

Would I soon join their ranks?

Would I exchange my stethoscope for an inmate number?

Could I persuade a jury of the truth—that I was a healer, not a criminal?

Standing in the shadow of that grim fortress, something shifted within me. Fear hardened into resolve. If they intended to take me, they would face all of me—my life's work, my devotion, my anguish, and above all, my truth.

This book isn't merely about my trial. It's about surviving fear. It's about a profession under siege. It's about physicians who uphold sacred oaths rather than taking deals. Ultimately, it is about what justice truly means when it knocks unexpectedly, cloaked in a white coat.

# Introduction

---

Tales of Physicians Caught in the Crosshairs of Federal Prosecution

Physicians are meant to heal, not to be hunted. Yet, in modern America, the very system that once revered doctors has turned against them, twisting regulations into weapons and transforming healers into criminals. The Controlled Substances Act, healthcare laws, and a labyrinth of federal statutes have ensnared countless physicians in a trap of legal peril, branding them as fraudsters when their only crime was dedication to their patients.

For over two centuries, doctors have stood as pillars of trust, ethics, and sacrifice. But today, they are vilified, prosecuted, and dragged into courtrooms like common criminals. Over the past 30 years, the relentless march of federal prosecutions has turned once-pristine white coats into prison uniforms. And I, Muhamad Aly Rifai, MD, was one of their targets.

I am a Middle Eastern, Muslim physician, an internist and psychiatrist, a researcher and entrepreneur. My life was built on the simple foundation of service to my patients and my country. I am a dedicated and caring healer.

Yet persecution was not new to me. I had already stared death in the face as a child, surviving atrocities that few could imagine.

In 1981, while in third grade in Aleppo, I sat on a school bus watching another bus, filled with high school students, stopped by the authorities. We sat frozen in horror as soldiers lined the students up against a wall and executed them all with machine gun fire. I still see their faces in my dreams. To this day, the nightmares persist, a haunting reminder that I, too, could have been among the dead.

I grew up knowing that fear was not a choice—it was a way of life. The disease of addiction plagued my father's side of the family, while depression ran rampant on my mother's. These biological predispositions intertwined with the trauma we endured, shaping me into a man who refused to crumble, no matter the adversity.

And so, when I found myself staring down the might of the U.S. federal government, accused, humiliated, and facing a lifetime behind bars, I did what I had always done. I fought.

In Doctor: NOT GUILTY, I expose the raw, unfiltered truth behind the legal war being waged against physicians. I lay bare the corrupt tactics of prosecutors, the soul-crushing brutality of federal investigations, and the high-stakes battles fought in cold, merciless courtrooms. Through my own ordeal and the struggles of other physicians who have walked through this fire, I unveil the dark underbelly of a system that no longer serves justice—but serves itself.

In telling my story, I will also recount episodes from my life that have made me the man I am today—not a victim—a fighter!

## A Survival Guide for Physicians Facing Federal Persecution

This book is not just a memoir of survival—it is a blueprint for those standing on the precipice of ruin. I had seen the legal system from the outside, working as an expert witness in psychiatric cases. But when I became the accused, I realized just how ruthless, relentless, and unforgiving the system truly is.

With the help of renowned legal warrior Paul Hetznecker and defense attorney Ronald Chapman II, I fought my way back from the brink. This book details that grueling war, providing tactical insights for physicians facing the unthinkable. I expose the deceptive strategies of prosecutors, the hidden weaknesses in federal cases, and the critical moves that can mean the difference between freedom and a life behind bars.

# Chapter 1

# United States of America

## v.

# Muhamad Aly Rifai

## Case No. 5:22-cr-00390

# My Battle for Survival

―――――

*"The essence of Government is power; and power,*
*lodged as it must be in human hands, will ever be liable*
*to abuse."*

— James Madison (Stansbury)

## "Baba! Baba!"

On the evening of April 17, 1947, Balkis Hibrawi carefully dressed her five children—Faez, Raya, Nadia, Najwa, and her youngest, six-year-old Faisal, my father,—in their finest clothes. Tonight was a moment of immense pride. The Ministry of Education had chosen their father, Mohammad Aref Rifai, the esteemed Director of Education, to deliver his renowned poem on Syrian independence at the National Library of Aleppo. His words had become a symbol of resistance, a melody of defiance woven into the fabric of a nation that had fought for its freedom from French rule.

The children, their hearts swelling with admiration, took their seats in the amphitheater, their young eyes fixed on the stage where their father would soon stand. As the murmurs of the crowd softened, Mohammad Aref Rifai ascended the podium, his presence commanding yet warm. He scanned the audience, found his children, and offered them a gentle nod—a silent reassurance, a bridge of love spanning the distance between them.

Then, with the grace of a master storyteller and the fire of a patriot, he began to breathe life into his verses. His voice, rich and unwavering, painted the struggle of a nation. Every word a brushstroke on the canvas of history. His poem honored the martyrs of the Great Syrian Revolution—those who had sacrificed everything so that Syria might stand free.

Yet, as his voice climbed the heights of passion, a sudden, invisible force seemed to take hold. His hand clutched at his chest, as if trying to contain a pain too vast to bear. His body wavered. Then, like a mighty cedar felled by an unseen wind, he collapsed to the ground.

A stunned silence descended upon the amphitheater. Then—chaos. Colleagues rushed to his side, among them his dear friend, Bahjat Shahabandar, who cradled him, desperately pleading for a response. But fate had already penned the final stanza of his life.

At just sixty-four years old, Mohammad Aref Rifai took his final breath on the very stage where he had poured out his soul for his country. He left behind a grieving widow, five orphaned children, and a legacy written in ink, sealed in sacrifice.

A cry of pure anguish tore through the silence.

"Baba! Baba!"

Little Faisal broke free from his seat, his tiny feet pounding against the cold floor as he ran to the podium. He clutched at his father's lifeless form, his sobs echoing through the great hall, a melody of sorrow that would never fade from his heart. In that moment, time stood still, freezing his grief into an eternal memory—one that would haunt him for the rest of his days.

Aleppo would never forget. What was once a day of joy—April 17, Syria's Independence Day—became a day of sorrow for the Rifai family. Instead of celebrating freedom, they mourned the loss of a father, husband, poet, and educator, a man who had given his final breath to the very cause he believed in.

As children, who never knew their grandfather, we would listen to my father, that young Faisal, now a man, tell us the story of his death as we gathered for family meals. But not just that story. That was just the epilogue to a life that was full, worthwhile, and giving. We grew up hearing and learning about a life of service, a life of dedication, and a life caring for others. Those stories became the foundation stones of our moral development. A man I never knew helped to make me the man I am today.

# The U.S. Constitution

## *Doctor Gangi*

On a frigid Tuesday morning, January 30, 2018, Dr. Pramela Ganji braced herself against the biting cold as she prepared for another day at the Federal Correctional Institution (FCI) satellite camp for women in Aliceville, Alabama.

Affectionately known as "The Doc" among her fellow inmates, Dr. Ganji, a Telugu-speaking physician of Indian descent, had been a revered family doctor in New Orleans, Louisiana. She graduated from Osmania Medical College in 1973, and completed her residency in family practice at St. Mary's Hospital in New Orleans.

Now in her late sixties, Dr. Ganji was ten months into a 72-month sentence for conspiracy to commit healthcare fraud—a charge she still struggled to comprehend. Her career, spanning over four decades without blemish, had been dedicated to patient care. Her patients adored her, and she had never faced any sanctions. The ordeal felt surreal, as if she had been thrust into a Kafkaesque nightmare—a stark reminder of Madison's warning that power, once placed in human hands, is susceptible to abuse.

That day, after assisting with meal preparation—a task she had taken on in the prison kitchen—Dr. Ganji joined the line for lunch. The menu featured baked chicken, sweet potatoes, black beans, and spinach. As she awaited her turn, memories of her involvement with Christian Home Health Agency flooded her mind. Toward the end of her career, she had collaborated with this hospice organization, referring patients and offering consultations. Unbeknownst to her, some employees had engaged in billing irregularities with Medicare, ensnaring her in a web of legal troubles. Despite the lack of direct evidence against her—no patient files reviewed, no patients interviewed—she was charged with healthcare fraud. The trial was a dystopian spectacle; 18 witnesses testified, none implicating her directly. Even the presiding judge expressed doubts about her guilt but left the decision to the jury, which ultimately convicted her. She was sentenced to six years in federal prison, followed by two years of supervised release, and ordered to repay $5,048,518 to Medicare. Her request to remain free during the appeal was denied, leading to her incarceration at FCI Aliceville.

Despite the daunting odds—less than 1% of federal convictions are overturned on appeal—Dr. Ganji, with her family's unwavering support, pursued justice. Her legal team argued the absence of concrete evidence and highlighted that witnesses had no direct knowledge of her involvement. They believed they had presented a compelling case to the conservative Fifth Circuit Court of Appeals, clinging to hope amidst adversity.

As Dr. Ganji finished her lunch on January 30, 2018, Warden Patricia Bradley approached her.

"Pramela Ganji, 34355-034," the Warden called out.

"Present," Dr. Ganji responded, adhering to protocol.

The Warden smiled warmly. "We've received an order for your release. Your sentence has been vacated. Congratulations, Doc."

Overwhelmed, Dr. Ganji stood in stunned silence. The Warden, breaking from customary formality, embraced her. The news was astonishing—a conviction overturned by the conservative Fifth Circuit Court of Appeals. The Warden explained that processing her release would take a day, setting her freedom for January 31, 2018. One more night in prison seemed a small price to pay for the justice she had long awaited. That evening, inmates and staff organized a celebration in her honor. Upon her release, Dr. Ganji chose to retire, focusing on her health and reconnecting with her three children, some of whom had followed her into the medical profession. She never returned to practicing medicine. Many people who are eventually proven innocent struggle to rebuild their lives after a wrongful conviction—scars refuse to heal, reputations remain tarnished, and memories of injustice haunt them. The stigma of a conviction lingers long after the verdict is overturned.

This ordeal exacted a heavy toll on Dr. Ganji. Her practice lay in ruins, and her once-respected name was overshadowed by controversy—all because prosecutors questioned her medical judgment.

Judges nationwide have begun to challenge such unjust prosecutions, recognizing that disagreements over medical practices do not equate to criminality. Most physicians strive to aid their patients and deserve the benefit of the doubt. Yet, as Madison warned, unchecked power in the hands of authorities too often leads to injustice.

Recognizing the delicate balance between medical practice and governmental oversight, Congress in 2010 added a subsection to the United States Code:

"Nothing in this subchapter shall be construed to authorize any Federal officer or employee to exercise any supervision or control over the practice of medicine or the manner in which medical services are provided..." (United States Code)

Physicians across the country have dedicated their careers to patient care, often making difficult decisions in complex medical and ethical landscapes. Yet, despite their commitment, many find themselves at odds with government regulators and legal authorities, facing allegations that challenge their professional integrity. In a system where power dictates justice, the consequences are often dire.

## My Case

In 2012, I established Blue Mountain Psychiatry in Easton, Pennsylvania, specializing in psychiatric care. We provided critical mental health care for elderly Medicare patients in nursing homes, using psychotherapy and telemedicine to reduce antipsychotic drug dependence. Our success was undeniable:

- CMS reported a historic reduction in psychotropic medication use.
- Pennsylvania saved an estimated $50 million in Medicare costs.

Yet, despite our success, the Department of Justice (DOJ) and Health and Human Services (HHS) launched an investigation. They claimed our services were fraudulent without consulting psychiatrists or coding experts.

On a November day in 2022, U.S. Attorney Jacqueline Romero and Assistant U.S. Attorney Joan E. Burnes announced:

"Lehigh Valley Psychiatrist stole from Medicare in a healthcare fraud scheme."

Despite the intimidation, armed raids, and false allegations, I refused to plead guilty.

In May 2024, I exercised my Sixth Amendment right to a public trial by jury. Twelve ordinary Pennsylvanians heard the evidence. Medical experts testified to my innocence. The jury deliberated for just a few hours before delivering their verdict:

NOT GUILTY.

Justice prevailed—but at a cost. My reputation was in tatters, my practice suffered, and years of my life were lost to a system that treats doctors as criminals. This is the very reality Madison foresaw—the inevitable abuse of power when left unchecked.

Physicians must defend themselves against wrongful accusations. The government often gets it wrong. The Sixth Amendment guarantees a jury trial, yet many doctors, fearing harsh sentences, surrender their rights.

Healthcare should be about patients, not politics. And yet, too many good doctors are sacrificed on the altar of bureaucracy.

The fight is not over. Medicine must be reclaimed by those who practice it, not those who prosecute it. If Madison's warning rings true, then we must remain vigilant, for power in human hands will always be liable to abuse.

The erosion of medical autonomy and the criminalization of standard medical practice have created an environment where physicians operate under constant fear—not of malpractice, but of prosecution. The Hippocratic Oath, once a guiding principle of ethical medical care, has now become a target for legal scrutiny. As more doctors find themselves entangled in federal investigations for decisions once deemed sound medical judgment, the question remains: Has the pursuit of justice been replaced by the pursuit of convictions? In Chapter 3, we will explore the legislative framework that has fueled this crisis, tracing the origins of modern healthcare fraud statutes and their unintended consequences for physicians across the nation.

# CHAPTER 2

# Hippocratic Oath—Criminal Statute?

---

*"Without Virtue there can be no liberty"*

**— Dr.Benjamin Rush**

## Duck and Cover

I grew up during one of the most turbulent periods in Aleppo's history. While many around the world know of the Syrian civil war that erupted in 2011, few remember the earlier conflict that scarred my childhood— the brutal civil war that raged between 1978 and 1983. During those years, the city of Hamah, once home to over 100,000 people, was reduced to rubble. The fear was omnipresent, a silent companion in our homes, our classrooms, and our dreams.

This war was not simply between armies. It was an insurgency led by the Muslim Brotherhood against the regime of President Hafez al-Assad, father of the recently deposed president. Both factions employed unforgiving tactics. Civilians—families like mine—were trapped between the blades of two merciless swords.

In 1981, when I was in third grade, I witnessed a horror that has never left me. Riding the school bus home, we came to a halt behind another bus, one carrying high school students. Soldiers stopped it, ordered every student off, and lined them against a wall. We children sat in paralyzed silence as the soldiers opened fire. The images are burned into my memory—the lifeless bodies, the silence that followed, the dreadful knowledge that we could have been next.

Only a month later, as our bus followed that same route, a spray of bullets tore through its side. I remember the scream of the metal, the holes punched inches from where I sat. I remember not screaming, not moving—just the ringing in my ears and the sound of my own heartbeat. These experiences didn't just scar me. They shaped the very core of who I am.

Trauma is a thread woven through the fabric of my family. On my father's side, addiction lurks in many forms. Alcoholism was common, though never named aloud. On my mother's side, depression cast a long shadow, with medication becoming a lifeline for many. These inherited burdens were intensified by the relentless tension and terror we all experienced growing up.

I became introverted, withdrawn. I trusted few and confided in fewer. We were devout Muslims, but even faith had to be practiced in secret. Attending Mosque risked suspicion of Brotherhood sympathies. Even our neighbors could not be trusted. People disappeared without explanation—sometimes taken by the regime, sometimes by the insurgents. Their absence was never questioned out loud.

Aleppo, one of oldest continuously inhabited cities in the world, has always risen from ruin, and perhaps that resilience found its way into me. Over time, the chaos and pain of my childhood transformed into something purposeful. I chose to become a psychiatrist—not to escape my past, but to understand it. To stand with others who carry invisible wounds. To offer something better than silence and fear.

My hometown, Aleppo, possibly inhabited since the sixth millennium B.C.E., once housed the world's first psychiatric hospital—Bimaristan Arghun—in operation from the 1400s to the 1900s. That legacy stayed with me. Amidst destruction, Aleppo had always cared for the wounded mind. I like to think that spirit, that compassion, is something I inherited. And it's what I now try to offer the world.

## The Sacred Origins of Medicine

Long before modern medicine was codified in university syllabi and federal handbooks, it was a spiritual vocation—an act of devotion grounded in service, humility, and a deep reverence for the Divine. The physician was more than a technician of the body; they were a mediator between suffering and healing, life and death, science and spirit. This sacred calling is most clearly captured in the historical essence of the Hippocratic Oath: not merely a pledge of ethical practice, but a solemn invocation of higher authority.

Hippocrates of Kos, often called the Father of Medicine, lived during the Classical Greek period in the 5th century BCE. In a world where disease was still widely attributed to divine punishment or imbalance of humors, Hippocrates introduced a revolutionary idea: that illness could and should be understood through observation, reason, and natural causes. Yet Hippocrates did not discard the spiritual or ethical dimensions of healing. On the contrary, he elevated them. His now-famous Oath was written to guide new physicians not just in their clinical skills, but in their moral character and sense of sacred duty.

## Hippocrates and His Oath

The Hippocratic Oath laid out the standards by which a healer should practice medicine—with humility, discretion, discipline, and above all, compassion. It emphasized the physician's duty to avoid intentional harm, to respect teachers, and to uphold confidentiality with patients. It was not merely a professional code, but a spiritual contract, rooted in reverence for life and the divine order.

The Oath begins:

> *"I swear by Apollo the Healer, by Asclepius, by Hygieia, by Panacea, and by all the gods and goddesses, making them my witnesses, that I will carry out, according to my ability and judgment, this oath and this indenture."*

And it ends:

> *"If I carry out this oath, and break it not, may I gain forever reputation among all men for my life and for my art; but if I break it and forswear myself, may the opposite befall me."*

This ancient commitment would shape the soul of medicine for centuries to come. Yet, as we shall see, its modern interpretation is no longer a shield—it has become a sword.

## Healing and Religion

In many traditions across the globe, healing has always been interwoven with spirituality. In Islamic tradition, the act of seeking a cure is itself a form of worship, an act rooted in Tawakkul (trust in God). The Prophet Muhammad (peace be upon him) famously stated, "Make use of medical treatment, for Allah has not made a disease without appointing a remedy for it." (Sunnah.com) Similarly, in Judeo-Christian contexts, healing is inseparable from prayer, faith, and divine intervention. The physician was seen as a vessel for God's mercy, a servant guided by compassion and humility.

The moral universe of medicine was thus cosmic in scale. The physician was to be ethical not because of fear of punishment or professional sanction, but because their actions echoed in eternity. Honesty, confidentiality, modesty, and a refusal to harm—even when asked to do so—were all spiritual mandates. To practice medicine was to walk a narrow path, watched over by divine judgment.

This understanding gave medicine its dignity. It placed enormous responsibility on the shoulders of the healer—not merely to treat the illness, but to protect the integrity of the healing act itself. Doctors were expected to align their intentions with sacred values, and to act as stewards of divine mercy on earth. Patients, in turn, trusted their doctors not only as experts, but as ethical beings called to a higher purpose.

## The Secularisation of Medicine

In the modern era, this relationship has been strained. Medicine has become increasingly secular, bureaucratic, and adversarial. The language of healing is now more likely to be found in legal documents than in sacred texts. The spiritual covenant has been replaced by contracts, policies, and compliance checklists. While this evolution brought advances in science and public health, it also left behind something essential: the soul of the profession.

Today, physicians are judged less by their compassion or intention than by their alignment with billing codes, guidelines, and administrative protocols. This shift has profound implications—not just for the integrity of medical practice, but for the spiritual and moral identity of those who serve in it.

In this context, the Hippocratic Oath—originally a sacred promise—is being reframed as a legal liability. Physicians who act in accordance with the ethical spirit of medicine may find themselves in conflict with the rigid frameworks imposed by regulatory systems. Compassionate care, once protected by spiritual tradition, can now be reinterpreted as criminal deviation.

What does it mean for a society when its healers are prosecuted for doing what they believe is right? When ethical nuance is replaced by legal absolutism? When the Divine calling to heal becomes entangled in the machinery of the state?

These are not hypothetical questions. They are the lived reality of many physicians today.

## A Case in Point: Dr. Stuart Gitlow

On the morning of Saturday, 17 March 2018, in the quiet stillness before sunrise, Dr. Stuart Gitlow was preparing for a day at his private practice in Woonsocket, Rhode Island. At 6:15 a.m., his routine was shattered by loud knocking at his door. When he answered, he was met by a team of armed FBI agents presenting a search warrant. Their mission: to investigate his clinical records. The physician, known for his national advocacy in addiction medicine and ethics, was given no prior warning. His office was raided. His home, disrupted. And yet, years later, no charges have been filed. No wrongdoing substantiated.

Dr. Gitlow is not an isolated case. Across the United States, physicians are increasingly targeted by federal agencies. Their best practices are reinterpreted as fraud. Their judgment is second-guessed by bureaucrats with no medical training. Lives are ruined. Careers are ended. All under the pretext of justice.

The Hippocratic Oath, once a sacred commitment to healing, has become a legal trap. Modern physicians swear to do no harm, to treat patients with respect, to avoid abuse, and to uphold ethical standards. But what happens when these very standards are weaponized? When ethical judgement calls are mischaracterized as criminal acts?

In 2023, at the American Medical Association House of Delegates, Dr. Gitlow stood and said:

"A doctor who can't be sued for malpractice because no patient was harmed can end up in federal prison for 20+ years because they prescribed off-guideline."

Representing the American Society of Addiction Medicine, his warning was not hyperbole. It was a sober assessment of the state of modern American healthcare. Physicians are increasingly prosecuted not for harming patients, but for diverging from bureaucratically defined 'norms'.

Meanwhile, the original Hippocratic Oath has been left behind by most medical schools. Its core tenets— to seek knowledge, protect life, do no harm, and avoid personal gain—are still vital, but its spiritual and moral undertones have been diluted. The spiritual roots of medicine, its relationship to the Divine, and the healing power of intention and prayer have been lost to a clinical, hostile bureaucracy.

Modern medical practice now demands not only compassion and knowledge, but legal vigilance. In this climate, even the most ethical, careful physicians can find themselves under federal investigation. Not because of patient complaints. Not because of harm. But because their treatment plans didn't align with administrative checklists.

We must ask ourselves: who defines care? Is it the physician at the patient's bedside? Or the prosecutor who has never held a stethoscope?

The spiritual bond between physician and patient—once grounded in trust, prayer, and ethical responsibility—is now too often replaced with suspicion, surveillance, and legal peril. The Divine calling to heal is under siege. And as Dr. Gitlow reminds us, it is long past time to push back.

# When Healing Becomes a Crime

Dr. Gitlow's experience is far from rare. The last two decades have seen a marked rise in criminal investigations into the conduct of medical professionals. In theory, this is about preventing fraud and protecting patients. In practice, however, it has often meant criminalising medical judgment and eroding the foundation of physician autonomy.

One of the key legal tools in this shift is the Health Insurance Portability and Accountability Act of 1996—HIPAA. Though widely known for its privacy provisions, HIPAA also introduced a lesser-known but far-reaching set of criminal statutes, codified in 18 U.S.C. §1347 and §1349. (Cornell Law School) These sections enable federal prosecutors to pursue healthcare fraud claims without requiring evidence of intent. A physician can be charged, tried, and sentenced not for knowingly committing fraud, but for making treatment decisions that deviate from bureaucratic standards—often under vague or subjective interpretations of what constitutes the "usual course of professional practice."

This legal framework has become fertile ground for prosecutorial overreach. A doctor may be indicted for prescribing a controlled substance "off-label," even if that prescription is medically sound and supported by clinical judgment. Entire careers can be dismantled by an unproven allegation, a misfiled code, or a billing error reinterpreted as conspiracy. The standard of proof has been watered down. The assumption of innocence is lost.

The most disturbing element is not just the potential for injustice—it is the effect on the very soul of medicine. Physicians now live with the constant threat of legal reprisal. The pressure to comply with administrative expectations overshadows their moral and clinical instincts. A treatment choice made in good faith can later be dissected in a courtroom, stripped of context, and presented as criminal evidence.

The story of Dr. Antonio Reyes Vizcarrondo from Puerto Rico offers a chilling example. Indicted on healthcare fraud charges, he was accused of submitting false claims. The Government claimed that Services Performed by this Doctor were billed for twice, once by him

(Lawfully) and another by the Hospital and the Staffing Agency. His was lawful (for which he was prosecuted for), the Hospital and the billing agency billed unlawfully. The hospital and agency did not have authorization to bill on his behalf. As a result it was they that were billing fraudulently.

The case threatened not only his freedom and livelihood, but his legacy as a respected community doctor. Fortunately, with proper legal and investigative support, the claims against him were ultimately withdrawn. The truth emerged: the fraud had been committed by a staffing company, not Dr. Vizcarrondo. But the damage to his reputation and well-being had already been done.

This is what modern prosecution looks like in the medical field: complex, aggressive, and all too often misplaced. A physician may work tirelessly, ethically, and compassionately for decades—only to find their decisions judged not by peers or patients, but by agents and prosecutors with limited understanding of medicine.

In 2010, amendments to the healthcare fraud statute further eroded the presumption of innocence by removing the requirement for prosecutors to prove specific intent. A physician can now be prosecuted even if they were unaware of the regulatory details they allegedly violated. Ignorance of the law may never have been an excuse, but ignorance of administrative coding standards, miscommunications with billing services, or well-intentioned deviations from "guidelines" are increasingly treated as federal crimes.

For many, the only choice becomes capitulation. The threat of lengthy trials, financial ruin, and harsh sentences drives physicians to accept plea deals—even when they know they are innocent. The fear of a "trial penalty" is real. And the cost is borne not just by the physician, but by their patients, families, and communities.

The deeper problem is one of cultural disintegration. The trust between doctor and patient, once rooted in a sacred calling, is collapsing under a regime of surveillance, suspicion, and state control. The doctor is no longer presumed to be a moral actor. They are watched, coded, and dissected.

In such an environment, it is no surprise that medical burnout is rising, that fewer students choose primary care, that independent practices are vanishing. The criminalisation of medicine is not just unjust—it is unsustainable.

## Returning to the Oath

The Hippocratic Oath was never perfect. It was born in a time with its own cultural and moral complexities. But its enduring relevance lies in its spirit: the commitment to protect, to serve, and to heal.

We must ask ourselves what kind of medicine we want to build in the 21st century. One ruled by fear, codes, and prosecution? Or one that revives the sacred trust between healer and patient? Physicians must not only be clinically competent but spiritually grounded and ethically courageous. They must be free to listen to their patients, follow their conscience, and serve with compassion—not fear.

Dr. Gitlow's words echo not just as a warning, but as a call to action:

"This is unacceptable... and it's time for us to push back."

To push back means more than protest. It means reform. It means restoring moral clarity to medical training. It means reasserting the doctor-patient relationship as sacred. It means advocating for laws that distinguish between malicious fraud and human error. It means remembering that healing is a Divine vocation—and that those who pursue it with honour should not be treated as criminals.

Let us return, not nostalgically but purposefully, to the oath. Not to preserve an outdated document, but to revive its heart. So that once again, medicine may be a calling of conscience, not a target of prosecution.

# CHAPTER 3

# Origins of investigations

---

*"And you were on the edge of a pit of the Fire, and He*
*saved you from it."*

— Quran 3:103

## Crossing Borders and Battling Shadows

The sun always seemed to shine on Amal Elementary School—at least
in my memory. From kindergarten through eighth grade, I walked its
hallways with a sense of purpose. I did well—earned high grades, raised
hands, proud nods from teachers. My parents were devoted, never
missing a teacher meeting, always hovering in quiet encouragement. My
early years were stable, framed by structure and expectations. But the
world beyond the school gates was anything but calm.

By 1987, Syria was simmering with political tension. Conversations
behind closed doors became quieter, glances became guarded. My
parents, sensing a storm on the horizon, made a choice that would
change the course of my life: they would emigrate to the United States.
I was to go ahead of them—alone.

At just 14, I boarded a flight to Texas, still clutching the Arabic of
my childhood and little more than a few words of English. I moved in
with my maternal uncle, Dr. Asad Sergie, a respected surgeon practicing
in the small town of Bay City. The transition was harsh, like stepping
from warm light into a foreign fog. Everything—from the food to the
language to the loneliness—felt alien.

But then came my cousin, Ali.

Ali was five years younger, full of energy and curiosity, and his presence became my anchor. He didn't care that my English was shaky or that I still dreamed in Arabic. We became inseparable. Through our conversations, video games, and schoolwork, the language began to settle into me. My tongue reshaped itself. Within a year, I was fluent—fluent and accentless. That transformation still surprises people. Ali would later become a dentist in Dallas. We remain close to this day, bound not just by blood, but by that shared chapter of adaptation and survival.

But America was not my final destination, not yet. I returned to Aleppo, drawn back to family, familiarity, and unfinished business. I enrolled at the Aleppo American College, a prestigious institution with high expectations. It was then, without warning, that my body began to betray me.

At first, it was subtle. Fatigue. Shakiness. Then came the weight loss—drastic and terrifying. My face grew gaunt, my eyes bulged unnaturally from my skull. I became a living ghost. The doctors feared the worst: thyroid cancer. It was 1986, just months after the Chernobyl nuclear disaster had unleashed a cloud of radioactive poison across Europe and into the Middle East. They suspected the fallout had reached Syria—and my body had paid the price.

The final diagnosis was Graves' Disease, a severe autoimmune disorder that ravaged my metabolism and appearance. My once-strong frame dwindled. My classmates, unsure and cruel in the way children can be, mocked and alienated me. I was no longer just a returning student—I was a target. I frightened even myself when I looked in the mirror. My thyroid doctor was Dr. Lester VanMiddlesworth who also became my mentor. (UTHSC)

But I endured.

I returned to the Aleppo American College and, despite the whispers and the bullying, pushed forward. The fire that had sparked in Amal Elementary—the hunger to learn, to rise, to fight—had not been extinguished. I studied hard, and I healed slowly. My teachers noticed. My grades soared. When graduation came, I stood near the top of my class—not just as a scholar, but as a survivor.

That chapter of my life—marked by continents, illness, and ridicule—set a precedent. It taught me that adversity was not the end of the road. It was the beginning of transformation.

## Divine Intervention

*"And We have made before them a barrier and a barrier behind them, then We have covered them over so that they do not see"*
*(Quran.com, Verse 36:9)*

Friday, May 3, 2024. It was supposed to be a turning point in the trial, and it was—just not in the way the government had hoped. Inside the courtroom, tension hung like a fog. The prosecution was prepared to unleash its most consequential witness, a registered nurse named Noreen Thomas. The lead prosecutor, Joan Burnes, believed Thomas would deliver a decisive blow—irrefutable proof of guilt. But as I recited verse 36:9 of the Quran in silent prayer, divine intervention arrived, unexpected and unmistakable.

Before Ms. Thomas could be sworn in, an unthinkable disruption unfolded. Despite court protocol strictly forbidding mobile phones, Burnes received a call—urgent, panicked. She stepped outside. When she returned, her face was pale, her composure fractured. Her home security system had notified her: intruders had attempted to break into her house. Her world, so meticulously ordered, was suddenly shaken. And so, despite the chaos, the court pressed forward. Ms. Thomas took the stand.

Her testimony began with confidence. She presented charts, figures, and what she claimed was airtight data: 100% fraudulent billing, calculated to deceive. But then came the cross-examination. My attorney, Paul Hetznecker, approached the podium and began, gently but deliberately, to unravel the narrative. What followed was a moment of legal and spiritual redemption:

Q: Do you know what the percentage is from 93 percent if you eliminate those five, what the percentage would be in terms of those claims denied?

A: Not off the top of my head, no. I would need to do the calculation.

Q: Me too. Ms. Thomas, this is a completely flawed report, is it not?

A: It's not accurate.

Q: So because it's not accurate, the data, that's, the basis for the conclusions, is not accurate, correct?

A: Correct.

Q: Therefore, the conclusions are not accurate, correct?

A: Correct.

Q: Therefore, the report is not accurate, correct?

A: Correct.

Q: And as you sit here now, would you have endorsed this report, knowing these flaws in the report, before testifying today?

A: I would not want to put my name behind something that was flawed like that.

Q: I understood. Because you have integrity about the work you do, correct?

A: Yes.

Q: And this work doesn't match your standard of integrity does it?

A: No.

Q: And this report would never go out, correct?

A: Correct.

Q: And it wouldn't be part of any further investigation done by the Federal Government or done by CMS, because it would never have gone out, correct?

A: Correct.

Q: And certainly didn't go to Dr. Rifai or Blue Mount Psychiatry, did it?

A: It did not.

In open court, under oath, the government's own expert disowned her testimony. The jurors watched closely. I could feel their eyes on me, not with suspicion, but with realization. The testimony meant to convict me had collapsed before them.

Three days later, Monday, May 6, 2024, I thought surely the government would yield. Surely, they would drop the case after such a dramatic defeat. But instead, they doubled down. Another witness—an employee named Candice Reagan—was called to the stand. She alleged fraudulent billing on November 23, 2017. Her story was vivid, detailed, damning. But again, the divine was present.

My attorney filed a motion. November 23, 2017, was Thanksgiving—a federal holiday. Offices were closed. Nursing homes were closed. There was no way any services could have been rendered that day, let alone billed. The judge reviewed the calendar and confirmed the obvious. The witness, and the government, had built a fiction. The jury saw it for what it was.

That date was one of the central pillars of the prosecution. With it gone, their case was crumbling.

On May 9, 2024, the jury returned. It took them only a couple of hours.

Not guilty. On all charges.

I sat still, humbled. Not elated. Not triumphant. Just still. Because I knew what had happened was not just law—it was divine mercy. The same mercy that had spared me in Syria in 1980, when I was nearly executed alongside other children. The same mercy that protected me from thyroid cancer after Chernobyl's radioactive cloud poisoned the air. The same mercy that spared my life in 2020, when a tire flew from a tractor-trailer and crushed my car—every part of it except the driver's seat.

I believe I am here for a reason. Not by luck. Not by chance. But by the will of the Divine. The court was merely the latest crucible.

My story is not just legal. It is spiritual. And it is far from over.

# The Tale of Dr. Paulus

It was a dreary, slate-gray day on March 5, 2020. The kind of day that hung heavy in the air, pressing on the mind like a warning of something about to shift. The television in the dayroom at the Beckley Federal Correctional Institution in West Virginia flickered constantly, broadcasting news of a novel respiratory virus making its way out of Wuhan, China. The rising panic of the pandemic was only beginning to spread in the U.S., but inside the walls of Beckley, where the passage of time was slow and cruel, Dr. Richard Paulus had more immediate concerns.

At 72 years old, Paulus was no longer the dynamic interventional cardiologist who had once commanded respect and admiration in Ashland, Kentucky. He was now Federal Inmate #18257-032, having surrendered his medical license in 2014 and had begun serving a 60-month prison sentence in June 2019. Accused and convicted of healthcare fraud, he had become yet another doctor ensnared in a vast web of federal scrutiny, compliance codes, and the evolving criminalization of medical discretion.

On that day in March, the quiet hum of the dayroom was broken by the sound of footsteps approaching. A prison counselor entered, clipboard in hand, his voice cutting through the silence with surprising formality: "Dr. Richard Paulus."

The name felt foreign in that setting. Paulus lifted his head, startled. "Yes, present."

The counselor offered an unusual smile. "Start packing your stuff, Doc. You're being released. Your verdict was vacated."

And just like that, after months in federal custody, the Sixth Circuit Court of Appeals had overturned his conviction. The judges had ruled that substantial judicial errors had occurred in the trial, mandating a new one. Within hours, Paulus found himself on the road home, returning to Ashland after nearly a year behind bars.

His was not a simple story of error and redemption. It was a case study in how federal investigations begin, how they gain momentum, and how, even when devoid of criminal intent, they can lead to devastating consequences.

Dr. Richard Paulus had arrived in Ashland in 1992, joining King's Daughters Medical Center (KDMC) and transforming its heart and vascular program into a regional hub. Patients from miles around sought care at the now-prestigious center. From 2008 to 2011, Paulus earned an average of $2.6 million annually. By the numbers alone, KDMC became one of the highest billing cardiac centers in the country, raking in $1.1 billion from Medicare for vascular procedures.

Those figures—grand, imposing, and tempting—raised eyebrows.

In 2008, an anonymous tip landed on the desk of the Office of the Inspector General for the Department of Health and Human Services (OIG-HHS). The claim? That Dr. Paulus was performing unnecessary stent procedures to inflate Medicare billing. It was the match that lit a decade-long fire.

The government began with a medical audit of several angiograms. Seven were denied reimbursement. A parallel path of investigation unfolded. In 2012, the Kentucky Board of Medical Licensure received a similar complaint. The Board, after reviewing cases forwarded by prosecutors, agreed: Paulus, they claimed, was diagnosing severe arterial blockages that simply didn't appear in the imaging.

Paulus disagreed. But the damage was done.

Though he had already retired, he voluntarily surrendered his license in November 2014, hoping to close the chapter. What he didn't know was that his own hospital had already turned against him. KDMC, under pressure, conducted an internal review, and quietly agreed to pay the federal government $41 million to settle allegations that it had submitted false claims.

The settlement included no admission of wrongdoing. But the moment KDMC's lawyers couldn't strike a similar deal with Paulus, the path became clear. The government moved forward with a full-blown criminal indictment.

In 2015, Paulus was indicted on one count of healthcare fraud and 26 counts of making false statements. The indictment alleged that Paulus had misrepresented the degree of stenosis (narrowing) in patients' coronary arteries—overstating blockages to justify unnecessary procedures. To the prosecution, this was not an error. It was a calculated deception.

Dr. Paulus hired high-profile defense attorney Robert Bennett—famous for representing President Bill Clinton during the Monica Lewinsky scandal. The case was relocated from Ashland to Covington, Kentucky, out of concern that local jurors might be biased due to the doctor's prominence.

The trial, which began in September 2016, became a spectacle.

The prosecution's strategy was clear: they would discredit Paulus's clinical judgment by comparing it against post-hoc reviews of angiograms. Their witnesses were top-tier cardiologists—Dr. Michael Ragosta of the University of Virginia and Dr. David Moliterno of the University of Kentucky—experts in cardiac catheterization. They testified that Paulus's readings fell well outside the range of acceptable interobserver variability.

The prosecution introduced financial records, pointing to Paulus's annual income and lifestyle. Their narrative suggested a man motivated by greed rather than patient care. To bolster their case, they emphasized billing patterns, volume of procedures, and statistical anomalies that made Paulus an outlier compared to his peers nationwide.

Paulus's team countered with testimony of their own. They argued that the images the prosecution's experts reviewed were compressed and pixelated versions of the original angiograms. More importantly, the defense pointed out that clinical decisions aren't made from still frames—they're made from moving images, patient histories, symptoms, and nuanced medical reasoning.

Several of Paulus's patients also testified. They described debilitating symptoms prior to treatment and significant relief following stent procedures. These were not hypothetical patients. These were real people, speaking to the quality of care they had received.

Yet the jury, confused and likely swayed by financial records showing Paulus's wealth, convicted him of one count of fraud and four counts of false statements. Eleven other counts were dismissed. The jury hung on the rest.

It was a partial win for the government.

But it didn't last.

In March 2017, Judge David Bunning granted Paulus's motion for acquittal. He ruled that the government had not provided enough evidence to prove beyond a reasonable doubt that Paulus had acted with fraudulent intent. A mistake—even a severe one—was not a crime.

The prosecution appealed.

In June 2018, the Sixth Circuit Court of Appeals reversed Bunning's decision, reinstating the conviction. They argued that deliberately inflating a diagnosis was a lie—and if done to bill for unnecessary procedures, it was fraud.

Paulus's legal journey, already exhausting, was about to enter another phase.

More revelations emerged. During the original trial, the prosecution had failed to disclose that KDMC had conducted an internal review of over 1,046 procedures. Of these 7% were problematic. The hospital had fought to keep those records sealed to avoid civil malpractice suits. And, crucially, the judge had held an ex parte meeting with prosecutors and hospital lawyers, excluding Paulus's defense team.

This was a constitutional violation.

The Sixth Circuit cited these procedural missteps and vacated Paulus's conviction in 2020. Their language was damning: "When a court rules on important issues without hearing from the defense, it risks making erroneous decisions that unfairly disadvantage the defendant. That's exactly what happened here."

Paulus's second trial began in November 2023. With his lead counsel, Robert Bennett, now deceased, attorney Hilary LoCicero took the reins. Much of the evidence from the first trial was excluded. No patient complaints, no hospital comparisons, and no testimony from the original trial.

The jury deliberated for five days. They found Paulus not guilty on one charge and were deadlocked on the others. Judge Bunning declared a mistrial.

In January 2024, the U.S. Attorney's Office finally relented. They dismissed all charges.

Dr. Paulus's saga had lasted 16 years.

His story illustrates the anatomy of federal healthcare fraud investigations. It starts with a complaint—anonymous or otherwise. It evolves into audits, reviews, peer assessments. When settlements can't be reached, it escalates into prosecution. In the absence of clear guidelines or a medical consensus, prosecutors turn disagreements into deception, errors into crimes.

This chapter of American medicine has blurred the lines between mistake and malice. For physicians like Dr. Paulus, it's not just their careers at stake. It's their freedom, their legacy, their very names.

And it can all begin with a single phone call.

## The Legal Minefield

The story of Dr. Richard Paulus offers only one view into the deeply intricate and often punishing world of healthcare fraud investigations. But it is by no means unique. In fact, the United States' regulatory framework surrounding healthcare is so vast and convoluted that even most federal criminal defense attorneys are not fully versed in its complexity. Only a small number of specialists—attorneys who live and breathe healthcare law—have the depth of knowledge required to navigate the intersection of criminal statutes, federal regulations, billing codes, and the administrative machinery of entities like the Office of Inspector General for Health and Human Services (OIG-HHS).

When the Department of Justice (DOJ), the OIG-HHS, the Drug Enforcement Administration (DEA), and other state law enforcement agencies open a healthcare fraud investigation, they often work with powerful teams and increasingly rely on data analytics and artificial intelligence to detect what they describe as "emerging fraud schemes." The term "scheme" itself is problematic. In my experience, I have found that many of the practices labeled as schemes were, in fact, accepted forms of medicine—methods misinterpreted out of ignorance or, worse, malice.

The DOJ maintains nine regional strike forces across the United States. These are specialized teams of prosecutors, FBI agents, and agency officials tasked with pursuing fraud cases at high velocity. What I learned through my own prosecution is that the moment you become aware of an investigation, time is already against you. Delay—whether out of fear, confusion, or misplaced confidence—can cost you everything. Early intervention, on the other hand, can sometimes redirect the course entirely.

Consider the case of Dr. Khan, his wife, and his partner. They were on the verge of facing both healthcare fraud and controlled substance charges. But with immediate legal action, the scope of the investigation was contained. That window for early intervention can be the difference between a settlement and a federal prison sentence.

So how do these investigations begin? Most often, they start with a simple complaint. The OIG-HHS operates a hotline where patients or employees can call to report perceived fraud or abuse. In my case, it began with a patient upset over a copayment. He believed he shouldn't have been charged and called the OIG hotline. The OIG, rather than investigating directly, passed the case to a Medicare Integrity Contractor—SafeGuard Services, LLC. These contractors conduct audits and, if suspicious activity is found, refer the case for criminal investigation by the DOJ.

Another route is the whistleblower, or *qui tam* lawsuit—cases filed under the False Claims Act by disgruntled employees or inside sources. These individuals may offer information in exchange for immunity or financial compensation. Once the DOJ is involved, a civil suit can quickly escalate into a criminal case, especially if the agency deems the conduct intentional or reckless.

Sometimes investigations stem from Medicare audits that appear administrative at first but later trigger criminal referrals. In 2017, my own audit followed this trajectory. We responded to a request for documentation with comprehensive records, supported by a healthcare attorney and an expert psychologist. Despite our thorough submission, we never received a response. Later, we learned that the audit had been redirected for criminal investigation without our knowledge.

The government claimed we had billed for psychotherapy services that were not rendered. Yet, no specific evidence was shared with us before the charges were brought. What followed was a cascade of misinformation, misinterpretation, and silence—until agents appeared with a search warrant.

I was fortunate to have a clinical social worker on staff who served as our point of contact. It was she who first spoke to the agents. Every medical practice, no matter how small, should have a written compliance policy, with clear protocols for responding to government inquiries and searches. These policies won't necessarily shield you from investigation—but they can demonstrate due diligence and reduce exposure.

Effective compliance programs are not window dressing. They can significantly reduce penalties under the U.S. Sentencing Guidelines and show that a practice took proactive steps to prevent fraud. The OIG lists seven essential elements: written standards of conduct, a compliance officer and committee, regular training, open lines of communication, consistent enforcement, routine audits, and a plan for corrective action.(Office of Inspector General)

The difference between a civil case and a criminal indictment often comes down to intent—or what the government interprets as intent. If you "knew or should have known" that a claim was false, the DOJ may pursue criminal charges. In my case, two former employees—a nurse practitioner and a billing manager—filed a sealed civil *qui tam* suit that continued even after I was acquitted. Once my criminal case ended, the DOJ unsealed the civil action to pursue it independently.

This pattern isn't rare. It's why physicians facing legal exposure need attorneys experienced in both civil and criminal healthcare litigation. These cases often run in parallel and feed off each other.

Sometimes, early legal strategy can prevent escalation. Dr. Yasin Khan and his partners at Lehigh Valley Pain Management Clinic faced a whistleblower complaint regarding improper billing for services rendered by non-physicians. Their attorney acted quickly, offering a settlement of $690,000—far above the value of the disputed services. In return, they avoided criminal charges, agreed to temporarily cease billing for "incident-to" services, and signed a five-year Corporate Integrity Agreement.

Contrast that with the case of Dr. Feng Qin, a New York cardiothoracic surgeon. After settling a civil case with the DOJ for $150,000 over allegedly unnecessary cardiac procedures, he found himself re-indicted after a nurse-turned-whistleblower came forward. Dr. Qin was later charged criminally for the same practices the DOJ had previously settled. Only after extensive litigation and the help of experienced defense attorneys were those charges dropped in favor of another civil settlement. Dr. Qin agreed to repay $800,000 and was excluded from Medicare until 2025. He now practices in China.

These stories illustrate the perilous and often inconsistent nature of healthcare fraud enforcement in America. The stakes are high, the timeline unpredictable, and the consequences life-altering. But through careful compliance, immediate legal counsel, and unwavering attention to the rules, it is possible to survive.

Sometimes, even win.

# CHAPTER 4

# Take the Fifth

---

*"Any lawyer worth his or her salt will tell the client in no uncertain terms to make no statement to the police under any circumstances"*

— Supreme Court Justice Robert Jackson in 1949 in Watts v. Indiana 338 US 49

## A Different Kind of Training

In 1988, my father began accepting contract work in the United States, including a significant project at the State University of New York in Binghamton. He traveled frequently between Syria and the U.S., straddling two worlds with a suitcase and a dream, until 2011 when the second Syrian Civil War made staying in Aleppo no longer viable. My parents left behind everything familiar and came to the United States permanently, joining the growing tide of families fleeing violence in search of peace.

By then, the trajectory of my life had already been set into motion. My older brother Aref had moved to Memphis, Tennessee, in 1989 to complete his residency in medicine. I followed him there the summer after high school, hungry to start my own chapter. The transition was jarring. The rhythm of American life was loud, fast, and unfamiliar. I took a job at FedEx's massive distribution hub, one of the busiest in the world. My shift began at 7 p.m., and from dusk until dawn, we worked. We unloaded twenty-to-thirty-ton cargo planes by hand, our backs strained, our fingers numbed by steel. Inside, we sorted and scanned endless parcels, racing against the clock to reload aircraft before takeoff. By 7 a.m., I would leave the airport bone-tired, clothes soaked with sweat, and feeling a new kind of pride. I was earning my keep in this strange new country—and learning discipline in its rawest form.

Despite the exhaustion, I carved out time to volunteer in the Emergency Room at the Veterans Affairs Medical Center in Memphis. There, I witnessed a different kind of struggle: the kind that happens when bodies fail and spirits bend. Veterans came in with wounds both visible and hidden. Watching them, helping them, I began to sense that I was called not just to help carry boxes, but to carry burdens. My fatigue was tempered by a rising clarity—I wanted to become a physician.

I returned to Aleppo and enrolled in a six-year medical program. To my surprise, the atmosphere had softened. The long shadow of fear that once loomed over our daily lives had begun to fade. I felt safe enough to attend mosque again, to walk the streets with less suspicion, to breathe. My studies became my sanctuary. Yet, every summer, I flew back to the United States—not to rest, but to learn. I worked as a lab technician at the University of Tennessee, contributing to neuroscience research involving rabbits and lab rats. The work was meticulous, clinical, and deeply absorbing. I handled biological agents, managed delicate instrumentation, and assisted in procedures that revealed the quiet mysteries of the brain. In those sterile labs, under the hum of fluorescent lights, my interest in psychiatry began to crystallize.

Meanwhile, I also completed Syria's mandatory military hospital training. Each summer before departing for America, I spent fifteen grueling days in the desert. Under the merciless sun, we drilled in sand and sweat, simulating emergency medical operations far from any hospital. We slept on cots, rationed our water, and worked in conditions that tested our endurance and forced teamwork. The desert, the FedEx tarmac, the Memphis lab—each environment was harsh in its own way, but each trained something different in me: stamina, coordination, patience, precision.

Looking back, especially during the harrowing days of the COVID-19 pandemic, I see how each of these experiences prepared me. God was weaving a path I couldn't yet see. The muscles I built unloading planes, the steadiness I practiced in lab work, the heat-hardened resilience I gained in the desert—all of it became part of the physician I would become. Not just technically trained, but spiritually forged. Prepared not just to treat illness, but to confront chaos with calm.

And like silence, training is its own kind of wisdom. You don't always realize its value until the moment demands it. You act—not because you've thought it through in the moment—but because you've been prepared to.

In law, in medicine, and in life, that readiness can be the difference between survival and ruin.

## The Power of Silence

The jury had only been out for less than an hour when they returned with a verdict—an ominous sign in most trials. For Dr. Michael Bahrami, it was a moment of dread. He stood accused in a one-count federal indictment: conspiracy to commit healthcare fraud. Two of his peers, fellow physicians, had already pleaded guilty to similar charges. They had admitted to accepting kickbacks from three Florida-based home healthcare agencies in exchange for patient referrals. Dr. Bahrami, however, held his ground. He had followed his attorney's advice to the letter: say nothing to investigators, speak no words to prosecutors.

Now he waited. Alone with his thoughts, his mind wandered to another moment of uncertainty—the day he fled Iran as a teenager during the political chaos that preceded the Islamic Revolution. At just 17, he arrived in the United States with little English, no money, and a determination to rise. He washed dishes as a busboy in Florida before enrolling at Rutgers New Jersey Medical School. From there, he completed his internal medicine residency at Capital Health Mount Sinai in Florida and a cardiology fellowship at Albert Einstein Medical Center in New York. By the time of his indictment, he was 59 years old and the father of two young children, ages five and seven. If convicted, he faced up to five years in federal prison.

But when the jury filed back into the Miami federal courtroom, they did not convict him. They found him *not guilty*.

As the verdict was read, his wife wept. His patients—many of whom had packed the courtroom in a show of unwavering support—cheered quietly, some in tears. The government's key evidence had come from more than 30 video recordings made by a cooperating witness. Yet Dr. Bahrami was never caught on camera taking money. His referrals were grounded in clinical need, not financial gain. The jury believed him. Silence had saved him.

This is not just a story of vindication—it is a powerful lesson in restraint. His decision to follow his attorney's advice, to hold his tongue when questioned, may have made the difference between a lifetime of achievement and a legacy destroyed. His choice became the pivot point that tilted the scales of justice back in his favor. In a legal system increasingly eager to criminalize clinical judgment, remaining silent is not only wise—it can be life-saving.

## Never Talk to the Police

The Fifth Amendment of the U.S. Constitution exists for a reason: to protect citizens from self-incrimination. If you take one piece of advice from this book, let it be this—*never talk to the police*.

By "police," I mean any investigative agent: FBI, DEA, OIG-HHS, state boards of medicine, or investigators from attorneys general offices. Not with an attorney. Not without one. Not ever.

It's not enough to simply stay quiet. In *Salinas v. Texas* (Legal Information Institute), the Supreme Court ruled that prosecutors may use silence against a defendant unless they explicitly invoke their right to remain silent. So if you're confronted, say clearly: *"I am invoking my Fifth Amendment right to remain silent."* Anything less, and that right may be lost.

Even with legal counsel, talking to prosecutors or investigators is fraught with risk. Just ask Senator Robert Menendez. In 2024, during an attempt to avoid indictment, his legal team presented prosecutors with a PowerPoint presentation. Some of the included statements were later interpreted as obstruction of justice. Though intended to prevent charges, it helped secure them.

In my own case, federal agents showed up at my door and told me they simply wanted to "clear up a few details." They insisted I had done nothing wrong. I was lucky enough to have legal counsel who advised me to stay silent. But countless others have made the mistake of talking, believing that truth will protect them. It won't.

Actor Alec Baldwin nearly lost his career after voluntarily talking to police following an accidental shooting on a film set. The conversation was hours long. Though he spoke freely, believing he was cooperating, those words were later used against him. (CBC) Martha Stewart, a cultural icon, was convicted—not for insider trading, but for making false statements to investigators. (EBSCO) Scooter Libby, Vice President Cheney's former chief of staff, wasn't convicted for leaking classified information. He was convicted for misleading federal investigators.(John D. Rogers)

Statements, even seemingly harmless ones, can be twisted. Even truthful words can be misremembered, distorted, or recast in the worst possible light. Federal agents are not neutral observers; their recollections—recorded on forms like FBI 302s, DEA-6s, or OIG OI-3s—are often the *only* version of the story that gets heard. And they are rarely kind. Often, they are summaries, not transcripts, infused with the investigator's interpretation rather than the interviewee's intention.

Let's talk about Dr. Ajeeb John Titus.

## The Case of Dr. Titus

It was just after 5 p.m. on a Thursday in March 2018. Dr. Titus, a respected family practitioner, was winding down his day when a long-term patient arrived late, asking for a routine prescription refill. The secretary had already left, but Titus stayed to help. What he didn't know was that another patient of his, recently arrested with illicit fentanyl patches, had named him as the supplier. Within a week, a narcotics investigator from the Pennsylvania Attorney General's office showed up.

"I just have a few questions," the agent said. "You're not in any trouble."

Dr. Titus agreed to a 45-minute interview. He answered truthfully, believing that honesty would protect him. On September 29, 2020, he was arrested.

The indictment quoted his own words, taken out of context. The narrative twisted a late patient visit into "meeting patients after hours for drug deals." It labeled him a "script writer." Never mind that Dr. Titus stored no controlled substances in his office. Or that his patient had a history of legal trouble. His own words became the case against him. He eventually accepted a plea deal and surrendered his license.

Had he not spoken? There would have been no statements to twist, no contradictions to exploit. His silence could have been the strongest shield.

## Never Talk—Especially When You're Innocent

General Michael Flynn—former National Security Advisor, retired Lieutenant General, and expert interrogator—believed he could talk his way out of a federal investigation. After all, he'd led military intelligence operations. But when FBI agents asked vague questions, his equally vague answers were spun into lies. He was indicted for making false statements. Not espionage. Not treason. False statements.

If a man like Flynn, trained in deception detection and interrogation, can be undone in a casual conversation, what chance does the average doctor have? (Stanford Law School)

Agents usually refuse to be recorded. Their written reports are the only record. Your actual words are irrelevant—it's their memory, their pen, and their report that will be entered as evidence. And if there's a discrepancy? It's their version that will prevail in court.

Even corporations aren't safe. The accounting firm Arthur Andersen was destroyed—not by fraud—but by an obstruction of justice charge for destroying documents during the Enron scandal. The conviction was later overturned, but the damage was done. The company collapsed. 100,000 employees lost their jobs.

Talking to law enforcement is not just risky—it's catastrophic.

## The Physician's Trap

Physicians are trained communicators. We convince patients to accept diagnoses, start treatment, undergo surgery. We build rapport. We trust our voices. But this very strength becomes a liability when facing criminal investigation.

In my trial, agents testified about a brief conversation in which I gave them my attorney's contact information. They then falsely claimed I made other incriminating statements—statements inserted into their testimony and entered into the record. I hadn't even spoken to them beyond giving my lawyer's name.

If you speak at all, even to provide your lawyer's name or ask about the investigation, it can be twisted and used against you. Always invoke your rights *verbally*. Say: *"I am invoking my Fifth Amendment right to remain silent and I want a lawyer."*

And don't waver. Don't get drawn into conversation. Don't attempt to explain or clarify. Don't assume that your education, your credentials, or your intentions will protect you. Silence is your shield.

## Final Word

Talking to law enforcement—even when you're innocent—can only hurt you. Don't believe that cooperation clears your name. Don't believe that silence implies guilt. Don't believe that prosecutors want your side of the story. What they want is evidence. And your words, however honest, however innocent, can and will be used against you.

Never talk to the police. Never talk to investigators. Never talk to prosecutors. Not once. Not ever.

Silence is not just golden. It may be the only thing that saves your life, your freedom, and your career.

It's the fifth. So here are *five* words to remember:

## SAY NOTHING AND SAVE EVERYTHING!

# CHAPTER 5

# May the Fourth Be With You

---

*"The nine most terrifying words in the English language are: I'm from the government, and I'm here to help"*

— Ronald Regan The President of United States

## The Road Less Traveled

Graduating from medical school should have been the triumphant climax of a long and arduous journey—but for me, it was just the beginning of a path shaped by humility, sacrifice, and purpose.

In 1996, I walked across the stage and received my medical degree, the culmination of a combined college and medical school program. I had also taken and passed both required United States Medical Licensing Exams—earning high marks that positioned me competitively for a residency program in the U.S. Everything seemed to point toward a conventional path. But then, life—guided perhaps by fate or divine providence—had something different in store.

Out of the blue, I received an unexpected offer from Kafait U Malik (my eventual professor) : a postdoctoral fellowship from the University of Tennessee. (UTHSC, "Profile") The faculty remembered me from my work as a laboratory technician and were impressed by my dedication and attention to detail. The position was backed by the United States Public Health Service and funded through the National Institutes of Health (NIH). It wasn't glamorous, nor was it lucrative. But it was meaningful.

The research focused on the neurochemistry of the brain, specifically the study of psychiatric illness—precisely the field I had dreamed of entering. While others pursued higher-paying clinical roles, I chose the quiet halls of a laboratory, trading prestige for purpose. I earned a fraction of what I could have in clinical practice, but I gained something infinitely more valuable: a deeper understanding of the very illnesses I hoped to one day treat. I remained in that fellowship until 1998, not for the paycheck, but for the promise of service.

By October 1997, I re-entered the world of residency applications. My heart was set on psychiatry, but cultural expectations tugged in a different direction. In my community, psychiatry carried a stigma. It was dismissed, misunderstood, even ridiculed. My parents—devout and traditional—worried about their son being labeled a "shrink." Out of deference to them and in observance of the religious virtues of honoring one's parents, I applied to a combined residency program in internal medicine and psychiatry at the University of Virginia, with training at Carilion Health System and the Veterans Affairs Hospital in Salem, Virginia.

This decision was not a compromise—it was a calling. It allowed me to serve both my family's hopes and my own conviction. It also gave me dual lenses through which to view health: the physical and the mental, the visible and the hidden. Little did I know how vital this dual training would become decades later, as I stood on the frontlines during the COVID-19 pandemic, caring for both bodies and minds.

My years at the University of Virginia were marked by intense study, long nights, and moments of breathtaking clarity. I earned scholarships and awards—including one from the American Psychiatric Association for research on severe mental illness, an honor bestowed upon only fifteen scholars nationwide. I threw myself into research with passion, publishing over twenty papers as a resident—an almost unheard-of feat. My focus was veterans' mental health, a population often forgotten, yet deeply deserving of care.

In time, my work was recognized by my mentors. I was selected as chief resident—not once, but twice. I completed the rigorous combined residency and emerged board-certified in Internal Medicine and Psychiatry. Later, I would add a third certification in Addiction

Medicine, retaking my board exams multiple times over the years to stay current in my practice.

My training director, a man not known for hyperbole, wrote in my recommendation: "He is the top resident trainee I have had in 25 years." I took that not as a badge of honor, but as a reminder: excellence isn't about titles or income—it's about commitment to healing.

I wasn't just learning to be a doctor. I was learning to become a servant—of my patients, of science, and of the country that had given me a new beginning.

# The Knock at the Door

Congressman Ron Paul said, *"The Fourth Amendment is clear; we should be secure in our persons, houses, papers, and effects, and all warrants must have probable cause. Today the government operates largely in secret, while seeking to know everything about our private lives—without probable cause and without a warrant."* (Edwards)

It was still dark when the silence of morning was shattered. On July 22, 2016, just before dawn, a convoy of black SUVs rolled up to the opulent home of Phillip Esformes. Federal agents emerged like a stormfront, clad in jackets marked with acronyms that signaled power—DOJ, FBI, HHS-OIG. Moments later, a similar team entered his nearby assisted living facility, a seemingly innocuous structure that also housed his business headquarters.

The agents had come armed not only with weapons but with a federal search warrant—an instrument of legal intrusion that would upend Esformes' world. By the time the sun fully crested the horizon, the agents had confiscated boxes of documents, computers, and—in a stunning breach of protocol—confidential communications between Esformes and his attorneys. Attorney-client privilege was trampled, yet the government plowed forward.

Esformes, though not a physician, was accused of masterminding one of the largest Medicare fraud operations in U.S. history—over $1 billion, they claimed. After a years-long investigation, multiple superseding indictments, and a prolonged trial, he was convicted in 2018. But even the force of that conviction couldn't mask the prosecutorial misconduct. A federal magistrate later acknowledged the government had crossed serious ethical lines during the search. Still, no charges were dropped. No officials were disciplined. Esformes remained imprisoned until President Donald Trump commuted his sentence on December 22, 2020. He walked free after more than a year behind bars—but the scars, both personal and legal, endured.

This story isn't just about one man. It's a siren call for every physician, every healthcare administrator, every practice owner. It's about what happens when the government knocks—and what you must know to survive it.

## When the Warrant Arrives

A federal search warrant isn't a polite inquiry. It's an invasion backed by law, strategy, and the full weight of the Department of Justice. When federal agents arrive, the message is clear: you're under investigation. And statistically, it's only a matter of time before an indictment follows.

Federal authorities often rely on sophisticated algorithms to identify billing anomalies. They label you an "outlier," but make no mistake—that's code for target. Your statistical deviation becomes their probable cause.

Even if charges are never filed, the mere presence of agents, the abrupt seizure of records, and the trauma of public exposure can be ruinous. Dr. Forrest Tennant, a decorated pain specialist and former editor-in-chief of Practical Pain Management, saw his life crumble under such pressure. In 2017, the DEA raided his home and clinic. Though no charges were ever brought, the relentless stress led to his retirement. He had spent a lifetime helping patients with chronic and terminal pain. After the raid, many of those patients were left stranded, some in agony, some without hope. One remarked, heartbroken, "Dr. Tennant was my last chance."

# Preparing for the Storm

Denial is the most dangerous mindset. Every practice—no matter how reputable or small—needs a robust response plan for raids and investigations. Who speaks to the agents? Who calls legal counsel? Who secures the EMR? Who documents everything? Failing to plan means planning for chaos.

On June 19, 2019, it was my turn. At precisely 9 a.m., all three of my practice locations were raided. The agents moved like clockwork, arriving before patients did, seizing equipment, accessing servers, and questioning staff. We had mentally rehearsed this moment, and our receptionist calmly requested copies of the search warrants. I was notified immediately and arrived at one office within minutes.

Despite the adrenaline pounding in my ears, I remained calm. I presented myself, invoked my Fifth Amendment rights, and provided my attorney's name and contact information. I did not answer their questions—but even that measured interaction was later twisted. In their official reports, agents inserted hearsay, misquoted me, and misrepresented my demeanor. In court, my attorney dismantled their testimony under cross-examination, exposing their fabrication. But the damage, as always, was real and chilling.

# Know the Boundaries

Search warrants have limits. They define who, what, where, and when. Agents are legally bound to stay within these confines. If they overreach, your only weapon is documentation.

In our case, agents accessed Dropbox—our cloud-based patient record storage—despite the warrant not specifying cloud services. We objected immediately but did not resist. That objection, filed by our attorney, became a crucial piece of our defense.

Document everything: what was taken, where they searched, what was said. If allowed, take photos or video. Ask for agents' names and badge numbers. Record timestamps. These notes may someday save your career.

## Shielding Your Team

During a raid, fear spreads like wildfire. Staff panic. They say too much. They think cooperation will protect them. It won't. Instruct them: they are not required to speak to law enforcement. Tell them to go home. Only designated personnel—ideally the practice owner or a senior executive—should interact with agents.

In our raid, employees were questioned without Miranda warnings. Some shared information that was later used against me. One agent's interpretation of an innocent comment became a cornerstone of their case. It took months to untangle the lies from the truth.

## Legal Warfare

Searches are governed by Rule 41 of the Federal Rules of Criminal Procedure. (federalrulesofcriminalprocedure.org) Most warrants expire in 14 days. But the damage begins instantly. The DEA and OIG have additional tools—administrative subpoenas, inspection warrants—that are just as invasive.

Improperly executed warrants can lead to suppression of evidence. But this is a legal battle, not a street confrontation. If agents exceed their authority, don't resist. Let them finish. Then fight in court.

As the Supreme Court stated in U.S. v. Leon, "Reasonable minds may differ" on what constitutes probable cause. But if a warrant is granted based on misleading or reckless information, it can be challenged—and sometimes overturned.

## When the Fourth Meets the Fifth

Silence isn't just your right. It's your salvation. Even polite pleasantries can be turned into "statements." My brief exchange—just a name, a lawyer, and a request for clarification—became a false narrative.

Esformes was railroaded after agents reviewed privileged communications. Tennant was never charged but lost everything. I was lucky. But only because I had prepared, remained silent, and fought back.

## Stand Ready

That knock on the door isn't just about collecting evidence. It's a moment of truth. It tests your preparation, your discipline, your resolve.

If you're not ready, you'll be at their mercy. If you are ready, you may still suffer—but you'll survive.

In the end, this chapter isn't about fear. It's about foresight. The Fourth Amendment is not just an abstract right. It is your line in the sand. Protect it.

Be ready.

# CHAPTER 6

# The Agents of Judgement

---

*We want to make sure that this great system is what will keep us safe will also keep us free."*

— **(Attorney General Nash, Minority Report)**

## The Touch of Love

Throughout my life, I had dedicated myself to the path of public service. From my earliest memories, school was not just a duty—it was a sanctuary, a calling. I worked constantly—whether in classrooms, hospitals, or research labs—driven by a hunger to serve, to heal, to contribute something meaningful to the world. For many years, I poured myself entirely into this mission. Love, I thought, could wait.

But then, during a brief visit home to Syria amidst my medical residency, everything changed. I met someone who would alter the course of my life—my sister's best friend, a young physician named Douha Sabouni. She had attended the same medical school I did, and when we spoke, something clicked. I remember the moment clearly: she said "hello," and the world, just for an instant, felt like it had paused. It wasn't dramatic or cinematic—it was quiet, simple, and undeniable. We spent those two weeks getting to know each other, two overworked medical minds discovering shared dreams, shared ideals, and a shared sense of purpose.

Her parents knew mine—they respected my family's name and reputation—and though they were traditional in their values, they offered their blessing. There was one condition: if the relationship were to proceed, it must do so within the bounds of engagement. I had no hesitation. I asked, and she said yes.

Our plans, like so many others in that era, were disrupted by the tragic events of September 11, 2001. I had intended to return to Syria just weeks after the attack, but international air travel was suspended. I wouldn't see her again until December. When I did, we wasted no time. We were married in a civil ceremony, and in the summer of 2002, shortly after graduating medical school, Douha joined me in Virginia. We were finally together, husband and wife, immigrants, and physicians building a life together in a land still new to both of us.

In 2003, we welcomed our first son, Nader. Douha, even in the early days of motherhood, did not let go of her dreams. Between late-night feedings and early-morning study sessions, she began preparing for her U.S. medical licensing exams. Two years later, our second son, Nabeel, was born. Douha took and passed her boards and built a remarkable career in obstetrics and gynecology. She founded her own practice in Easton, Pennsylvania, and quickly became known for her compassionate care and technical brilliance. She embraced innovation with open arms, pioneering the use of robotic-assisted surgeries to treat gynecological disorders and introducing aesthetic medical treatments to support women suffering from urinary incontinence and post-menopausal issues.

What always impressed me—what continues to impress me—is not just Douha's medical skill, but her heart. Her patients are not cases or numbers to her. They are stories, hopes, and lives. And in her, they find someone who listens.

Together, we've built more than a home—we've built a shared vocation. Medicine is not just a job for us. It's a devotion. We've stood by each other through years of training, hardship, and joy. Through war, relocation, childbirth, career changes, and, in my case, prosecution. And still, we rise every morning with the same commitment: to care for others. In January 2013, we welcomed our third child Zayd.

Douha remains my life partner, not only in marriage, but in mission.

# The Agents of Judgment

"Pre-crime"—a term born in the dystopian imagination of science fiction writer Philip K. Dick—once seemed like a far-off fantasy. In his short story *The Minority Report*, Dick painted a chilling future where suspects were arrested before crimes were committed, based on predictions from a trio of psychics. When Steven Spielberg brought the tale to life in the 2002 film starring Tom Cruise, audiences were captivated and disturbed in equal measure. But what once belonged to the realm of fiction is now creeping into our lived reality. I referenced the problems with this area in a recent blog. (Rifai)

From *Blade Runner* to *A Scanner Darkly*, *Total Recall* to *The Man in the High Castle*, Dick's body of work has often foreshadowed unsettling truths about surveillance, control, and the erosion of individual freedom. His narratives have become cultural touchstones—haunting warnings wrapped in futuristic fiction. With each adaptation, the cautionary elements of his stories have grown increasingly prophetic, reflecting real-world anxieties about predictive policing, mass surveillance, and the dangers of an all-knowing state. Today, the machinery of the modern government employs sophisticated tools to monitor, predict, and prosecute—not unlike the mechanisms envisioned by Dick decades ago.

In this emerging surveillance state, the Office of Inspector General (OIG) stands as one of its most potent enforcement arms. Established in 1976, OIG was tasked with eliminating waste, fraud, and abuse in federal health programs such as Medicare and Medicaid. With approximately 1,600 personnel and oversight over more than 100 Department of Health & Human Services (HHS) programs, its reach is broad and invasive. Its central mission may be noble in name, but its methods often raise constitutional red flags, particularly in the world of healthcare, where clinical judgment is easily misconstrued as criminal deviation.

Enter the agents: Stephanie Yeager. Andrew J "AJ" Timonere. Police Officer Gretchen Kraemer. Austin Lastoskie. These are not just names etched in a report or scribbled in a warrant—they are instruments of the state, wielding extraordinary power with little oversight. Their entrance into a physician's life transforms ordinary clinics into crime scenes. Their questions are not invitations to dialogue but traps set within the narrow confines of presumption. When they arrive, the presumption of innocence is already crumbling.

When the agents arrive, they do not enter quietly. They bring with them the weight of the federal government, the authority of law, and the unspoken assumption that if they are knocking, you must have done something wrong. It is not a polite inquiry; it is the beginning of a narrative where you are no longer a professional, a healer, a scientist. You are a suspect.

I remember the day well. The morning light had barely crept into the windows when the sharp knock rattled the doorframe. There was no question of ignoring it. When I opened the door, there they stood: OIG agents in dark jackets, badges flashing like coins of condemnation. Behind them, a team moved with practiced coordination. They presented a search warrant with the clinical detachment of those who have done this many times before.

The lead agent introduced herself—Stephanie Yeager. Calm, methodical, polite in the way one might be when informing a man that his house is on fire. She informed me that this was part of an ongoing investigation. No accusations were made aloud, but the implication hovered thick in the air. I asked to see the warrant. She handed it over, and I scanned it, trying to suppress the rising tide of panic. It all looked official. Cold. Precise. Devastating.

I gave them the name and contact information of my attorney. I invoked my Fifth Amendment right and said that I would not answer questions. Still, they searched. Still, they gathered. Agent Andrew Temonere moved through the clinic with deliberate steps, collecting documents and devices with the efficiency of someone who knew exactly what he was looking for. I wanted to ask him what he thought he'd find—but I knew better than to speak.

Even silence can be twisted. Later in court, the agents claimed I had made statements—casual comments, offhand remarks—that painted me as guilty. But I had said nothing of substance. The record had become a fiction, built not from transcripts, but from memory, interpretation, assumption.

And this is the danger. When agents arrive, they do not come seeking truth. They come seeking confirmation. Their minds are made up. Every item seized is evidence. Every silence is guilt. Every word you do say, no matter how benign, is another thread in the noose.

So I stood silent. I watched. I made notes. And when they left, I called my attorney and began the long, arduous process of defending a life's work from the erasure of suspicion.

The agents will not remember your years of service. They will not weigh your intentions. They will not give you the benefit of the doubt. They will take what they can carry, and they will leave behind a crater. And then, they will write the story—unless you fight to tell your own.

## Rat in the Maze

Among the cluster of agents who entered my life during the investigation, none stood out quite like Austin Lastoskie. On the surface, he was calm, reserved, methodical—a man who asked questions with surgical precision and took notes with the detachment of someone assembling a machine. What I didn't realize at the time, and only learned much later, was that Agent Lastoskie wasn't just a field investigator—he was a trained behavioral analyst. This changed everything in hindsight. He hadn't come to gather facts; he had come to study *me*. To interpret my tone, my pauses, my posture. To sift every word through a psychological sieve designed to detect deception or guilt—even when none was present.

The realization struck me like a second interrogation. While I had assumed our exchanges were procedural, they were actually performative—tests of behavior against a template of presumed guilt. His questions weren't neutral probes; they were chess moves in a game I hadn't agreed to play. Understanding this retrospectively added another layer of disquiet to my experience. When your every gesture becomes data, every silence an admission, the very act of breathing under investigation becomes suspect. And the agent across the table isn't just watching you—he's profiling you.

# The Methodologies of Behavioral Analysis in Investigations

Behavioral analysis, particularly within law enforcement, draws upon interdisciplinary frameworks spanning psychology, criminology, neuroscience, and even linguistics. At its core, the methodology involves the systematic observation and interpretation of human behavior to assess intent, deception, or risk. While popularized by television dramas, real-world behavioral analysis is far more clinical and nuanced, relying less on intuition and more on structured indicators.

One widely used framework is the Behavioral Analysis Interview (BAI), a non-accusatory interview technique developed to assess truthfulness. The method involves establishing a behavioral baseline through innocuous questions and then monitoring deviations in verbal and non-verbal cues as sensitive subjects are introduced. Practitioners trained in BAI are taught to observe micro-expressions, shifts in posture, eye movement, speech rate, and even respiration patterns. According to Inbau, Reid, and Buckley, deviations from the baseline, when considered in clusters rather than in isolation, may indicate deception or withholding of information. (Inbau et al.)

Another cornerstone method is the use of Statement Validity Analysis (SVA), which evaluates written or verbal statements for internal consistency, contextual embedding, and sensory detail. SVA practitioners are trained to detect cues such as cognitive load, emotional leakage, or lack of spontaneity—all potential flags for coached or fabricated narratives.

The FBI's Behavioral Analysis Unit (BAU) pioneered the integration of psychological profiling into federal investigations. This includes the classification of behavior types, development of offender typologies, and use of risk matrices to predict escalation or recidivism. Today, this analytical ethos extends beyond profiling unknown offenders and is applied increasingly to "insider threat" detection, especially within healthcare, cybersecurity, and financial fraud cases. Behavioral analysis is not always overt; it is often part of silent assessments during interviews, surveillance, or even courtroom proceedings.

However, the effectiveness of behavioral analysis is not universally accepted. A 2016 review published in *Legal and Criminological Psychology* by Meissner et al. found that professional lie detectors—including law enforcement agents—often perform only marginally better than chance. Even experienced investigators may be susceptible to confirmation bias, interpreting ambiguous behavior in ways that support their existing suspicions. (Swanner et al.)

Moreover, a growing body of research suggests that behavioral indicators are culturally variable and deeply context-dependent. A person avoiding eye contact may be perceived as deceptive in Western settings but respectful in others. The danger lies in mistaking cultural or emotional responses for criminal cues.

When behavioral analysis is embedded within a legal context— particularly one involving healthcare professionals or immigrants unfamiliar with the American justice system—it can become a tool not of insight but of entrapment. The psychological stress of facing federal investigation alone can cause behavior that mimics deception: stammering, fidgeting, avoiding eye contact. Yet these reactions are as likely to reflect fear as guilt.

What's more, practitioners of behavioral analysis often operate with limited checks and balances. Unlike forensic evidence, which must meet evidentiary standards, behavioral assessments can be filed in reports without the subject's knowledge and without an opportunity for rebuttal. Once written down in an agent's notes, those impressions— however flawed—can shape the entire trajectory of a case.

## Exposing the Problem

Attorney Paul Hetznecker, a renowned constitutional law professor and civil rights advocate, has spent decades fighting this creeping erosion of civil liberties. His work has focused on challenging government overreach, particularly where due process and civil protections collide with the modern surveillance state. Hetznecker has argued forcefully that our society has become too comfortable with preemptive justice— where a person can be deemed guilty by an algorithm, flagged by a pattern, or condemned by the bias of an investigator. "Pre-crime," he says, "is no longer just a futuristic fantasy. It's the lived experience of countless Americans—judged not for what they've done, but for what the system fears they might do." (Hetznecker)

This shift is further complicated by the rise of data-driven behavioral analytics—technologies that claim to predict fraud or criminal behavior by identifying statistical anomalies in data. These systems comb through mountains of electronic medical records, billing histories, and prescription logs, flagging anyone who deviates from the norm. On the surface, it seems scientific. Objective. Impartial. But beneath that veneer lies a cascade of flawed logic. A 2022 study warned that data-driven fraud detection methods are prone to producing false positives. (Kumaraswamy et al.)

These systems do not interpret context, nuance, or clinical complexity. They do not understand that two physicians may approach patient care differently yet both ethically. Instead, they flag deviations, feed the alerts to investigators, and initiate scrutiny that can upend lives.

What follows next is one of the most dangerous psychological forces in any investigatory process: confirmation bias.

## Confirmation Bias: The Invisible Hand in Investigations

Confirmation bias is one of the most persistent and dangerous cognitive pitfalls in human reasoning, especially when it infiltrates legal and investigative processes. In essence, confirmation bias is the tendency to search for, interpret, and recall information in a way that confirms one's preexisting beliefs or hypotheses, while disregarding or undervaluing evidence that might contradict those beliefs. This psychological phenomenon has been widely documented across disciplines, from behavioral economics to cognitive science and law enforcement.

As early as the 1960s, researchers like Peter Wason identified how individuals selectively gather information that supports their assumptions, even in controlled laboratory settings (Explorable. com). In real-world settings, particularly those involving high-stakes investigations, the effects can be catastrophic. Confirmation bias affects us in all walks of life and is looked at in detail in a paper published in 1998. (Nickerson).

In law enforcement, confirmation bias often emerges once a suspect has been identified. Investigators may consciously or unconsciously shape the narrative to support that suspect's guilt. Neutral evidence is seen through a distorted lens, while contradictory evidence is dismissed or minimized. This tendency has been explored in legal psychology, particularly in the work of Dror and Charlton, who showed that forensic analysts were more likely to interpret ambiguous fingerprints as matches when told they came from a prime suspect. (Dror et al.)

The implications for healthcare fraud investigations are profound. When agencies like the Office of Inspector General (OIG) or the Drug Enforcement Administration (DEA) initiate probes into a physician's practice, the decision to investigate often stems from statistical anomalies or complaints—but the investigation itself is guided by human interpretation. Once suspicion is cast, every chart, prescription, or patient interaction can be reinterpreted through the lens of presumed guilt. Even compliance efforts may be viewed cynically as attempts to conceal wrongdoing.

This cascade of biased reasoning can lead to unjust prosecutions. The danger lies not in malice, but in method. Investigators may sincerely believe they are pursuing justice, but their reliance on flawed heuristics turns their inquiry into a self-fulfilling prophecy.

Reducing confirmation bias requires systemic changes. Blind reviews, taint teams, rigorous evidentiary standards, and independent oversight are tools that can help ensure fairness. Additionally, investigators should receive training not just in law and procedure, but in cognitive science, to better understand their own fallibility.

In a justice system that prizes due process and impartiality, acknowledging and mitigating confirmation bias isn't optional. It is essential. Because when guilt is assumed rather than proven, we don't just fail the accused—we fail the very principle of justice itself.

Once a physician is flagged, the investigative process shifts. Investigators, often unconsciously, begin looking not for the truth—

but for evidence that supports the flag. Every action, every chart entry, every administrative oversight becomes potential proof of guilt. This tendency has been well-documented in psychological literature. Confirmation bias is pervasive, especially in high-stakes decision-making. Investigators are human—they filter ambiguous evidence through their preexisting assumptions.

Officers are more likely to interpret evidence negatively if they believe a suspect to be guilty. (Meterko and Cooper) This isn't malice; it's cognitive wiring. But in the context of federal healthcare investigations, where the consequences are dire, it becomes catastrophic.

Confirmation bias warps the collection of evidence. Witness statements are shaped to fit the narrative. Innocuous conversations are reframed as conspiratorial. Physicians who speak to agents—hoping to clarify, to help—often only provide more fodder for suspicion. Their words are transcribed through the lens of guilt, their intentions irrelevant. And in court, the agent's notes—not the actual statements—carry the most weight.

## The Negative Halo Effect: When One Flaw Defines the Whole

In the theater of law enforcement and justice, perception often trumps reality. One of the most deceptive psychological phenomena that skews those perceptions—especially in high-stakes investigations—is the negative halo effect, also known as the "horn effect." It occurs when a single negative attribute or trait disproportionately influences how a person is judged overall, coloring neutral or even positive traits in a darker light.

Coined in social psychology by Edward Thorndike in 1920, the halo effect originally described how people assumed individuals with positive traits (like attractiveness or charisma) must also be intelligent or competent. The reverse—the negative halo—has equally powerful and damaging implications, especially when applied in contexts of power, judgment, and authority. (McCormick)

In criminal investigations, particularly in healthcare fraud or medical misconduct, this effect can lead agents, prosecutors, and jurors to see a physician's actions through a distorted lens. If a practitioner is alleged to have made a single billing error or has received even one patient complaint, that solitary mark can overshadow decades of ethical service, humanitarian work, or academic excellence. An untidy office becomes a "lack of oversight." A high volume of prescriptions becomes "reckless behavior." An assertive demeanor turns into "aggressiveness" or "noncompliance." One mark of suspicion becomes a total indictment of character.

Even simple things like the perceived attractiveness of an individual can affect how everything done by that person is viewed. Attractive defendants are often perceived more favorably, leading to more lenient sentences, whereas less attractive individuals may face harsher judgments. Also, if a suspect possesses a trait deemed socially undesirable, witnesses or investigators might unconsciously attribute additional negative qualities or guilt to that person, potentially compromising the objectivity of the investigation. (Noor et al.)

In legal and regulatory environments, the danger is compounded. Once investigators or prosecutors identify a physician as a potential wrongdoer, the human brain's natural inclination toward cognitive consistency takes over. As described by social psychologist Leon Festinger in his theory of cognitive dissonance, individuals will go to great lengths to align new information with their existing beliefs—even if it means distorting the facts. This creates a perfect storm: one red flag triggers the negative halo, and confirmation bias cements it.

The agent sees what they expect. The prosecutor builds a narrative around guilt. The jury feels the weight of suspicion before hearing the defense. In the case of healthcare professionals, years of altruistic service can be eclipsed by a single irregular billing code or a misinterpreted conversation with a patient. As legal scholar Barbara O'Brien noted in her work on cognitive bias in the courtroom, these distortions are rarely malicious but nearly always unconscious—and thus more dangerous. (O'Brien)

The negative halo effect also leads to "spillover bias" in the courtroom. Jurors who see a physician charged with fraud may unconsciously assume incompetence in other areas: poor bedside manner, negligence in diagnosis, or lack of concern for patient welfare.

This kind of character contamination is not just unjust—it actively undermines the presumption of innocence.

To mitigate the impact of the negative halo effect, legal systems must adopt safeguards. Judges should be vigilant in excluding prejudicial evidence unrelated to the charge at hand. Investigators must be trained in cognitive bias and encouraged to maintain objective records. Defense attorneys should educate juries about these psychological pitfalls and highlight the accused's full professional history, not just the cherry-picked negatives.

In a world where perception increasingly shapes legal reality, it is essential to ask: are we seeing the truth, or simply a shadow cast by one flaw? The negative halo effect turns complexity into caricature. Justice demands we see more.

## Presumption of Innocence?

These forces create a system where justice is not pursued but guilt is presumed. And once presumed, the machinery of enforcement is rarely stopped.

For the accused, this is a nightmare. The investigative spotlight doesn't just illuminate—it burns. It sears through reputations, careers, families. And often, the agents believe they are doing the right thing. They believe they are catching the bad guys. That belief—however sincere—is precisely what makes confirmation bias so insidious. Because it turns flawed assumptions into absolute truths. It turns due process into a performance. And it turns the innocent into targets.

The original press release regarding my prosecution, issued on November 14, 2022, and its updated version released on October 28, 2024, violate multiple sections of the United States Department of Justice Manual, including Sections 1-7.310, 1-7.400, 1-7.500, 1-7.610, and 1-7.710. Notably, both versions of the press release failed to include the standard disclaimer: *"The charge is merely an accusation, and the defendant is presumed innocent until proven guilty."*

By omitting this critical disclaimer, the Government infringed upon my due process rights, specifically the presumption of innocence. This omission is particularly troubling given that in the twenty press releases preceding my case, all defendants were granted this fundamental protection through the inclusion of the disclaimer. Furthermore, in twenty additional press releases published after mine, the same presumption of innocence was consistently afforded to all other defendants.

Only Dr. Rifai—a Muslim defendant of Middle Eastern descent—was denied this essential safeguard.

The Government bears full responsibility for all communications to the media. Section 1-7.310 of the Justice Manual states: *"Each of the 93 United States Attorneys will exercise discretion and sound judgment, consistent with this Policy, as to matters affecting their own district... The United States Attorney has responsibility for all matters involving the local media."*

It is neither sound judgment nor consistent with Department policy to deprive me of my due process rights and the presumption of innocence. In doing so, the United States demonstrated a serious lapse in discretion and exhibited what can only be described as "moral obliquity," indicating that this prosecution was vexatious and pursued in bad faith.

This isn't just about surveillance. It's about storytelling. Because once the system decides you're the villain, it starts writing your story. And you—the protagonist of your own life—are silenced, reduced to a case number, a data point, a defendant.

We must ask ourselves: Can there be justice when the script is written before the facts are gathered? What hope does truth have when those tasked with uncovering it arrive with conclusions already drawn?

This chapter is not merely a warning—it is a plea. A call to remain vigilant in the face of creeping authoritarianism dressed in the language of efficiency and safety. It is a reminder that in the age of algorithms, surveillance, and pre-judgment, justice must be fought for—not assumed.

Innocence must not only be proven. It must be defended from the very first knock at the door. Because when the agents arrive, they bring with them more than questions. They bring a story. And unless you fight to reclaim it, it won't be yours to tell.

# CHAPTER 7

# When the Watchdog Barks at the Innocent

---

*"Terror is nothing but prompt, severe, inflexible justice."*

— Maximilien Robespierre

## Time at the National Institute of Mental Health; United States Public Health Service

Near the end of my residency, I had the opportunity to present a pioneering research paper at the American Psychiatric Association conference. After my presentation, I was approached by the Clinical Director of the National Institute of Mental Health (NIMH) in Bethesda, Maryland. Impressed by my work, he extended an offer for a two-year assignment under the Department of Health and Human Services and the United States Public Health Service. Though I had offers from private practices offering four to five times the salary, I chose instead to serve the public health mission of my new homeland. It was a decision guided not by compensation, but by a deeper calling—a belief that public service should prevail over personal financial gain.

The position at NIMH marked a high point in my early career. It provided me with the extraordinary opportunity to collaborate with some of the country's most distinguished medical minds, including Dr.

Anthony Fauci. Our offices and laboratories were located on the same floor of the NIH Clinical Center, and our professional relationship grew into a personal friendship. I had the chance to present several cases to Dr. Fauci, exploring the psychiatric dimensions of infectious diseases. This collaboration not only broadened my understanding of the intersection between psychiatry and immunology but also prepared me—years in advance—for the public health challenges that would emerge during the COVID-19 pandemic.

My time at NIMH also placed me at the forefront of innovative psychiatric research. I participated in early studies exploring the use of ketamine, an anesthetic, as a potential treatment for severe depression. The results were promising, and even now, years later, I continue to use ketamine therapeutically for patients with treatment-resistant psychiatric conditions. I was also involved in groundbreaking work investigating the effects of magnetic stimulation on the brain. That research contributed to what would later become FDA-approved treatments for major depressive disorders, such as Transcranial Magnetic Stimulation (TMS). These experiences reinforced my commitment to scientific advancement rooted in real-world clinical impact.

As my tenure at NIH came to a close, I was recruited by Lehigh Valley Hospital and Health Network in Bethlehem, Pennsylvania. In 2006, I assumed a senior leadership role as Head of the Inpatient Unit and Psychiatric Emergency Services. This transition allowed me to shift from research to direct community care—developing and implementing innovative service models that addressed long standing gaps in psychiatric treatment. My focus became clear: to bring high-quality, cutting-edge care to the patients who needed it most, regardless of background or circumstance.

The thread running through all these chapters of my professional life is simple yet enduring: a belief in service over status, innovation over inertia, and compassion over convenience. Whether in the halls of NIH or on the front lines of a community hospital, that mission has remained constant.

# The Terror

Robespierre's infamous justification of revolutionary terror is often read as an artifact of history, a relic of a time when the guillotine symbolized moral clarity enforced through violence. But the sentiment endures in subtler forms. In this chapter, we encounter its modern equivalent—not in the execution square, but in the bureaucratic corridors of federal enforcement. Today, the tools are different: search warrants, spreadsheets, sealed indictments. But the principle remains disturbingly familiar—justice that is "prompt, severe, inflexible" often forgets to ask if it is also just.

# Modern Echoes of Robespierre's Justice: Presumption Over Proof

Robespierre's chilling assertion finds unsettling resonance in modern legal practices where the machinery of justice often acts in anticipation, rather than in response, to actual wrongdoing. One such example is the use of material witness statutes in terrorism-related cases. Following 9/11, dozens of individuals were detained not for crimes committed, but for their perceived future value to prosecutions. These detentions—often without formal charges—were justified under the guise of national security. Yet in many cases, the evidence was scant, and the accusations were rooted more in ethnic profiling or circumstantial associations than in concrete wrongdoing. One notable case was that of Abdullah al-Kidd, an American citizen and former University of Idaho football player. (ACLU) He was arrested and held for over two weeks under a material witness warrant, despite never being charged with a crime. The government claimed he was needed to testify in another case, but no testimony was ever requested. His detention was later ruled as an abuse of power, and al-Kidd spent years seeking legal redress. Here, the state exercised its power swiftly and severely, privileging control over accuracy—Robespierre's "inflexible justice" applied in peacetime law.

Another instance is the aggressive use of civil asset forfeiture laws, where property is seized based on suspicion of involvement in criminal activity, even when the owner has not been charged with a crime. In jurisdictions across the United States, law enforcement agencies have confiscated homes, cars, and bank accounts with minimal due process, often forcing innocent people into protracted legal battles to reclaim their property. Consider the case of Tyson Timbs, a recovering addict from Indiana who used his father's life insurance money to purchase a Land Rover. (Constitutional Accountability Center) After being convicted of a drug-related offense, the state seized his vehicle—valued at more than four times the maximum monetary fine for his crime—under civil forfeiture. Timbs took his case all the way to the U.S. Supreme Court, which ruled in his favor, determining that the seizure was grossly disproportionate and violated the Eighth Amendment. This case underscores the danger of punishment without proportionality and highlights how the burden can unjustly shift to the citizen to prove innocence. It is a policy deeply reminiscent of Robespierre's paradigm—where speed and certainty override the safeguards of investigation and trial.

Annie Lee Moss became a symbol of the dangers of presumed guilt during the height of the McCarthy era. (Aloe and Weinberg) A quiet, middle-aged African American woman working as a communications clerk at the Pentagon, Moss was accused of being a member of the Communist Party based on her name appearing on a list provided by an informant. The evidence was thin—there was confusion about whether it was even the same Annie Moss—and she was given no opportunity to confront her accuser or examine the source of the allegations before being suspended from her position.

When she finally appeared before Senator Joseph McCarthy's committee in 1954, her composed demeanor and professed patriotism cast doubt on the accusations. Notably, her case gained public attention when journalist Edward R. Murrow spotlighted her plight on national television, exposing the committee's overreach and lack of credible evidence. Though she was ultimately reinstated and later exonerated, the ordeal left her reputation bruised. Moss's case stands as a sobering reminder that in times of political fear, even the most unassuming individuals can become targets of a justice system warped by presumption rather than proof.

Finally, we have my area—healthcare fraud investigations where data anomalies are treated as definitive indicators of criminal intent. Algorithms flag providers based on statistical outliers, triggering audits, suspensions, or even indictments with little context considered. In such cases, medical professionals are presumed guilty for deviating from a bureaucratic norm, regardless of clinical necessity or patient complexity. Prosecutorial narratives are often built before any interviews occur. The result is a justice process inverted—where judgment precedes inquiry, and defense becomes the burden of the accused. This modern "prompt justice" sacrifices nuance for numbers, punishing professionals not for crimes committed, but for fitting a suspicious profile.

This form of injustice is widespread. So much so that it finds expression in art and literature. Don't read the next two paragraphs if you haven't read or seen the works mentioned—I hate spoilers.

John Steinbeck's *Of Mice and Men* offers a haunting portrayal of presumed guilt through the character of Lennie Small—a gentle man whose mental disability makes him vulnerable to misunderstanding and fear. When Lennie unintentionally kills a woman, the community does not wait for facts, context, or explanation. He is hunted down as a threat, his guilt presumed by virtue of his difference and the panic it evokes. Like so many others in history and modern justice, Lennie's fate is sealed not by proof, but by fear—a mirror of how easily suspicion can eclipse truth.

In The Fugitive (1993), starring Harrison Ford and Tommy Lee Jones, Dr. Richard Kimble is wrongfully convicted of murdering his wife, despite a lack of solid evidence. He escapes custody and goes on the run—not only to clear his name, but to uncover the real killer. The justice system, meanwhile, operates under the assumption of his guilt, relentlessly pursuing him without entertaining the possibility of error. The film dramatizes the peril of institutional certainty, echoing how narratives of guilt can become self-reinforcing, regardless of the truth. Like other stories of wrongful accusation, *The Fugitive* reminds us that the presumption of guilt often leaves little room for actual justice.

This chapter is the lived echo of this ideology. It details how a healthcare professional dedicated to service became a target of data-driven assumptions, and how systems meant to protect the vulnerable instead turned on those who serve them.

When suspicion becomes policy, when algorithms replace inquiry, and when punishment precedes proof, we are no longer safeguarding justice—we are staging it. Here, in this story, terror wears a badge and holds a subpoena. And just like in Robespierre's vision, it calls itself virtue.

## From Theory to Reality: A Case Study in Pre-Crime Healthcare Enforcement

The previous chapter examined the structural biases, cognitive distortions, and surveillance-driven culture that now permeate federal healthcare investigations. Concepts such as confirmation bias, the negative halo effect, and the misuse of behavioral analysis were explored not in abstraction, but as the emerging norm in oversight systems once built to protect. Now, we turn from theory to lived experience.

What follows is not hypothetical. It is not an imaginative extension of science fiction, nor a philosophical exercise in civil liberties. This is the story of what happens when a physician becomes the subject of a flawed algorithm, when data is stripped from clinical context, and when enforcement agents pursue prosecution over understanding. It is the human cost of the systems described in Chapter 6. It is also a meditation on what we risk losing—not only justice, but compassion, nuance, and trust in the institutions meant to protect us.

I am a caring physician, an immigrant, and an entrepreneur who fled war-torn Aleppo, Syria, to dedicate my life to healing. I built clinics in underserved communities, pioneered telepsychiatry before it became mainstream, and treated patients who had nowhere else to go. My ethos was rooted in service, resilience, and equity. But in 2019, everything I had built came under siege—triggered by a federal investigation led by people who never spoke with me, never saw my practice, and never attempted to understand the context in which I worked. One name stood out among them: Special Agent Stephanie Yeager of the Office of Inspector General for the Department of Health and Human Services (OIG-HHS).

The Office of the Inspector General was born from the ashes of public mistrust. Instituted by Congress through the Inspector General Act of 1978, it was designed to serve as an internal watchdog—rooting out fraud, waste, and abuse in federal agencies. In theory, it was a noble structure: impartial, transparent, and accountable. But over time, that vision gave way to something more opaque. Today, the OIG-HHS is not simply an audit body—it is an enforcement engine, often operating with little external oversight and substantial prosecutorial influence. With over 1,600 employees and sweeping authority, its reach is vast, and its judgment, at times, dangerously unchecked.

During the tenure of Daniel Levinson, who led the office from 2004 to 2019, the agency pivoted dramatically from evaluative oversight to aggressive enforcement. On paper, the metrics were staggering—$25 billion in recoveries in a single year. (OIG) But numbers can be deceiving. For healthcare professionals, especially those in complex specialties like psychiatry, the enforcement-first approach became a sword of Damocles. Routine billing mistakes, nuanced documentation discrepancies, or even high volumes of care for severely ill patients began to trigger audits, raids, and criminal referrals. What should have been peer-reviewed evaluations were increasingly reinterpreted as fraud indicators.

These evolving policies led to a cultural transformation inside the OIG—where once there was reflection, now there was reactivity. Investigators began seeing themselves less as neutral evaluators and more as hunters. Their work became defined not by clinical insight, but by how many charges they could build and how large their recoveries were. The deeper ethics of care, so central to medicine, were discarded in favor of prosecutorial ambition.

That transformation was more than procedural. It changed the very character of interactions between healthcare providers and federal authorities. Where once dialogue and correction were possible, there was now silence and suspicion. Where a phone call or clarification would once have sufficed, there now came subpoenas and raids.

Stephanie Yeager began her OIG career in the Office of Evaluation and Inspections (OEI). Her focus was technical: reports on Medicare drug pricing discrepancies, inconsistencies among Medicare Administrative Contractors, and patterns in billing data. Reports such as OEI-03-13-00450 (Murrin) and OEI-03-11-00640 (Levinson) had the veneer of objectivity. But their methodology—data-driven yet context-agnostic—created models that rarely accounted for the human stories embedded in care. These reports, rather than guiding best practices, became tools used to flag outliers as fraudsters. Outliers not because of criminal intent, but because they served sicker patients or used new, evolving technologies to meet unmet needs.

She was neither a clinician nor a policy expert. But in 2015, after completing a brief stint at the federal law enforcement training center, Yeager joined the OIG's enforcement division. Within just a couple of years, she was supervising raids, directing subpoenas, and interpreting spreadsheets as legal evidence. This transition—from analyst to law enforcement—should have triggered ethical and procedural guardrails. Instead, it became the norm. Investigators like Yeager carried the power of the state with the perspective of data analysts and the tunnel vision of performance metrics.

Her record before joining the enforcement team was already fraught. In a 2012 report she led (OEI-03-12-00550) (Levinson), the Centers for Medicare & Medicaid Services (CMS) rejected her interpretation of payment rules. CMS explicitly stated: "CMS does not concur with this recommendation." (Levinson) That should have raised concerns. Instead, her career advanced. Her inclination to read noncompliance into every irregularity became an asset.

That same inclination brought her to my door.

On December 13, 2021, federal agents executed a search of my clinics in Easton, Stroudsburg, and Palmerton. No warning. No prior dialogue. Agents ignored Public Health Emergency protocols that the very Department of Health and Human Services was actively promoting. Patients were turned away mid-session. Long-time staff stood frozen in disbelief. And yet, behind the spectacle was not a criminal network or organized deception—it was a billing model misunderstood, a patient population underserved, and a care delivery model misread through the sterile lens of algorithms.

The government alleged overutilization. But in mental health—particularly with complex, comorbid, or treatment-resistant patients—high utilization is often synonymous with ethical care. The very patients least likely to access services are the ones who require the most. What the agents flagged as excessive was, in fact, deliberate, evidence-based, and medically documented care. But context had been excised. In its place stood columns and rows of data, interpreted without expertise in psychiatry, addiction, or trauma.

The raid didn't just disrupt my practice—it ruptured something deeper. The implicit social contract between physician and patient, between professional and regulator, between healer and institution, was torn. My patients, many of whom struggled with trust to begin with, were retraumatized. My staff, loyal and compassionate, became wary. And I, who had spent decades building bridges, found myself branded as a suspect.

It also destabilized a model of care designed precisely for the vulnerable. Our clinics were purpose-built to serve those most often overlooked—immigrants, trauma survivors, individuals with co-occurring disorders. The very structure of our operation, including high-touch follow-up and intensive documentation, had always been a strength. Under investigation, it became our weakness. What was once seen as care became painted as overuse. What was once lauded as innovation was now suspect.

Once the indictment dropped, the consequences were immediate and brutal. Insurance contracts vanished overnight. Professional referrals dried up. Staff morale plummeted. And though the presumption of innocence remained enshrined in legal theory, in practical terms, I had already been convicted. The emotional toll was immense. The financial toll, devastating. The reputational damage was incalculable.

Years passed. The legal process dragged on. But eventually, the case began to collapse—not due to procedural technicalities, but because the evidence, when properly examined, did not support the allegations. During trial, Yeager and her colleague, Special Agent Andrew "AJ"

Timonere, testified. Under cross-examination by constitutional law expert Paul Hetznecker, their composure eroded. Contradictions surfaced. Their investigative assumptions—never validated by clinical experts—were exposed. Neither agent had engaged in a cost analysis, nor consulted mental health practitioners. What they had done was interpret deviation as deception.

Timonere, though a Certified Fraud Examiner and former forensic accountant for the FBI, admitted on the stand that he had conducted no financial analysis of my practice's operations. Millions were spent on this investigation—on manpower, legal proceedings, and institutional resources—yet not one hour was spent reviewing the actual cost structure of my clinic. The metrics that mattered were indictments and headlines—not truth.

Their unraveling in court was not theatrical—it was inevitable. In a system that prioritizes presumption over proof, it takes only one principled cross-examination to reveal how thin the scaffolding truly is. They were "Hetzneckered"—undone not by tricks, but by facts.

But the damage had already been done.

Further complicating the government's case was the involvement of Officer Gretchen Kraemer, an undercover officer who had posed as a patient. When the time came to testify, her recollections were vague, and recordings were missing. She admitted key portions of the surveillance—on which the case heavily relied—had been lost or were never recorded properly. Discrepancies between her narrative and the clinical record became too significant to ignore. Even the DEA's attempt to revoke my license based on this interaction was dismissed by an Administrative Law Judge. But the shadows these efforts cast cannot be erased.

My story is not an isolated event. It is emblematic of a systemic failure to distinguish between vigilance and overreach, between accountability and punishment. The OIG was never meant to function as a law enforcement agency in its own right. Yet today, its agents operate with powers often indistinguishable from prosecutors, and sometimes, with even fewer checks.

This convergence of data, suspicion, and unchecked enforcement has built a machine that no longer pauses to reflect. It rewards speed, aggression, and statistical wins. But oversight without empathy, and justice without nuance, breeds not trust—but terror.

If we are to restore integrity to this system, meaningful reform must follow. We must:

1. **Re-establish boundaries between analysis and enforcement.** The firewall between evaluation and prosecution must be restored and rigorously maintained.

2. **Implement clinical peer review in all medical fraud cases.** Data must not supersede medical judgment without professional vetting.

3. **Guarantee due process in fact and form.** Practitioners must be given a genuine opportunity to correct misunderstandings before facing punitive action.

4. **Measure agents by the quality of justice, not quantity of indictments.** Metrics should reflect outcomes, integrity, and proportionality—not raw enforcement figures.

5. **Include cultural competence and trauma-informed training for investigators.** A system blind to human diversity and suffering cannot deliver fair outcomes.

6. **Create pathways for restorative correction over punitive destruction.** Before indictments, there must be avenues for clarification, restitution, and resolution.

7. **Increase transparency around investigative protocols.** Public understanding of how investigations are launched and conducted is essential for accountability.

8. **Establish an independent review body to monitor the OIG.** Oversight of the overseers is critical to restoring public trust.

Healing cannot begin with apologies alone. It must begin with accountability. And accountability must begin with us—the professionals, the lawmakers, and the public—demanding that oversight once again be rooted in fairness, not fear.

The systems we create reflect our values. If those systems reduce professionals to case numbers, and justice to algorithms, we have lost our moral compass. But if we listen, if we reform, if we lead with humility, we can reclaim what has been lost.

Let Chapter 7 stand not only as a testimony, but as a turning point. The systems described in Chapter 6 were never meant to be permanent. We have the power to reimagine them—more ethical, more accurate, more human.

Because in the end, justice is not a formula. It is a choice.

# CHAPTER 8

# The Lawyers

---

*"Lawyers are from Mars, doctors are from Venus."*

— James Owen Drife, MD, FACOG, Professor of Obstetrics
and Gynecology

## Innovation in Telehealth and the Commitment to Service

Following my training at the National Institute of Mental Health, where cutting-edge research and forward-thinking practice defined every day, I brought that spirit of innovation to my next chapter in the Lehigh Valley, Pennsylvania. At a time when telemedicine was still an emerging concept—long before its widespread acceptance—I implemented one of the region's first telehealth psychiatric services. In 2007, using basic video conferencing technology, I provided psychiatric consultations to patients in rural and underserved parts of Pennsylvania. These communities, often overlooked in discussions of mental health access, were in desperate need of continuity in care. Telehealth allowed us to bridge that gap—quietly, effectively, and with dignity.

During this period, Douha had completed her medical exams and began her residency in Obstetrics and Gynecology at St. Joseph's Hospital in Paterson, New Jersey, about an hour from our home. Her schedule was rigorous—residency in any specialty is grueling, but OBGYN brings a particular intensity. Night calls, early-morning shifts, and constant readiness were her norm. While she committed herself fully to her training, I balanced a demanding clinical load with the primary responsibilities of raising our children. Our days began before sunrise—dropping off the children at daycare at six a.m. sharp, then heading directly into inpatient rounds at the psychiatric unit. It was a rhythm built on dedication and shared sacrifice.

Our decision to settle in the Lehigh Valley was more than practical; it was deeply symbolic. Syria, our homeland, is a land of inventors and artisans. Cities like Aleppo and Damascus are among the oldest continuously inhabited cities on Earth, rich with history and innovation. That spirit lives in Syrians across the world. Steve Jobs, whose father was Syrian, once named Apple's intelligent assistant "Siri" in homage to his heritage. Comedian Jerry Seinfeld often credited his Syrian grandmother's storytelling and humor for shaping his worldview. In this lineage of resilience and imagination, Douha and I found pride and purpose.

We bought a modest home in the Lehigh Valley, hoping to grow our roots in this quiet corner of America. Almost immediately after our purchase, the real estate market collapsed. For more than a decade, the value of our home remained below the mortgage balance. But we continued our payments—not out of financial obligation alone, but because we believed in building a life with integrity. Through recessions, early-morning routines, and professional hurdles, we stayed the course.

Douha completed her residency and began practicing as an attending physician in obstetrics and gynecology, serving women and families with the same commitment she had carried through her training. I continued my work with Lehigh Valley Health Network until 2011, deepening my clinical practice while continuing to explore innovative ways to make care more accessible.

Looking back, these were not just years of endurance. They were years of purpose. They were about more than surviving a housing crash or managing a hectic schedule. They were about living out the values we brought from Syria—tenacity, innovation, service—and embedding them in the American story we were working to build.

# Choosing Counsel

In the complex and often unfamiliar environment of the criminal justice system, particularly at the federal level, the selection of legal counsel is not simply a matter of hiring a service provider—it is a strategic decision that can determine the outcome of the case and the course of the physician's professional and personal life. For doctors facing serious allegations such as healthcare fraud, violations of the Controlled Substances Act, or related federal crimes, the stakes are extremely high: a conviction could result in imprisonment, revocation of medical licensure, exclusion from federal healthcare programs like Medicare and Medicaid, significant financial penalties, and permanent reputational harm.

Choosing an attorney under these circumstances requires careful analysis, not only of credentials but also of actual litigation experience, particularly in federal courts. Many physicians, unfamiliar with the legal system, may be tempted to choose an attorney based on superficial factors—such as a high ranking on Google, an aesthetically pleasing website, or a claim of a personal connection to prosecutors or judges. However, these should not be the primary considerations. Instead, the focus must be on objective, verifiable evidence of competence in handling healthcare-related federal criminal matters. This includes experience in cases involving the False Claims Act, anti-kickback statute violations, unlawful prescribing, billing fraud, or DEA registration violations.

A critical first step is to examine whether the attorney has a track record of taking healthcare-related cases to trial—not simply negotiating plea agreements. Physicians should inquire about how many healthcare fraud or controlled substances cases the attorney has handled, how many of those went to trial, and what the outcomes were. This information is not always readily available on law firm websites, but it can often be found through PACER (Public Access to Court Electronic Records), which contains filings and decisions in federal court cases. A defendant can look up an attorney's name in PACER to see the nature and number of cases they've worked on, providing valuable insight into the attorney's experience and credibility.

Additionally, board certifications, such as those from the National Board of Trial Advocacy (NBTA), and memberships in relevant associations like the National Association of Criminal Defense Lawyers (NACDL) or the American Health Law Association (AHLA), may indicate a commitment to professional standards, but these are not substitutes for direct experience in federal criminal healthcare litigation. Physicians should ask for references—past clients or co-counsel—and may even request a consultation to discuss a potential strategy, not just logistics or pricing.

Another important criterion is the attorney's understanding of the medical profession itself. While a lawyer cannot be expected to have a clinical background, those who have represented doctors and healthcare entities extensively will often have a working knowledge of medical billing practices, clinical workflows, peer review processes, and the role of regulatory bodies such as the DEA, CMS, and state medical boards. Attorneys who regularly work with healthcare professionals are more likely to be able to identify when conduct that seems questionable on the surface is actually compliant with medical standards or customary practice. This insight is critical to crafting an effective defense.

Communication style and responsiveness are also key considerations. In high-stakes criminal matters, delays in communication can cost opportunities to mitigate risk, respond to subpoenas or pretrial motions, or submit documentation to avoid escalation of charges. Physicians should assess whether the attorney is accessible, clear in their explanations, and proactive in outlining the next steps. During the consultation, attention should be paid to whether the attorney is listening carefully and asking relevant, probing questions—or simply offering reassurances without specific information.

Fee structure is another area where physicians must be cautious. Some lawyers offer flat-fee arrangements that may seem cost-effective, but these can sometimes incentivize early resolution by plea rather than taking the time to prepare for trial. Others charge hourly and provide detailed invoices for each aspect of case preparation. Understanding how an attorney charges and how those fees align with the expected scope of the case—from investigation through potential trial—is critical to ensuring you receive adequate representation.

Finally, the physician should feel confident that the attorney is willing and able to challenge the government's case—not merely guide them through a plea. Prosecutors often present evidence in a manner designed to overwhelm or intimidate. A good defense attorney must be able to critically evaluate discovery material, bring in expert witnesses, file motions to exclude prejudicial evidence, and develop a robust theory of defense.

In sum, the process of selecting an attorney for a federal criminal case involving a physician is not about finding the most pleasant or well-advertised representative. It is about identifying someone who is both strategically capable and substantively experienced in healthcare law and federal litigation. The attorney must be well-versed in the intersection of medicine, regulation, and criminal law, and they must have demonstrated the willingness to fight vigorously, intelligently, and ethically on behalf of clients in similar positions.

## The Crucible of Connection

Embarking on this journey requires more than finding a legal representative with a polished demeanor or a reassuring smile. The quest is for an advocate who embodies the duality of mentor and challenger—someone unafraid to probe deeply, question relentlessly, and unearth the bedrock of truth beneath layers of accusation. This dynamic mirrors the relationship between a sculptor and marble; only through vigorous chiseling does the masterpiece emerge. Transparency becomes the chisel in this analogy. Whether you stand steadfast in your innocence, acknowledge shades of culpability, or bear the weight of guilt, unvarnished honesty with your attorney is the cornerstone upon which your defense is built.

In the labyrinthine corridors of federal indictments, where routine medical decisions are often painted with the brush of criminality, your attorney must be the torchbearer illuminating the path to justice. They should possess the acumen to dissect the prosecution's narrative, challenging each assertion with surgical precision. An admission of "Yes, I did this," met with the attorney's discerning "But does this constitute a crime?" can pivot the case from condemnation to exoneration.

## Navigating the Maze: Selecting Your Legal Champion

The odyssey of selecting legal counsel is fraught with potential missteps and mirages. In an era where digital landscapes are dotted with alluring advertisements and self-aggrandizing proclamations, the discerning seeker must look beyond the veneer. Personal referrals, the whispered endorsements of trusted confidants, often lead to treasures hidden beneath the surface. A federal public defender, though sometimes overlooked, may possess a trove of experience and a track record of tangible successes that outshine their private counterparts.

Seek an attorney whose tenacity is matched by their courtroom prowess, whose experience is not just measured in years but in the depth and breadth of trials undertaken. However, be mindful that the pool of attorneys seasoned in federal criminal trials is receding, much like a shoreline eroded by the relentless tides of plea bargains and settlements. The statistics are sobering: from approximately 3,800 federal criminal trials in 2010 to fewer than 1,750 in 2022. This decline not only affects defense attorneys but also the prosecutors and judges, leading to a collective atrophy in trial experience.

## The Alchemy of Experience and Specialization

The legal arena is not a monolith; it is a mosaic of specialties and nuances. Thus, securing an attorney with a proven record of trial victories, particularly in the realms of healthcare fraud and controlled substances, is paramount. Even if an attorney's portfolio lacks a specific focus on healthcare, this gap can be bridged by enlisting a cadre of healthcare investigators.

In my odyssey, I discovered such a synergy in Pennsylvania with Paul Hetznecker, a legal artisan whose craftsmanship in defense strategies is unparalleled. To fortify our arsenal, we enlisted Ronald Chapman II, Esq., LLM, whose expertise in healthcare law acted as the keystone in our arch of defense. Chapman's integration of the Chapman Consulting Group infused our strategy with a depth of investigative prowess that proved invaluable.

## *Paul Hetznecker: The Advocate*

Paul Hetznecker's narrative deviates from the archetypal legal lineage. His genesis was not in the hallowed halls of long standing legal dynasties but in the nurturing embrace of a family devoted to community and mental health. His father, Dr. William "Bill" Hetznecker, was a luminary in community psychiatry, whose work illuminated the path for countless underserved children and families in Philadelphia. His mother, Noreen, was a beacon of advocacy and education, whose resilience in the face of blindness did not dim her contributions but rather cast them in a more inspiring light.

Paul's formative years were steeped in an environment where questioning the status quo was not just encouraged but expected. This intellectual ferment led him to the University of Massachusetts Amherst, where he immersed himself in the study of constitutional law and civil rights. His journey continued at Temple Law School, where he honed his skills in the crucible of mock trials and fervent debates.

As a public defender, Paul carved a niche representing those marginalized and maligned, taking on cases that others deemed unwinnable. His defense of a paramedic wrongfully arrested during the 2016 Democratic National Convention is emblematic of his commitment to justice. The case ascended to the Third Circuit, where Paul's advocacy not only secured his client's exoneration but also reinforced the principles of accountability within federal law enforcement agencies.

## *Ronald Chapman II: The Strategist*

Ronald Chapman II's trajectory is a tapestry woven with threads of military discipline, prosecutorial insight, and a profound commitment to justice. As a former military prosecutor and Marine Corps veteran,

Chapman's approach to defense is both strategic and unyielding. His attainment of a Master of Laws in Healthcare Law is not merely an academic accolade but a testament to his dedication to mastering the complexities of healthcare litigation.

One illustrative case in Chapman's repertoire involved defending a urologist with affiliations to esteemed institutions like Johns Hopkins and the Mayo Clinic. Accused of operating multiple pill mills, the physician faced a maelstrom of legal peril. Through a trial that unfolded over a grueling month, Chapman's defense was a masterclass in dismantling the prosecution's edifice, brick by brick. The culmination was not only an acquittal but also a subsequent civil triumph that compelled the government to return $6 million seized assets, a David-and-Goliath victory in the modern legal arena.

Beyond the courtroom, Chapman's voice resonates in academic halls and professional symposiums. His lectures at Harvard, presentations in Washington D.C., and engagements with various state medical societies underscore his role as both a thought leader and a sentinel in the field of healthcare law. His adept navigation of interactions with federal agencies—the DOJ, DEA, FBI, OIG-HHS, and FDA—further cements his reputation as a formidable advocate for healthcare professionals under scrutiny.

## The Synergy of Collaboration

The confluence of Paul Hetznecker's local acumen and Ron Chapman II's specialized expertise, augmented by the investigative might of the Chapman Consulting Group, forged a defense team that was both dynamic and resilient. This collaboration was not serendipitous but the result of deliberate and discerning selection—a process I wish to illuminate for others traversing similar tribulations.

# The Art and Science of Legal Defense

In the intricate dance of legal defense, the attorney must be both artist and scientist—crafting narratives that resonate with human emotion while meticulously deconstructing the prosecution's arguments.

This duality demands a profound understanding of the client's circumstances, motivations, and the nuanced details of the case. It is a symphony of legal knowledge, psychological insight, and strategic execution, with the defense attorney conducting a delicate orchestra of facts, law, and human empathy. Paul Hetznecker, in my case, was precisely that kind of maestro. His cross-examinations were not mere procedures; they were performances—methodical, intense, and often devastating to the prosecution's case. He exposed contradictions like a jeweler revealing flaws in a seemingly perfect diamond, unraveling expert testimonies, discrediting hostile witnesses, and leaving the jury no option but to doubt.

Each day in court felt like watching a master at work—Paul pacing steadily, voice measured yet commanding, eyes scanning the courtroom with the vigilance of a hawk. He listened more than he spoke, and when he spoke, it was with the gravity of a man who understood that every word could shift the scales of justice. He carried within him the legacy of his parents—a father who healed minds and a mother who, despite losing her sight, helped others see. Their influence lived on in Paul's tireless defense of those marginalized by the system.

The courtroom was not the only place where Paul's brilliance shone. His scholarly inclinations found an outlet when he became an adjunct professor at Arcadia University, teaching courses on civil rights and surveillance. His lectures were said to be passionate, wide-ranging, and grounded in real-world experience. He did not merely teach law— he illuminated its power, its pitfalls, and its potential for redemption.

## The Psychological Battlefield

It cannot be overstated: the psychological toll of being a physician accused of federal crimes is profound. It tears through every layer of identity, shredding reputations and rupturing families. During this time, your attorney becomes not just a legal guide, but a surrogate anchor—a stabilizing force in the chaos. A defense lawyer must understand the emotional and mental state of a healthcare professional whose world has been upended. This is why Paul's familiarity with psychiatry, shaped by his family background, became more than an intellectual asset—

it was a source of human understanding, empathy, and composure in the storm.

Paul knew when to push, when to pull, and when to simply stand beside me in silence. That intuition is rare. It's what made his advice so valuable and his presence so reassuring. When he told me not to speak to federal agents under any circumstances, I listened. That single piece of advice proved pivotal: the government never had a statement from me to twist or weaponize. Silence became my shield. Paul had handed it to me.

# On Red Flags and Warnings

When selecting legal counsel in medical cases—particularly those involving allegations of healthcare fraud, unlawful prescribing, or regulatory violations—there are several warning signs that should immediately raise concern. One of the most significant red flags is a lack of experience with healthcare-related cases. Attorneys who have not previously handled matters involving the False Claims Act, Anti-Kickback Statute, Stark Law, Controlled Substances Act, or medical licensure issues are unlikely to understand the nuances and regulatory complexities that healthcare professionals face. This can seriously impair their ability to mount a credible defense.

Closely related is the issue of limited or no experience in federal court, especially if your case is being prosecuted by federal authorities. Some lawyers may advertise themselves as criminal defense experts yet have never taken a federal case to trial. If an attorney emphasizes plea deals over litigation without having the skill or readiness to go to trial, that is a critical vulnerability. Physicians need lawyers who are not only willing but capable of defending them at trial, if necessary.

Be wary of vague promises or exaggerated claims. Any attorney who guarantees an outcome—such as claiming you will not go to prison or that the case will definitely be dismissed—is not being honest. Similarly, statements like "I know the prosecutor" or "I have a good relationship with the judge" may sound reassuring but are meaningless when not backed by a clear legal strategy and demonstrable experience.

It is also important to verify the attorney's track record. Don't just rely on their website or advertising materials—search for actual cases they've handled using PACER (Public Access to Court Electronic Records) or state court databases. If they can't provide examples of similar cases or references from past clients, it's a sign to be cautious. A qualified attorney should be transparent about their history and capable of speaking directly about how they've handled cases like yours.

Another red flag is evasive communication. If an attorney avoids or deflects your direct questions—especially about case strategy, billing, or who will be working on your case—that's a concern. Some lawyers may try to impress with legal jargon while sidestepping the specifics. A competent attorney should be able to explain your situation in clear, accessible terms and be transparent about your options.

Physicians should also be cautious of lawyers who recommend an early guilty plea before even reviewing discovery materials or conducting an independent investigation. This suggests either a lack of diligence or a preference for quick resolutions rather than a strong defense. An effective lawyer should want to examine the evidence, consult experts, and understand the full context of your clinical decisions before advising on a course of action.

Poor communication or unavailability is another serious concern. If your lawyer routinely fails to return calls or emails in a timely fashion, doesn't keep you updated on developments in your case, or seems too busy to give your matter the attention it deserves, your defense will suffer. High-quality representation requires active engagement, not just in the courtroom, but in the day-to-day management of your case.

Billing practices can also reveal deeper issues. Be alert to unclear or overly complex fee structures, especially large flat fees that are not tied to defined milestones or levels of service. While some flat fees are reasonable, they can also incentivize lawyers to settle cases early without fully investigating or preparing for trial. Hourly billing may offer greater transparency, but it's also important to ensure that you're not paying for unnecessary associates or redundant work.

A good healthcare defense attorney should be comfortable working with subject-matter experts—whether forensic accountants, medical consultants, or billing specialists. If a lawyer seems reluctant to bring in external support or believes they can handle all technical aspects on their own, they may not be prepared to build a comprehensive defense, especially in complex fraud or prescribing cases.

Another common misstep is choosing an attorney who seems overly friendly with prosecutors or judges and uses that as their main selling point. While professional courtesy between legal professionals is expected, relying on personal relationships instead of strategy, knowledge, and preparation is not only misleading—it's dangerous. Such relationships rarely offer any meaningful advantage and may deter your attorney from being aggressive when necessary.

Before committing to representation, always check the attorney's professional standing. Look for any history of disciplinary action by the state bar, and read reviews from past clients—particularly those who had similar charges. Issues like negligence, poor communication, or ethical violations should not be overlooked.

Also, pay close attention to how the attorney treats your concerns. If they dismiss your questions, minimize the severity of the case, or impose a cookie-cutter defense approach without learning the details of your specific situation, it's a signal that they may not provide the individualized attention your case demands.

Clarify the team structure as well. Some firms advertise a high-profile partner but assign cases to junior associates or contract attorneys. Make sure you understand who will be preparing motions, handling discovery, negotiating with the government, and—if it comes to it—representing you in court.

Lastly, it's vital that your attorney understands the wider professional implications of your case. This includes knowledge of how a criminal charge might affect your medical license, DEA registration, hospital credentials, or ability to participate in federal insurance programs. If your attorney shows no awareness of these issues or doesn't coordinate with licensure or administrative counsel, they may be leaving major parts of your defense unaddressed.

In a legal landscape where physicians face complex and often high-profile charges, avoiding these red flags can be the difference between a well-managed defense and an irreversible professional downfall.

# The Financial Maze: Flat Fees vs. Hourly Billing

Attorney fees are another minefield. Some attorneys charge a flat fee with the intent of resolving the case quickly—often through a guilty plea. Why? Because trial is expensive, risky, and exhausting. A flat fee that doesn't account for the Herculean labor of trial preparation may incentivize lawyers to do less, not more.

Flat fees offer predictability. You pay one set amount for the legal representation, regardless of how much time the attorney ends up spending on your case. For many physicians, this can be reassuring— especially when facing an open-ended investigation or criminal proceeding where the duration and complexity are difficult to forecast. Flat fees can also reduce the anxiety of being "on the clock" every time you speak with your attorney. In some cases, a well-structured flat fee agreement can foster trust and prevent disputes over billing.

However, flat fees can carry hidden risks. Some attorneys may offer a flat rate that only covers early-stage representation—for example, pre-indictment counsel or negotiation with the government—but does not extend to motions practice or trial. If the case proceeds further than expected, clients may find themselves having to pay a second fee for trial representation. Worse, there are instances where flat fees unintentionally incentivize attorneys to push for early pleas rather than investing the necessary time and resources to prepare for trial. If the fee isn't calibrated to the possibility of litigation, the attorney may quietly steer the client toward settlement simply to avoid uncompensated effort.

By contrast, hourly billing is transparent and reflects the actual time invested in the case. For complex matters—especially those that require forensic review, expert consultation, or extensive motion practice—hourly billing ensures that the attorney is compensated for the work performed. It can be particularly useful in cases that evolve in complexity, where unforeseen issues arise and require substantial legal attention. With proper documentation, clients can track how their funds are being used, and they often have more leverage in shaping the scope of the work being performed.

The downside to hourly billing is cost unpredictability. Legal defense in a federal healthcare case can run well into six figures, and without a clear cap, clients may find themselves overwhelmed by the cumulative hours billed. It also places pressure on every interaction—each phone call, each email, each review of documents contributes to the running total. This may discourage some clients from maintaining regular communication with their attorney or from seeking clarity on issues unless absolutely necessary, which can hinder the attorney-client relationship.

In my case, Paul offered a flat fee. But he wasn't the kind of lawyer to take shortcuts. He poured himself into my defense with the dedication of a craftsman who knew his reputation—and my future—were on the line. That said, many experienced lawyers prefer hourly billing for good reason: defending a federal criminal case is time-intensive. Long nights, weekends lost, dozens of pre-trial motions, witness interviews, expert consultations—these efforts add up. Clients must understand this, and lawyers must be transparent about their structure and intent.

It is a bitter irony that many physicians—who spend their lives mastering their field—end up placing their fate in the hands of attorneys with little understanding of healthcare law. Some are sold on flash rather than substance. But in this arena, where precision matters, where one misstep can cost years of freedom, your lawyer must be more than competent—they must be exceptional.

## A Word on Communication

In the red flags above, I mentioned poor communication. Effective communication with your attorney is not just helpful—it is essential. An attorney who fails to return your calls or emails, who ghosts you for days at a time, is signaling one of two things: they are overwhelmed, or they are indifferent. Neither is acceptable. A good attorney may not respond instantly to every message—nor should they—but they will respond thoughtfully and in a timely manner, focusing their time where it best serves your defense.

Yet clients, too, have a responsibility. During moments of panic, it's easy to flood your attorney with texts and emails, desperate for reassurance. But such behavior can cloud strategy, waste resources, and derail momentum. Communication must serve the goal: trial preparation and acquittal. Think of it as a chess game—every move must be deliberate, not reactionary.

## Beware the Siren Song of Promises

Finally, beware the most dangerous trap of all: attorneys who make promises. There are no guarantees in federal criminal defense. No one—not the most brilliant lawyer, not the most connected firm—can promise acquittal or immunity from jail. Any suggestion otherwise is not only unethical—it's a lie.

In my journey, I heard it all. "Plead guilty, and you won't do time." "This prosecutor's easy to work with." "Your case is unwinnable—don't even try." Each promise, each pessimistic prophecy, was ultimately unfounded. I learned that the best attorneys don't make promises. They make plans. They do the work. They fight.

And so, I leave you with this: in the harrowing process of federal prosecution, the selection of your attorney is the most consequential decision you will make. It is your only real weapon. Choose wisely. Consult others. Study case records. Ask questions that demand honest answers. And above all, trust your instincts.

Your freedom may depend on it.

# CHAPTER 9

# The Prosecutor

---

*"Not all doctors charged with healthcare fraud are guilty,*
*but many choose not to fight."*

— David Oscar Markus, JD and Mona Markus, JD

## Overcoming Adversity and Standing for Principle

In 2011, I was recruited to serve as Head of the Department of Psychiatry at Blue Mountain Health System, a rural healthcare network in Pennsylvania. What I found upon arrival was a system in need of transformation—fragmented services, overstretched resources, and a patient population underserved in mental health. Through relentless dedication and long hours, I spearheaded a series of reforms that revitalized the department. During my tenure, the system's psychiatric service revenue doubled, and more importantly, patients in these isolated communities began to receive the quality care they had long been denied.

But progress often provokes resistance. Despite my success, I faced a profound ethical and personal challenge. The hospital's CEO began requesting controlled medications—opioids and other regulated substances—for himself, his romantic partners, and even their children. These individuals did not meet any legitimate clinical criteria for such prescriptions. The requests were not merely informal; they were accompanied by veiled inducements—promises of lucrative long-term contracts worth millions. My answer was simple and unwavering: no. I would not compromise my medical integrity. Instead, I escalated my concerns, formally notifying the hospital's board of directors and its chief medical officer.

The retaliation was swift. The CEO threatened to terminate my employment. I responded in writing, reiterating that I had reported his conduct to the board. What followed remains one of the most harrowing moments of my professional life. In a public setting, the CEO turned to hospital staff and declared, "This Middle Eastern terrorist is publicly threatening me." The words struck like a blow—not just to me personally, but to the values I believed American institutions were meant to uphold. It was not only an attack on my character, but a weaponization of race and heritage in a space that should have stood for healing and ethics.

I filed a lawsuit for wrongful termination. The litigation was emotionally and professionally taxing, but I insisted on one key condition: that the proceedings not be buried in confidentiality. I wanted the public to see what had happened—not for vindication, but for truth. In time, the CEO was dismissed, and the hospital system—already strained by poor governance—collapsed into bankruptcy. It was ultimately absorbed by a larger health network. The Honorable Judge Jeffrey L. Schmehl presided over the case and its settlement. Though the financial outcome was modest, I accepted it, knowing that the larger victory lay in preserving my ethical integrity.

This chapter in my life serves as a testament to conviction in the face of coercion. I did not bend to pressure, nor barter ethics for advancement. I did not allow racism to define me or money to silence me. In the end, my principles remained intact—unbought, unshaken, and unafraid.

# Federal Prosecutor

The figure of the federal prosecutor occupies a central, often misunderstood, position in the machinery of American justice. More than simply the government's lawyer, the prosecutor acts as investigator, strategist, spokesperson, and gatekeeper to the vast and intimidating power of the Department of Justice. The choices prosecutors make—whom to indict, what charges to bring, when to go public, and when to push for a plea—can shape, or shatter, lives. For professionals like physicians, whose reputations and licensure depend on public trust and regulatory approval, the prosecutor's discretion is not just powerful; it is existential.

In my case, this role was embodied by Assistant United States Attorney Joan E. Burnes, who operated within the Eastern District of Pennsylvania. Her credentials were solid: a BA from Syracuse University and a JD, magna cum laude, from Temple University. After private practice in Philadelphia, she entered public service as a federal prosecutor, building a reputation for pursuing complex white-collar cases. Her approach to my prosecution reflected many features of federal enforcement: institutional momentum, strategic media engagement, and a near-presumption of guilt.

From the moment I was targeted, the machinery of the state moved with precision. The first signal came not from a courtroom, but from a press release. With the cooperation of the U.S. Attorney's media office, Burnes released a statement that labeled me a Medicare thief and a fraudulent psychiatrist. The language was sharp, inflammatory, and deeply misleading. While the allegations would eventually be contested in court—and many would collapse—the damage was immediate and irreversible. Patients canceled appointments. Peers distanced themselves. Professional relationships vanished overnight.

That's the unspoken goal of federal press strategy: not just to inform the public, but to cripple the defendant's support system. In the digital age, a government press release is as good as a conviction in the court of public opinion. And prosecutors know it. Unlike defense attorneys, who are ethically bound to protect client confidentiality, prosecutors face fewer constraints when issuing public statements, especially before trial. The Justice Manual offers guidelines, but these are often treated as flexible suggestions rather than binding standards. For defendants, especially physicians, these early public narratives create the steepest uphill battle.

Federal prosecutors operate in a culture where success is measured not just by verdicts but by headlines. Convictions are trophies; plea deals are chalked up as efficient wins; media coverage is proof of impact. Rarely do the nuances of a case—intent, context, mitigating factors—receive fair weight. The binary of guilt and innocence is often flattened into a public narrative of criminality long before any jury deliberates. This isn't a flaw of the system; it is the system.

The statistics are chilling. Federal data shows that more than 97% of all criminal convictions in the United States are the result of plea deals.(Johnson) Only a tiny fraction of defendants ever go to trial, and fewer still are acquitted. This lopsided reality isn't a reflection of overwhelming guilt across the population; it is a symptom of systemic pressure. Prosecutors have an entire arsenal of tools designed to make trial seem not only risky, but reckless. Charge stacking, financial pressure, threats of enhanced sentencing, and even targeting of associates are all tactics designed to crush a defendant's will to fight.

Another frightening statistic related to plea bargaining is that many innocent people plead guilty to lesser crimes in order to avoid the risk of the more severe punishments associated with the crimes they are originally charged with. A study of DNA exonerations conducted by the Innocence Project found that 11% of exonerated individuals had pleaded guilty. While it is difficult for a variety of reasons to estimate the number of innocent people who have pleaded guilty, most studies likely undercount wrongful convictions. (americanbar.org)

I was explicitly warned that if I did not accept a plea, I could face decades in prison and massive financial penalties. These threats were not empty—they were codified in the charges brought against me. Each billing entry, each administrative action, was framed as a separate count. This is the reality of modern federal prosecution: the same conduct can be subdivided into dozens of alleged crimes. Even if the facts remain constant, the punishment expands exponentially. It's a tactic designed less to reflect justice than to incentivize capitulation. It is only when you are faced with this for real that you feel the pressure to give in and escape the potential horrors of decades in prison.

There is nothing new in this tactic. The practice of plea bargaining in the modern American justice system bears an uncomfortable resemblance to the psychological tactics used during the medieval Inquisition. In both systems, the accused is placed in a position where fear—not justice—becomes the principal driver of confession.

During the Inquisition, the accused were shown the instruments of torture: racks, iron boots, and thumb screws. While these tools were not always used, their mere display served a calculated purpose—to instill dread and extract submission. Inquisitors knew that pain, or the threat of it, was often more persuasive than proof. The confessions they obtained were less a measure of guilt than a testament to human vulnerability.

In today's courtroom, the tools are different but the effect is eerily similar. Defendants are shown the "instruments" of modern punishment—decades-long sentences, mandatory minimums, and the near-certainty of conviction should they dare go to trial. With over 97% of federal convictions secured through plea deals, the system effectively replaces deliberation with coercion. The choice is often stark: plead guilty to a lesser offense or face a punitive sentence far greater than the crime warrants. Like the inquisitorial rack, the modern plea deal operates not as an expression of justice, but as an engine of fear.

Another unsettling tactic was the suggestion—subtle, yet unmistakable—that if I refused to cooperate, my colleagues or employees might come under scrutiny. These kinds of implications, unspoken in the courtroom but conveyed in meetings or legal correspondence, are designed to erode a defendant's sense of control. Suddenly, the stakes are not just personal. They become collective. The pressure to surrender intensifies when it's tied to the potential suffering of others.

This tactic—suggesting that harm may befall others if the accused does not comply—has been used throughout history to break resolve. During Stalin's Great Purge in the Soviet Union, it was common for NKVD interrogators to hint, or state outright, that failure to confess could result in the arrest or execution of a spouse, sibling, or child. The accused, many of whom were innocent, often capitulated not out of guilt but from the unbearable pressure of knowing that others—especially the vulnerable—would suffer for their resistance. In some cases, entire families were destroyed not by the act of dissent itself, but by the psychological torment of watching one's integrity weaponized against their loved ones. That same pressure—quietly deployed, never written, but always understood—remains one of the most effective tools of coercion. When the cost of resistance expands beyond oneself, the temptation to surrender grows almost irresistible

In this environment, choosing to fight becomes an act of rebellion, perhaps even insanity! Most physicians, under pressure from family, peers, and even some defense lawyers, are urged to plead. They are told to cut their losses, preserve what little remains, and avoid the catastrophic consequences of a full-blown trial. But surrendering to fear does not always serve justice. In my case, I chose to resist, not because I was naïve, but because I knew the truth was on my side. And I knew that allowing fear and pressure to dictate my future would be the real loss.

Burnes, like many prosecutors, had faced high-stakes trials before. One of her most well-known cases was that of Dr. Dorothy June Brown, an educator accused of misappropriating millions of dollars in public charter school funds. The case was a media sensation, painted as a classic tale of greed in public education. But the reality was far more complex. Dr. Brown was a pioneer in charter education, and many of the financial arrangements targeted by prosecutors were longstanding, contractually based agreements. The case dragged on for years, ending in a hung jury and a partial acquittal. Eventually, Dr. Brown was deemed unfit to stand trial due to cognitive decline, and the charges were dismissed.

This case, though unrelated to mine in substance, revealed much about Burnes' approach: persistent, high-profile, and determined to push a case through regardless of the toll it took on the defendant. Her methods reflected a broader trend in federal prosecution, where the pursuit of conviction can take precedence over proportionality and compassion.

Perhaps the most surreal example of prosecutorial discretion came in a case Burnes led against a Pennsylvania man accused of illegally selling protected turtles online. The defendant, dubbed the "turtle man of Levittown," was subjected to surveillance, GPS tracking, and a multi-agency investigation more befitting a narcotics ring than a wildlife offense. Despite causing no demonstrable harm to the environment, he was sentenced to six months in prison. The irony, of course, was that thousands of turtles continued to die on New Jersey roads due to automobile traffic—an issue no federal agency seemed eager to prosecute.

This pattern—of prioritizing symbolism over substance—appeared again and again. Prosecutions became performative exercises in deterrence. In my own case, it seemed that I had been selected not because of the severity of my actions, but because of the visibility of my role, the timing of my services, and the opportunity to make an example. I became a symbol, not a person. My name was added to the ledger of cautionary tales federal agencies use to demonstrate toughness.

But what often goes unseen is the psychological toll this approach takes on defendants and their families. Months turn into years. Legal costs mount. Your name becomes synonymous with guilt in every article, every legal notice, every whispered conversation in professional circles. Prosecutors like Burnes, equipped with institutional prestige and legal immunity, operate without fear of consequence, while the defendant lives every day in a state of legal siege. Each court date is a public performance. Each government filing, no matter how misleading, is accepted as gospel until it can be painstakingly rebutted in court—if the defendant survives that long.

In the federal system, even innocence does not guarantee protection. The burdens of proof, the rules of evidence, and the sheer length of proceedings mean that truth is often delayed—sometimes indefinitely. Prosecutors know that delay favors the government. Defendants lose resources, stamina, and support. They move from hospitals to courthouses, from clinics to legal consultations, and often, into emotional despair. Prosecutors do not have to win every trial—they only need to win the pretrial battle of attrition.

In reviewing my case, I discovered that the very framework guiding prosecutorial conduct—the Principles of Federal Prosecution, codified in the Justice Manual—provides significant leeway. These guidelines outline when federal charges are warranted, but they also allow for interpretation based on subjective assessments: whether the prosecution serves a substantial federal interest, whether there's sufficient evidence, and whether non-criminal alternatives exist. These conditions are meant to safeguard against arbitrary indictments, but in practice, they are applied unevenly. The criteria become a set of rhetorical boxes that, once checked, justify the full force of federal prosecution, no matter how flimsy the factual foundation.

And even when the underlying conduct is legal—or at worst, administrative error—prosecutors can pursue charges under overlapping statutes with vague language, such as mail fraud or conspiracy. These catch-all tools grant prosecutors the power to pursue individuals aggressively, even when direct harm is absent or unproven. It becomes less about whether the conduct was criminal and more about whether it can be made to look criminal in the eyes of a jury. It's a game of framing, narrative control, and strategic pressure.

As a physician, my world was built on evidence, protocol, and outcomes. I assumed, naively, that the legal world functioned similarly. But what I found instead was a performance space—one in which prosecutors like Burnes wrote the first act, cast themselves as heroes, and painted the accused as villains, long before any judge entered the scene. And when the curtain finally lifted in court, the defendant was already forced to act from a position of weakness.

I learned that justice, in the federal system, is not a straight line. It is a labyrinth, constructed and controlled by those with the power to dictate its terms. Prosecutors play the role of gatekeeper, architect, and sometimes executioner. Their choices define not just the outcome of a case, but the lives of everyone touched by it. And unless more attention is given to the unchecked reach of their authority, the scales will remain tipped against those who most need protection.

As the statistics show, most don't fight. But I did. And that made all the difference.

# The Senator and the Scalpel

In the dark theatre of American justice, where presumption of innocence often dies at the courthouse steps, the prosecution of Senator Ted Stevens stands as a brutal reminder that power offers no immunity from prosecutorial overreach. Stevens was no ordinary defendant. A World War II veteran, the longest-serving Republican senator in U.S. history, and a key architect of Alaska's statehood, he wielded influence few physicians could dream of (Congress.gov). And yet, in 2008, he stood alone, indicted on seven felony counts for allegedly failing to disclose gifts related to home renovations—a narrative simplified for soundbites, weaponized for headlines.

What followed was not a trial in pursuit of truth, but a campaign built on omission and distortion. The Department of Justice withheld critical exculpatory evidence, including FBI interview notes that contradicted their own witness's testimony, and a memo in which the same witness said that Stevens had explicitly instructed all renovation bills be paid in full. These facts never reached the jury. The prosecutors curated a version of events designed not for justice, but for conviction. It worked—until the truth clawed its way to the surface.

After Stevens lost his seat and his reputation, a whistleblower within the DOJ revealed the misconduct. An independent investigation confirmed what defense counsel Rob Cary had long suspected: the government had buried the facts. (Johnson) Judge Emmet Sullivan, no stranger to the contours of institutional abuse, declared it one of the most "profound breakdowns in the fair administration of justice" he had ever witnessed.(Toobin) One prosecutor, Nicholas Marsh, took his own life. The others continued their careers. Stevens died in a plane crash in 2010, his name still tethered to a case that should never have been brought.

I learned of Stevens's ordeal through Cary, who later encouraged me to write this book. He had chronicled the case in *Not Guilty: The Unlawful Prosecution of U.S. Senator Ted Stevens* (Cary), laying bare a prosecutorial system that bends rules and buries truths. Reading it was like peering into a mirror. What had happened to a senator in Washington had happened to me in a small-town clinic. And what happened to me has happened to countless physicians across America—especially those who treat the vulnerable, the addicted, the underserved. The same tactics appear again and again: suppress evidence, control the narrative, pursue the case with tunnel vision and theatrical flair. It is not about justice. It is about winning.

Physicians are not indicted for crimes; they are indicted for optics. Chart notes become crimes. Billing codes become conspiracy. Medical discretion becomes "outside the standard of care." Prosecutors paint us as reckless, greedy, or deviant, and the public believes it—because they are meant to. Few juries understand the nuance of medical judgment. Fewer still see the buried audits, the patient stories that exonerate, the context that matters. Prosecutors bank on that ignorance. And they win.

Ted Stevens had the Senate floor. I had my license, my oath, and the weight of a community. Neither shield proved enough. If they could distort a senator's life so completely, what hope does a physician have when standing alone against the machinery of federal prosecution? That question haunts every courtroom. It echoes in every indictment of a doctor whose only mistake was practicing medicine in a system that punishes judgment and criminalises ambiguity.

But like Stevens's story, mine is not a surrender. It is a record. A warning. And a call.

Because if doctors remain silent, if we do not speak, if we do not write—we feed the silence that wrongful prosecutions thrive in. Stevens did not live to see his name fully restored. But his case was a turning point. It reminded some judges, some journalists, and some citizens that the government is not infallible. That prosecutors can—and do—get it wrong. That justice, delayed and deformed, still matters.

And so I write, not just for myself, but for every physician caught in this system. For those who walked into courtrooms with truth on their side and left with shackles around their wrists. For those who never made it to trial. For those who are still too afraid to speak.

We must tell our stories. Because when we do, justice no longer belongs solely to the prosecutors. It belongs to the people they tried to silence.

# CHAPTER 10

# To Plea or Not to Plea: What to Know About Plea Deals

---

*"People plead guilty or admit to crimes they didn't commit for various reasons. Certain interrogation procedures produce high rates of false confessions."*

— Eric Schneiderman, Attorney General of New York (2011–2018)

## Choosing Service Over Status – The Path Less Taken

By the close of 2012, I had reached another turning point. After years of leadership at Lehigh Valley Health Network, and following the principles instilled in me during my time with the National Institute of Mental Health and the United States Public Health Service, I chose to embark on an independent path—one that would allow me to practise medicine on my own terms. That December, I founded Blue Mountain Psychiatry, a private clinic rooted in ethical, evidence-based psychiatric care, and anchored in the values I had always held close: scientific integrity, innovation, and compassion.

From the outset, my practice was future-facing. We incorporated telepsychiatry long before it became standard, reaching patients in underserved rural communities across Pennsylvania. At a time when access to care was fragmented, we were building bridges. We also adopted novel treatment modalities—among them, transcranial magnetic stimulation (TMS) and the supervised use of ketamine—for individuals battling treatment-resistant depression and other severe psychiatric conditions. These approaches were not only clinically effective but, in many cases, life-saving.

January 2013 brought more than professional growth—it brought personal joy as well. That month, my wife Douha and I welcomed our third son, Zayd. Despite the demands of running a growing clinic and managing complex caseloads, I remained committed to my family and to my calling. Our home in the Lehigh Valley became a place of growth, reflection, and purpose.

Yet with recognition and visibility came new opportunities—some more tempting than others. In early 2013, international recruiters approached me with a proposal: to relocate to the Gulf States, specifically Qatar or the United Arab Emirates, to serve as a chief psychiatrist and national wellness ambassador. The offer was nothing short of extraordinary. Douha and I travelled multiple times to the region to meet with stakeholders, senior health officials, and even members of the leadership in Qatar. They were impressed by our combined credentials and saw in us a couple who could help transform their national mental health infrastructure. For our contributions, they offered a salary of $1.5 million annually.

It was a crossroads—one many in my position might have seen as a dream fulfilled. The financial security, the status, the lifestyle; all of it beckoned. I spent months in deliberation. But as I wrestled with the decision, another honour arrived. In February 2014, I was informed that the American Psychiatric Association and the Pennsylvania Psychiatric Society had jointly selected me for the Psychiatric Leadership Award—an accolade reserved for practitioners who demonstrated visionary leadership in the field. My early adoption of telehealth and novel treatment strategies had not gone unnoticed.

That award, which I accepted in May 2014, affirmed something deeper than prestige. It was a reminder of the path I had already chosen—to remain in service to a community often overlooked, and to continue the leadership trajectory that had placed me on course to become President of the Lehigh Valley Psychiatric Society, and later, a potential candidate to lead the Pennsylvania Psychiatric Society.

And so, I declined the offer from Qatar.

To some, walking away from tenfold income might seem irrational. But to me, it was clear. I had been trained by the best, and I had committed myself to a philosophy of care that prioritised access, dignity, and public good over financial gain. My service in the United States Public Health Service Civilian Corps was not merely a line on my CV—it was a pledge. A pledge to serve not only when it was easy, but also when it mattered most.

As it turned out, that decision became profoundly significant just a few years later. When the COVID-19 pandemic struck, I was here—in Pennsylvania, embedded in a network of care, leading a practice prepared for remote service delivery and equipped with the tools to provide stability in a time of national crisis. Had I chosen differently, I would not have been in position to help the thousands of patients who turned to us during those harrowing months.

Looking back, I see not just a fork in the road, but the subtle hand of Providence. Our paths are not only shaped by ambition, but by the moments in which we choose service over spectacle, humility over hubris. My decision to remain grounded—to commit to rural America, to build systems of care where they were most needed—was never about rejecting opportunity. It was about recognising a higher one.

## Plea Dealing

The modern American justice system operates, overwhelmingly, through plea deals. According to the U.S. Department of Justice and the American Bar Association, over 97% of criminal cases are resolved without trial, via negotiated pleas.(Vera Institute of Justice) These agreements may appear practical—an efficient way to ease congested court calendars—but their implications can be ethically fraught. Particularly in federal healthcare fraud cases, where defendants face staggering numbers of charges and the threat of decades-long sentences, plea deals are often a form of psychological coercion.

This chapter examines the case of Drs. Ashis Rhakit and Jayati Gupta Rhakit, a married couple who ran Ohio Cardiology Associates, with clinics in Cleveland, Parma, and Strongsville. Though ultimately acquitted, their experience highlights how federal agencies can use plea leverage and legal pressure in place of proven guilt.

The Rhakits were flagged for investigation because their practice had some of the highest billing rates for cardiac diagnostics in Ohio. They specialised in cardiology and pain management—a combination that drew suspicion in an era of opioid scrutiny. Undercover FBI agents and confidential informants were dispatched to act as patients. Their goal? To entrap the Rhakits into overprescribing medications and ordering unnecessary tests.

On January 24, 2018, the U.S. Attorney's Office for the Northern District of Ohio charged the couple with conspiracy, healthcare fraud, making false statements, and violating the Controlled Substances Act. The charges alleged that the doctors exaggerated or fabricated patient symptoms (chest pain, palpitations, and shortness of breath) in order to justify tests including cardiac catheterisations, echocardiograms, carotid scans, and EKGs. The government claimed that benzodiazepines and pain relievers like tramadol were prescribed without medical necessity, solely to encourage patient return visits.

Over the course of the investigation, the charges ballooned from 24 to 87 counts, through the use of superseding indictments. This tactic, standard in federal prosecutions, increases pressure on defendants to accept a plea—a psychological weapon more than a legal necessity. Despite this, the Rhakits refused to plead guilty and proceeded to trial in July 2021.

The prosecution's case unfolded over seven weeks. They presented 45 witnesses, including four confidential informants, an undercover FBI agent, medical experts, and insurance company representatives. Secret audio and video recordings were played in court. The government's narrative was that the Rhakits ran a seven-year scheme of overtreatment and overprescription.

But the defence mounted a comprehensive and aggressive rebuttal. Lead attorney Frank Baez, representing Dr. Ashis Rhakit, deployed a clear strategy: "You can't trust the message if you can't trust the messenger." Under intense cross-examination, government witnesses were revealed to have been offered leniency, cash payments, or sentence reductions in exchange for their cooperation. It also emerged that the FBI instructed informants to lie about experiencing pain to obtain prescriptions. Some of those informants were facing their own pending charges.

Even more concerning, the FBI was found to have misrepresented witness interviews in official records. Perhaps most damning of all, prosecutors elicited courtroom testimony from patients who denied experiencing symptoms documented in the Rhakits' charts—despite medical records from unrelated providers confirming those same symptoms had been reported.

The government's press release, issued prior to acquiring complete medical records, had publicly declared the Rhakits guilty of ordering unnecessary tests over a seven-year period. (Justice.Gov) This assertion was made before sufficient evidence existed to support the timeframe—an example of prosecutorial overreach that ultimately damaged the case.

As their case unravelled, the defence demonstrated that investigators pursued vulnerable patients with chronic illness or memory impairment to bolster the case. Charges were piled high by finding patients with dementia and then telling them they had been subjected to unnecessary procedures—a claim these patients were hardly qualified to evaluate.

Over three weeks, the defence painted a different picture: this was a case of competing medical opinions. The FBI and Department of Justice had pursued the case without proper clinical knowledge. Their medical experts were offering hindsight judgment on complex decisions made in real time by physicians caring for patients with overlapping cardiac and anxiety-related symptoms.

After ten weeks of testimony, the jury deliberated for two full weeks. The result: not guilty on 50 counts. On the remaining 37, the jury failed to reach a verdict. There was not a single conviction. (Blake) The case stands as a rare, remarkable rejection of a sweeping federal prosecution.

Stunned, prosecutors eventually agreed to drop the remaining charges in exchange for a civil settlement. The doctors paid $600,000, but the agreement included no admission of guilt. The government continued to maintain that the Rhakits had provided unnecessary tests; the Rhakits maintained their complete innocence. The settlement preserved plausible deniability on both sides.

This case underscores the dangers of plea deals when used as a tool of coercion. Had the Rhakits accepted a plea—as many would have under the threat of 87 felony counts—they would have lost their licenses, reputations, and likely faced imprisonment. Instead, they stood firm and prevailed.

- Over 97% of U.S. criminal cases are resolved through plea agreements, not trials.
- Superseding indictments often serve to pressure defendants rather than present new evidence.
- In this case, informants were incentivised to fabricate or exaggerate.
- The FBI instructed patients to lie and kept flawed records.
- Medical expert testimony was often based on second opinions, not definitive wrongdoing.
- Jury scepticism of prosecutorial conduct was decisive in the outcome.

The Rhakits' experience is a cautionary tale for any professional in the crosshairs of a federal investigation. It also prompts larger questions: when prosecutors act like judges, and when investigators manufacture narratives before gathering facts, can any plea deal truly be called voluntary?

## Why Would an Innocent Person Take a Plea Deal? Understanding the Unthinkable

Imagine being accused of a serious crime you didn't commit. You know you're innocent, yet your lawyer advises you to accept a plea deal.

It seems illogical—why would anyone admit guilt if they are innocent? The reality is far more complex and troubling than it appears on the surface.

The criminal justice system in the United States is heavily reliant on plea bargains. Over 97% of criminal cases are resolved without ever going to trial, often through plea deals. These agreements can seem pragmatic for the guilty, allowing reduced sentences or lesser charges in exchange for an admission of guilt. But what happens when someone who is innocent feels they have no choice but to plead guilty? This blog post explores the many reasons why innocent individuals accept plea deals and how the system, as it currently operates, can lead to devastating miscarriages of justice.

## The Harsh Reality of Pre-Trial Detention

One of the most coercive elements in the criminal justice system is pre-trial detention. When someone is arrested, they may be denied bail or unable to afford it. This leaves them incarcerated, sometimes for months or even years, before their trial even begins. Jails are overcrowded, dangerous, and psychologically damaging. Under these circumstances, even an innocent person may choose to plead guilty to a lesser charge simply to get out and return to their family, job, and life.

This tactic is especially powerful when the time served awaiting trial is longer than the sentence offered through the plea deal. For someone who has already spent months in jail, a guilty plea with a short or time-served sentence becomes a way out—even at the cost of their record and reputation.

## The Threat of the "Trial Penalty"

The "trial penalty" refers to the fact that those who go to trial and are convicted often receive significantly harsher sentences than those who accept a plea deal. This discrepancy puts enormous pressure on defendants to plead guilty, even if they are innocent.

Consider the psychological toll: prosecutors may threaten decades in prison, while a plea deal might carry a few years, probation, or even just a fine. Faced with such a daunting choice, many defendants opt for the safer route, fearing the consequences of a trial loss—despite their innocence.

## Overcharging and Prosecutorial Leverage

Prosecutors often use a strategy known as "overcharging," where multiple charges are filed, some of which may be exaggerated or unsupported. This inflates the potential punishment and gives the prosecution significant leverage in plea negotiations. An innocent person, overwhelmed by a laundry list of charges and facing years or decades in prison, may feel compelled to plead guilty to a lesser count just to avoid catastrophic sentencing.

## Inadequate Legal Representation

Many defendants rely on overworked public defenders who manage dozens, sometimes hundreds, of cases simultaneously. These attorneys often don't have the time or resources to fully investigate each case. When presented with a plea deal, they may recommend accepting it simply to avoid the risk of trial—particularly if the case is weak but the stakes are high.

While most public defenders are dedicated professionals, the system often sets them up to fail. The volume of cases, lack of funding, and systemic pressures can lead to advice that prioritizes expedience over justice.

## Coercion and Manipulation

Some innocent people are manipulated into accepting plea deals by tactics that border on coercion. Police and prosecutors might suggest that their friends or family members could face consequences if they don't cooperate. Others are told that pleading guilty will result in a better deal now than they could ever hope for later. The implication is clear: accept this offer or face the wrath of the system.

In some extreme cases, plea deals are offered with the explicit condition that the defendant must waive their right to appeal or even to assert their innocence in public. This tactic not only silences the accused but also erases any possibility of rectifying a wrongful conviction later.

## Psychological Pressure and Desperation

The psychological toll of being accused, incarcerated, and threatened with years behind bars can be immense. Depression, anxiety, and hopelessness are common among defendants, particularly those who know they're innocent. Under such pressure, a plea deal can appear as a lifeline—a way to end the nightmare.

Young defendants and individuals with mental health challenges are especially vulnerable. Lacking the maturity or support to fully understand the implications of a plea, they may make decisions that haunt them for the rest of their lives.

## The Collateral Consequences of a Guilty Plea

Accepting a plea bargain requires an admission of guilt, regardless of whether the defendant actually committed the offence. This admission is not merely procedural—it carries significant long-term consequences. A guilty plea, even if taken under pressure, becomes a matter of public record and can have a lasting impact on your reputation, relationships, and future prospects.

One of the most immediate consequences is the creation of a criminal record. This record is accessible in background checks and may severely limit future opportunities. Employment prospects, housing applications, and access to financial services can all be negatively affected by the presence of a conviction, even if the plea was part of a negotiated settlement.

Additionally, entering into a plea agreement often means waiving critical legal rights, including the right to appeal. Many defendants are unaware that by accepting the terms of a plea deal, they effectively limit or relinquish the opportunity to seek a new trial—even in cases where new evidence later emerges. This can leave individuals permanently burdened by a conviction, despite potential proof of innocence.

Sentencing conditions tied to plea deals can also be burdensome. These may include probation, community service, or significant fines. While such terms might appear more lenient than the potential outcome of a trial, they still carry implications that can disrupt a person's personal and professional life for years.

Beyond formal sentencing, there are often collateral consequences. These can include restrictions on employment, limitations on travel, and the loss of voting rights or firearm ownership. Such repercussions may extend well beyond the duration of the sentence itself, making it vital for anyone considering a plea to consult with a qualified criminal defence solicitor before making any decision.

The stakes are even higher for non-citizens. A guilty plea to certain charges can trigger serious immigration consequences, including detention, removal proceedings, or outright deportation. It is essential for individuals in this position to speak in confidence with a lawyer, under the protection of attorney-client privilege, before accepting any deal.

Some professions—such as healthcare, law, or finance—require licensing through regulatory bodies that may consider criminal convictions when evaluating eligibility. A guilty plea may therefore jeopardise a person's career or prevent them from entering certain fields entirely.

Moreover, obtaining an expungement or having a record sealed becomes significantly more difficult following a guilty plea. Expungement is a legal process that limits public access to criminal records, but not all jurisdictions allow it after a plea bargain has been entered. This means that the stain of a conviction could remain permanently visible.

In certain jurisdictions, a felony conviction through a plea deal can also result in the loss of civil rights, such as the right to vote, serve on a jury, or own firearms. These rights may not be automatically restored even after the sentence has been completed, and regaining them can require a lengthy and complex legal process.

Finally, there is the enduring impact of social stigma. Even when the plea is the result of legal strategy rather than actual wrongdoing, the public perception of guilt can damage personal relationships and standing within a community. For many, this social penalty may be one of the most painful and enduring aspects of the plea process.

## Toward a More Just System

The prevalence of plea deals is not inherently unjust. When used correctly, they can serve both the accused and society. But safeguards must be put in place to ensure that innocent individuals are not coerced into pleading guilty.

Reforms could include:

- Increased transparency in plea negotiations
- Judicial oversight to ensure pleas are truly voluntary
- More funding for public defenders
- Eliminating mandatory minimums and reducing trial penalties
- Providing post-conviction relief for those who plead guilty under duress

We must also shift public perception. Pleading guilty should not automatically equate to actual guilt. Recognising the pressures that lead to coerced pleas is the first step in fixing a deeply flawed aspect of our justice system.

## Conclusion

When someone pleads guilty to a crime, the common assumption is that they must have committed it. However, the past few decades have revealed that this belief is frequently misplaced. In fact, nearly 12% of the 375 individuals exonerated through DNA evidence in the United States since 1989 had originally pleaded guilty to serious offences they did not commit. (Innocence Project) More broadly, data from the National Registry of Exonerations shows that 18%

of all known exonerees entered guilty pleas despite their innocence. (guiltypleaproblem.org) These statistics highlight a troubling reality: the plea bargaining system can and does lead innocent people to admit guilt.

The question, "Why would an innocent person take a plea deal?" has no simple answer—but many heartbreaking ones. In a system where time, money, fear, and pressure determine outcomes more than truth, the innocent often find themselves caught in a cruel dilemma. As we work toward a more equitable justice system, we must remember that every plea deal comes at a cost—and sometimes, that cost is justice itself.

# CHAPTER 11

# The Judge

---

*"Judges are like umpires. Umpires don't make the rules,
they apply them. The role of an umpire and a judge is
critical. They make sure everybody plays by the rules, but
it is a limited role. Nobody ever went to a ball game to
see the umpire"*

— Chief Justice John Roberts, The United States Supreme Court.

## Continuing Innovation in Psychiatry

Innovation was never a marketing slogan—it was, and remains, the lifeblood of my clinical practice. At Blue Mountain Psychiatry, which I founded in 2012, our mission was clear from the start: to provide compassionate, evidence-based care tailored to the unique needs of each patient. But we were also driven by something deeper—a commitment to restoring patients to a state of true remission, not just management. That commitment led us to adopt some of the most advanced psychiatric treatments available, long before they were considered mainstream.

From its inception, Blue Mountain Psychiatry was designed to be different. We focused on serving individuals suffering from treatment-resistant psychiatric illness—those whose symptoms had not improved with traditional medications. For these patients, standard approaches offered little hope. We aimed to change that.

Having trained at the National Institute of Mental Health in Bethesda, Maryland, I was fortunate to work on some of the earliest research into the use of ketamine as a treatment for severe depression. Our team at the NIH saw firsthand how a medication originally used as an anaesthetic could, under careful supervision, alleviate profound and enduring psychiatric suffering. Many of my former colleagues would go on to partner with Johnson & Johnson to develop a branded formulation of ketamine. Meanwhile, I returned to Pennsylvania determined to make this treatment accessible.

Blue Mountain Psychiatry became the first practice in the greater Lehigh Valley to offer ketamine therapy for patients with severe, treatment-resistant depression and anxiety. Unlike the inflated pricing structures seen in larger metropolitan centres, our ketamine treatments were offered at modest, community-accessible rates. By 2022, we had treated over 250 individuals with this innovative therapy—many of whom had exhausted every other available option.

But our innovations did not end there.

We were also the first psychiatric practice in the region to introduce Transcranial Magnetic Stimulation (TMS)—a non-invasive treatment that uses magnetic fields to stimulate targeted areas of the brain involved in mood regulation. (Saini et al.) While the science behind TMS had been developing for years, it was largely underutilised in community practice. At Blue Mountain Psychiatry, we adopted deep TMS, an advanced version capable of reaching further into brain structures, offering relief for patients who couldn't tolerate medication or for whom no medications had worked.

Researchers have found that TMS significantly reduces core PTSD symptoms such as avoidance, anxiety, and somatization. (Basil et al.) Patients also showed overall clinical improvement, as measured by the Clinical Global Impression Scale. (Busner and Targum)

Many of our patients—particularly those affected by long-term depression and anxiety—were struggling financially. For them, we offered care regardless of ability to pay. Treatments that cost thousands elsewhere were provided free of charge or on a sliding scale. Innovation, we believed, should not be a privilege for the few—it should be a right accessible to all.

At the same time, our region was facing the growing shadow of another public health emergency: the opioid crisis. In the early 2010s, its effects began to ripple through the Lehigh Valley, devastating families and overwhelming existing resources. I felt called to act.

I volunteered to serve at the newly established Lehigh County Center for Recovery, the region's first inpatient drug and alcohol rehabilitation centre. There, I offered psychiatric evaluations and medical treatment to individuals in the early stages of addiction recovery. To strengthen my ability to serve this vulnerable population, I pursued additional training and became board-certified in Addiction Medicine by the American Board of Addiction Medicine—joining my existing certifications in Psychiatry and Internal Medicine.

For ten years, from 2013 to 2023, I served in this role, treating more than 5,000 patients struggling with substance use disorders. I saw firsthand how trauma, mental illness, and lack of resources could intersect to entrench suffering. Yet I also witnessed how compassionate, informed care could change lives.

This work was not glamorous. It was not lucrative. But it was necessary.

Every new service or therapy we introduced at Blue Mountain Psychiatry was driven by the needs of our patients. We brought science out of academic journals and into real lives—offering ketamine when few dared to, deploying TMS before most had even heard of it, and standing with our community in the darkest days of an addiction epidemic.

We didn't just believe in innovation—we lived it, one patient at a time.

# The Judge

In the intricate ballet of the American criminal justice system, the judge stands not merely as a neutral referee, but as a pillar of the courtroom. With each ruling, each instruction, and each measured word, a federal judge can shape the very course of a trial. The stakes are enormous. A single decision can tip the balance between conviction and acquittal. Yet for all their power, judges operate under immense responsibility—

to uphold the law, protect the Constitution, and, most importantly, ensure that justice is not only done, but seen to be done.

My case was heard in the United States District Court for the Eastern District of Pennsylvania, a jurisdiction steeped in legal history and precedent. The man overseeing the proceedings was the Honourable Jeffrey Louis Schmehl. I had first encountered Judge Schmehl during my civil litigation against Blue Mountain Health System years earlier—a case involving wrongful termination, discrimination, and breach of contract. Back then, he had struck me as measured and fair, someone who listened more than he spoke. When I learned he would also preside over my federal criminal case, I felt cautious optimism. I knew this man. I had seen him in action.

Federal judges in the United States are a breed apart. Unlike state judges, who are often elected, federal judges are appointed by the President and confirmed by the Senate. Their appointments are for life. They do not campaign. They do not answer to voters. They are insulated from the shifting winds of public opinion, precisely to protect their independence. Judge Schmehl was appointed in 2013 by President Barack Obama and confirmed by a unanimous vote of 100–0 in the U.S. Senate—a rare display of bipartisan confidence in an era of division.

Born in Reading, Pennsylvania, in 1955, Schmehl graduated from Dickinson College and earned his law degree at the University of Toledo. After practising privately and serving as Berks County's solicitor, he rose through the ranks to become President Judge of the Berks County Court of Common Pleas before his federal appointment. His career was marked not by flash or notoriety, but by steady, dedicated service.

In court, Judge Schmehl brought a quiet authority. He didn't need theatrics. His power came from procedure, precedent, and presence. He ruled with precision, spoke with clarity, and conducted the courtroom with a deep sense of decorum. I didn't always agree with his rulings—particularly those related to the admissibility of key evidence—but I could never accuse him of bias or hostility.

Jury selection, one of the most critical phases in any trial, was handled with care. Schmehl asked the right questions, seeking to eliminate bias before it had a chance to taint the case. His courtroom was disciplined but not cold. He allowed both prosecution and defence to speak freely, but he never let things spiral out of control.

One particularly important pre-trial motion addressed a piece of evidence that could have irreparably prejudiced the jury against me. My legal team fought hard to exclude it, and while Schmehl did not rule entirely in our favour, he found a middle ground—admitting the evidence but with limitations that protected my right to a fair trial. That decision demonstrated what I came to see as his defining quality: balance.

Throughout the proceedings, Schmehl delivered jury instructions with great care. He didn't simply recite legal boilerplate—he explained the law in plain language, ensuring that jurors, many of whom had never set foot in a courtroom, understood the gravity of their task. He was patient. He was precise. And he was deeply respectful of the burden placed upon the jurors.

Outside my case, Judge Schmehl's influence was equally notable. He presided over the high-profile mistrial of former union leader John Doherty. (Tanenbaum) When that jury reported they were hopelessly deadlocked, he declared a mistrial—a difficult but necessary call. He also ruled in the early stages of *Groff v. DeJoy*, a case that later reached the U.S. Supreme Court and reshaped religious accommodation in employment law. While the Supreme Court ultimately reversed his decision, the case exemplified the complexity and gravity of the matters that come before federal judges. (Vogue and Sneed)

Federal judges shape the legal landscape with every decision. Their opinions become part of the judicial record. They interpret the Constitution. They rule on motions that can either expose injustice or mask it. And while they cannot create law, their interpretations often define it in practice. There are currently over 670 U.S. district court judges and 179 appellate judges. Each holds immense power over the lives of the individuals who come before them.

I felt fortunate that Judge Schmehl presided over my case. He brought empathy without sentimentality. He treated me not as a defendant, but as a person—a person whose future rested in the balance. His experience as both a public defender and private attorney informed his judicial philosophy. He understood the law from both sides of the aisle, and that understanding translated into fairness.

His temperament, too, was exemplary. He never raised his voice. He never belittled counsel. He was, as one hopes all judges to be, the calm centre of the storm.

In testimony before the Senate Judiciary Committee, Schmehl named three essential attributes for a good judge: courtroom experience, judicial temperament, and a strong work ethic. He demonstrated all three throughout my trial. But more than that, he embodied the ideal of justice—not the harsh, retributive kind, but the principled, deliberative kind our system aspires to uphold.

That system is far from perfect. Judges can make mistakes. They can be reversed on appeal. They can, despite their best intentions, allow injustice to pass through their courtroom doors. But when a judge like Schmehl sits on the bench—someone with integrity, restraint, and a genuine commitment to justice—there is hope. Hope that the system can work. Hope that truth can prevail.

The gavel is not a weapon. It is not a shield. It is a tool—used not to silence, but to create order, to mark transitions, and, in the best cases, to deliver justice. In the courtroom of Judge Jeffrey Louis Schmehl, I saw that ideal realised.

And for that, I am grateful.

## A Judiciary Betrayed: The "Kids for Cash" Scandal

Judges, though, are human. Regrettably, not all are as principled as Judge Jeffrey Louis Schmehl. While some uphold the law with impartiality and integrity, others succumb to ambition, bias, or greed. The power conferred by the bench is immense—decisions made in courtrooms can alter lives, destroy careers, or, in some cases, steal childhoods. Nowhere is that abuse of power more vividly illustrated than in the "Kids for Cash" scandal, a case that unfolded just one county over from where I practiced. It remains one of the darkest chapters in American judicial history—a cautionary tale of what happens when justice is commodified, and when the very people entrusted to protect the vulnerable become the architects of their harm.

In the early 2000s, Luzerne County became the epicentre of a judicial crisis that would reverberate nationwide. Two sitting judges— Mark Ciavarella and Michael Conahan—engineered a scheme to close the county-run juvenile detention facility and reroute children into private, for-profit institutions in exchange for nearly $2.8 million in kickbacks. This wasn't a policy failure; it was an intentional monetisation of juvenile justice. (The Associated Press)

What made the scandal especially personal was that both Ciavarella and Conahan were known to Judge Jeffrey Schmehl—then a circuit judge—before his elevation to the federal bench. Their proximity to honourable colleagues underscores how corruption doesn't always operate in shadows. Sometimes, it walks the same corridors as integrity.

The mechanics of their scheme were simple and devastating. Minor infractions—truancy, schoolyard arguments, adolescent defiance— were met with disproportionate punishment. The goal was to keep the beds full and the money flowing. Children became pawns in a profit-driven pipeline. In response, the Pennsylvania Supreme Court vacated nearly 4,000 juvenile convictions, acknowledging the scope of harm inflicted by a judiciary that had failed its most vulnerable. (Juvenile Law Center)

Justice eventually came, but slowly. In 2011, Ciavarella was convicted of racketeering, money laundering, and related offenses, and sentenced to 28 years in federal prison. (Associated Press) Conahan pleaded guilty and received 17.5 years. Yet even this resolution bore controversy. (FBI) In December 2024, President Joe Biden commuted Conahan's sentence, prompting public outcry and renewed scrutiny over accountability in high office.

This was not an isolated scandal. It was a symptom of a deeper vulnerability in the justice system—a vulnerability that allows power, when left unchecked, to transform public service into personal gain. When justice becomes transactional, when liberty can be exchanged for profit, the courtroom ceases to be a forum for truth. It becomes a marketplace. And in that marketplace, it is always the powerless who pay the highest price.

# Other Cases: When Judges Become Defendants

The misconduct of Ciavarella and Conahan was particularly shocking because of the scale and brazenness of their scheme. But they are far from the only judges to betray the bench. American legal history holds other examples—some quieter, others equally dramatic—of how those entrusted to uphold the law can themselves fall prey to ambition, arrogance, or entitlement.

## *Judge Harry E. Claiborne: Convicted in Office*

Appointed by President Jimmy Carter in 1978, Judge Harry E. Claiborne served on the U.S. District Court for the District of Nevada until he was convicted in 1984 of filing false tax returns. Remarkably, Claiborne refused to resign, forcing Congress to act. In 1986, the U.S. Senate convicted him on three of four articles of impeachment, making him the first federal judge in history removed from office for crimes committed while sitting on the bench. (United States Senate) His case remains a landmark example of how criminal conduct at the highest levels of the judiciary can be met with constitutional accountability—albeit reluctantly.

## *Judge Alcee L. Hastings: From Impeachment to the House of Representatives*

Judge Alcee Hastings, appointed in 1979 to the U.S. District Court for the Southern District of Florida, was charged just two years later with soliciting a bribe in return for judicial leniency. Though acquitted in criminal court in 1983, a subsequent judicial inquiry found that Hastings had lied under oath. He was impeached by the House in 1988 and convicted by the Senate in 1989, resulting in his removal from the bench. (Marcus) In an extraordinary twist, Hastings went on to launch a political career, serving nearly three decades as a U.S. Congressman from Florida until his death in 2021.

# Parallels for Physicians: Public Trust and the Weight of Scrutiny

The stories of Ciavarella, Conahan, Claiborne, and Hastings may unfold in courtrooms, but their implications reach far beyond the judicial system. For physicians—especially those working in politically or medically sensitive fields—these cases carry a haunting resonance. Just as judges can find themselves weaponized by their own system, so too can doctors be criminalised not for malpractice, but for professional decisions recast through the lens of suspicion.

A physician's version of "improper conduct" might be an aggressive treatment plan, a non-standard prescription, or a misunderstood billing entry. Prosecutors, like rogue judges, can manipulate ambiguity, frame narratives, and paint complexity as culpability. The stakes—licenses, reputations, even liberty—are just as high.

These judicial scandals serve as more than historical anecdotes. They are cautionary tales. They remind us that those with power—whether behind a gavel or a stethoscope—must be vigilant not only in their conduct, but in defending their integrity against institutions that may fail to protect it.

# Chapter 12

# The Sixth Amendment on Trial –
# A Doctor's Reckoning with Justice

*"Justice must not only be done, but must also be seen to be done"*

— Lord Hewart, Rex v. Sussex Justices, [1924] 1 KB 256.

*"In all criminal prosecutions, the accused shall enjoy the right to a speedy and public trial, by an impartial jury..."*

— Sixth Amendment to the United States Constitution

## Psychiatry, Leadership, and a Time of Crisis

It was 2016 when I received a call that would quietly shift the course of my professional journey. The leadership at Easton Hospital had a vision: to establish an inpatient psychiatric unit—a sanctuary for those in crisis. They asked me to lead it.

The decision did not come lightly. An inpatient unit is more than walls and beds—it is, at its best, a place of healing for those whose minds have turned against them. And in that quiet corner of the hospital, I saw possibility. I brought to the ward the same intensity I had always brought to my work—an insistence on both humanity and science, on psychotherapy as well as pharmacology. I used newer medications, modern approaches, and above all, a deep respect for the people in our care. These patients were not broken. They were simply in pain. And pain, with time and care, can soften.

The community responded. Families reunited with their loved ones—stabilised, restored, returned home. The media took notice. I gave interviews to local radio, to television, to NPR affiliates. Not for vanity, but because I believed this: when mental illness is seen, named, spoken of—it loses its shame. That, too, is healing.

Later that year, I was elected President of the Lehigh Valley Psychiatric Society. The role was expected to last one year. Instead, I served four—because the world changed.

When the pandemic came, it came for our minds as much as our lungs. Fear, isolation, grief—all of it fed the silent pandemic of mental illness. And suddenly, our profession was asked to pivot overnight. I became the voice people turned to for telepsychiatry—for bringing help through a screen when face-to-face wasn't safe. Local stations aired my guidance. I trained psychiatrists across Pennsylvania, not for recognition, but because there was no time to wait.

I remember the early weeks vividly. The late-night calls, the patients trapped in silence, and the practitioners unsure how to help without a room to sit in. I helped them build those rooms in the digital world—rooms of trust, compassion, and care. And I asked for nothing in return.

Some days, I miss the quiet of those hospital corridors. The ritual of walking into a room, sitting beside someone in pain, and saying, "You're not alone." But I know those words echo still, even over Zoom. And I know that leadership—real leadership—is not about titles or terms. It's about presence. It's about showing up when the world unravels.

## The Sixth Amendment

The words of the Sixth Amendment shimmer with promise, but for most physicians caught in the web of federal healthcare fraud investigations, those words have lost their weight. I know this not from theory, but from standing on the edge of that cliff myself. I have seen colleagues fall—not from guilt, but from the bravery of demanding their day in court. The Sixth Amendment promises a public trial. But in America today, that trial has become a gamble—a relic recited more often than it is realised.

## Trial by Jury: Right or Ruin?

Once the soul of our justice system, jury trials have become museum pieces—spoken of with reverence, yet rarely seen in the wild. The Sixth Amendment says we're entitled to them. Reality says otherwise. A 2023 Pew report laid it bare: less than 1% of federal criminal defendants were acquitted at trial. (Gramlich) Nearly 90% percent pled guilty. (Gramlich) Not because they were guilty—but because the alternative was a freefall into oblivion. In this landscape, the choice to stand trial isn't brave. It's suicidal.

This didn't happen by accident. It's the product of design—what legal scholars now call "the trial penalty." It's a punishment for daring to exercise your constitutional rights. Say no to a plea deal, and you'll face charges multiplied like hydra heads, sentences stretched by prosecutorial alchemy. Innocence becomes irrelevant. Efficiency is the new justice.

I lived this truth. One morning, the agents came. No warning. No courtesy. Just silence and badges. They moved through my clinic like it was a crime scene, lifting charts, questioning motives, drawing conclusions in ink while I stood mute with disbelief. They told me I was a fraud—not because I stole, but because I treated patients in ways that confounded billing algorithms. They called judgment criminal. They made medicine a codebook. And when I said no to a plea— because I hadn't done what they claimed—they showed me the real cost of saying no.

## The Anatomy of a Trial Penalty

There is a name for what nearly broke me—what breaks so many before they ever set foot in a courtroom. The National Association of Criminal Defense Lawyers called it out in their chilling report: *The Trial Penalty: The Sixth Amendment Right to Trial on the Verge of Extinction.*

(NACDL) What they described, I lived. The numbers are brutal. If you plead, you might serve five years. If you go to trial, that same set of facts—those same accusations—can swell into a twenty-year sentence. Same crime—different cost. The price? Your courage.

Fraud cases are especially prone to this legal inflation. The sentencing guidelines are merciless spreadsheets: rigid, mechanical, unyielding. They don't ask why you did something, or whether harm was real. They calculate theoretical losses, assign enhancements like extra weight on a drowning man, and call it justice.

Here's how the machine operates: A physician is accused of billing fraud. The plea offer comes early—five years, maybe less. Refuse it, and the government's tone shifts. Suddenly, you're not just a doctor who billed unconventionally. You're a leader of a conspiracy. You obstructed justice. You abused a position of trust. They stack charges like bricks, building a wall between you and your life. That five years becomes fifteen. Or twenty.

I heard the offer. I did the math. They told me—plainly, coldly—that if I chose trial, if I insisted on facing a jury, they would bury me in enhancements and new counts. They would "supersede" the indictment, add more charges, raise the stakes. It wasn't a negotiation. It was extortion with a human face.

And this is what we now call the justice system—not a trial, but a threat. Not a right, but a risk. Not a courtroom, but a calculator.

In essence, this process is pursued to get as many convictions processed as quickly as possible at minimal cost. Clearly, it is not about justice or fairness.

# Case Study: Michael E Fletcher, MD and Kendall Hansen, MD

The names Michael Fletcher and Kendall Hansen should be etched into the mind of every physician who dares to practice medicine with autonomy. They jointly ran a clinic in Alabama. Both were charged—overprescribing opioids, billing fraud, the usual script. Both stood before juries. But only one walked away.

Dr. Fletcher was sentenced to three years of probation, including 10 months of home incarceration with an ankle monitor. Prosecutors had asked for a nearly three-year prison sentence. (Bentley) Dr. Hansen was acquitted. The difference? It wasn't in the medical records. It wasn't in the conduct. It was in the courtroom's invisible variables: strategy, jury makeup, narrative control.

In Fletcher's trial, the government rewrote his story. They turned chronic pain care into drug dealing, a clinic into a crime scene. Expert testimony that could have contextualized his decisions was buried under prosecutorial showmanship. Fletcher's defense lacked experience in the terrain of medicine-as-crime. The jury heard only one voice—and it was not his.

Hansen, by contrast, had Chapman Law Group behind him—a team fluent in the dialect of healthcare law. They reframed the allegations with surgical precision: standard of care, peer review, clinical discretion. They reminded the jury that medicine is not math. That treating pain is not profiting from it. That intent matters. The jury listened—and they chose not to destroy a man's life. (Chapman II)

As my own trial loomed, I studied their stories like scripture. What shielded Hansen that Fletcher lacked? Was it geography? A more perceptive jury? A judge who didn't lean? The line between prison and freedom is thinner than we want to believe. Sometimes it's no line at all. Sometimes it's luck in a suit and tie.

I remember the moment my attorney, Paul Hetznecker, returned to the defense table after delivering his closing. He looked at me—not with confidence, not with despair, but with brutal honesty. "They have enough to convict you," he said. "And they have enough to acquit you. Just pray."

## When Justice Became Arithmetic

The Sentencing Reform Act of 1984 was supposed to bring order. (Congress.GOV) Fairness. Predictability. Instead, it delivered cruelty by algorithm. Its legacy—the U.S. Sentencing Guidelines—turned justice into an equation. One where intent weighs heavier than consequence. Where numbers matter more than nuance.

In fraud cases, the metric isn't what was taken. It's what *might* have been. "Intended loss," they call it. Not actual harm. Not real money. A billing discrepancy stretched over time, across patients, across charts—it becomes millions on paper. No need to prove theft. No need to show injury. The number is enough. And with that number, sentencing escalates like a fever.

Then the enhancements come, stacked like bricks on a man's back. "Abuse of trust"—because I was a physician. "Special skill"—because I had training. "Obstruction"—because I refused to confess to a lie. Every piece of my identity—my education, my ethics, my insistence on innocence—was rebranded as evidence against me.

And if you own a firearm—even legally, even locked away—it adds more years. Not for use. Not for threat. Just for presence.

They offered me a deal. Years in prison, wrapped in a bow of lesser charges. And I thought about it. God knows I did. But in the end, I feared a silent compromise more than a public battle. I feared surviving as someone I wasn't.

So I said no. I stood before a jury. I risked everything.

And by grace—or fate—or stubborn truth—I walked free.

## The Truth About Loss: When a Number Becomes a Weapon

In the courtroom where my freedom once trembled on the edge of a verdict, I learned that numbers don't just tell stories—they can destroy them. There's one number in particular: *intended loss*. It doesn't measure what was taken. It measures what the government says *you meant* to take. Not fact, not proof—just projection. Just theory. It is imagination, sharpened into a blade, and wielded by prosecutors to turn honest confusion into crime.

When I was indicted, they told the world my fraud totaled over a million dollars. One million! That number echoed like a gunshot through the press, through the courtroom, through my life. But what did Medicare actually pay? A fraction of that. No theft. No harm. But to the Department of Justice, it was never about what happened. It was about what *might have* happened. What they could say I intended. And with that imagined loss, they built enhancements like scaffolding—years stacked on years, decades conjured from shadows.

That is the dark arithmetic of federal sentencing: you're punished not for what you did, but for what they *think* you wanted to do.

And then, in 2022, the Third Circuit Court of Appeals finally said: enough.

In *United States v. Banks*, the court declared a truth so basic, it should never have required litigation: *loss means actual loss.* (Cornell) Not the prosecutor's fantasy. Not the agency's spreadsheet. But real, measurable harm. It was a rare moment of clarity in a system that so often rewards distortion. The court cited *Kisor v. Wilkie*, affirming that deference to bureaucratic interpretation ends when the meaning is clear—and "loss," they said, is clear.

Had I been tried in the Third Circuit—in Pennsylvania, or New Jersey, or Delaware—that ruling would have changed everything. *Banks* would have stripped the prosecution of its most powerful fiction. It would have forced the jury to weigh what *was*, not what *might have been*. Instead, in my jurisdiction, I faced the full fury of the imagined. They extrapolated. They speculated. They turned my billing practices into a thought crime and held it up as gospel truth.

I remember the moment it hit. The prosecutor clicked to a slide—a number, bright and brutal: $1 million. It felt absurd. It felt obscene. Like being accused of stealing a mansion because you walked past the gate. No context. No explanation. Just numbers—cold, swollen, merciless.

The truth? I was serving underserved patients. Providing psychiatric care where few others would. The billing irregularities weren't fraud—they were paperwork missteps in a maze of red tape. But that didn't matter. Once they had their number, I ceased to be a doctor. I became a case file. A cautionary tale.

That's the difference between *actual loss* and *intended loss*. It's not a technicality. It's the difference between justice and vengeance.

And I wonder—how many other doctors would have stood and fought, had they not been staring down numbers pulled from the sky?

How many pled guilty not because they were, but because the system made the risk of innocence too steep to bear?

*Banks* offers a lifeline. But justice shouldn't be a postcode lottery. If fairness matters, then truth—not speculation—must rule our courts.

I chose to fight. I stood in that courtroom and took the risk. And by some miracle, I was acquitted.

But too many don't survive that choice. Too many are swallowed by the numbers.

Let *Banks* be more than a precedent.

Let it be a reckoning.

## Sometimes You Don't Have to Go to Trial

In the long shadow of the courthouse, where justice is often a matter of endurance, sometimes the smartest move is not to fight on the battlefield—but to challenge the war itself.

The case of Dr. Bart Gatz is a masterclass in legal precision—and a reminder that even in a system tilted toward prosecution, the Constitution still has sharp edges.

Dr. Gatz was no rogue operator. He was a respected physician—until the government came for him. Two felonies. A conspiracy, they said. Kickbacks for prescribing a certain drug. The charges were filed on August 28, 2020—just days before the statute of limitations would slam shut. But the filing wasn't what it appeared to be. Instead of going through a grand jury, as the Constitution demands, prosecutors filed what's known as an *information*—a charging document usually submitted only with the defendant's agreement. But Dr. Gatz had given no such consent. No waiver. No nod. And yet, the charges moved forward.

Then came the clockwork: on the final day before the statute of limitations expired, at precisely 6:33 p.m., the government served him. The timing wasn't coincidence. It was strategy. It was delay disguised as due process.

When grand juries reconvened—after a long COVID-induced hiatus—the government tried to dismiss the case *without prejudice*, planning to bring it back properly, with a new indictment. But the court saw through the maneuver.

Judge Donald M. Middlebrooks didn't flinch. He ruled that the government's tactical dance around the statute of limitations was not clever—it was unlawful. To permit it, he wrote, would be to sanction gamesmanship over fairness, expedience over principle. He dismissed the case *with prejudice*. (Weaver) Final. Irrevocable.

And just like that, Dr. Gatz was free.

He never had to face a jury. Never had to sit through opening statements or cross-examinations. Because his team understood something too often forgotten: trials are not always the battlefield. Sometimes, the real war is procedural. Constitutional. Tactical.

This wasn't a loophole. It was a safeguard. A boundary drawn by the Founders, for moments exactly like this.

Justice was done—not by argument, but by insisting the rules *mean* something. That the law must not be bent, even when bent for convenience.

It's a lesson that every physician, every defendant, every citizen should remember: sometimes the bravest move isn't to fight harder—it's to stand still and point at the line they've crossed.

## Sudipt Deshmukh, MD: When They Call It Murder

Sometimes they don't accuse you of fraud. Sometimes, they call it murder.

Dr. Sudipt Deshmukh wasn't running a pill mill. He was a primary care doctor in New York, treating chronic pain, trying—like so many of us—to help patients navigate the thin line between relief and dependence. But when a handful of those patients died from opioid overdoses, the government didn't just point a finger. They drew a sword.

They charged him with manslaughter. Homicide. They didn't just come for his license—they came for his life.

It was an unprecedented move: to hold a physician criminally liable for the biological consequences of treatment, to convert causality into culpability. It was, in every way, a death penalty case cloaked in a white coat.

Dr. Deshmukh didn't run. He didn't fold. With Chapman Law Group and CCG Healthcare Law at his side, he went to trial—knowing full well the stakes. The jury heard everything: the accusations, the nuances, the medicine. And in the end, they said what the government would not: this was not murder. This was medicine.

He was acquitted. Completely. Unconditionally. (Chapman)

But victory in court does not always mean victory in life. The damage was already done. His practice collapsed. His name was dragged through the headlines. The emotional wreckage, the years of uncertainty, the fear of a lifetime behind bars—they don't go away just because the jury says *not guilty*.

What if he had pled guilty? He might have served ten years. A number with an endpoint. A kind of surrender. But instead, he faced down a life sentence—and reclaimed his freedom.

The question isn't just how he won.

The question is why he ever had to fight that battle in the first place.

# The Tale of Another Name—Like Hansen: Steven R. Henson, MD

Some names stay with you—not because they won, but because they endured.

Dr. Steven R. Henson was a physician from Wichita, Kansas. Not a rogue. Not a villain. A doctor who, like so many of us, practiced in the gray zones of pain management—zones the law would later pretend were black and white. He ran the Kansas Men's Clinic, and in 2019, he was sentenced to life in federal prison. Life. For prescribing opioids—oxycodone, methadone, alprazolam—outside what the prosecution deemed "legitimate medical purpose." Cash payments. After-hours visits. The government said he fed the opioid crisis. The court agreed. (Marten)

But then the law changed.

In *Ruan v. United States*, the Supreme Court delivered a seismic ruling: that to convict a physician under the Controlled Substances Act, the government must prove—not guess, not presume, but *prove*—that the doctor *knowingly* acted without authorization. Intent. Mens rea. The cornerstone of criminal law, restored at last to the doctor-patient relationship.

On that basis, the Tenth Circuit vacated several of Dr. Henson's convictions. The jury in his trial had been given flawed instructions— ones that assumed guilt where *Ruan* now demanded doubt. Suddenly, the unthinkable became possible: retrial, reconsideration, release. (Hamm)

I met him during that interlude—while I was still awaiting my own verdict. He had been freed from prison temporarily, and I saw something in him that haunts me to this day: a man breathing air he never expected to taste again. Just being out—for a year or so—was, for him, a kind of miracle. A sliver of heaven.

I owe him more than I can say. His story steadied me.

In May 2024, facing the risk of another life sentence at retrial, Dr. Henson made a choice. He pled guilty—to conspiracy, to distribution, to money laundering. The plea deal came with a five-year sentence. Five years instead of life. A grim trade, perhaps—but one that gave him certainty. One that let him imagine the other side of a prison gate.

His case is no easy parable. There was conduct the courts condemned. But there was also context—missing from headlines, absent from indictments. And there was evolution: the law shifting beneath his feet, too late to undo the damage, but just in time to grant a lesser fate.

Dr. Henson's journey reminds us how fragile the line is between medicine and crime. It reminds us how juries, judges, and journalists can misread what happens in an exam room. It reminds us that legal standards are not fixed—they move, they grow, they sometimes correct themselves.

But by then, a life has already been altered beyond recognition.

His story is not just cautionary—it's instructive. Not just tragic— but human.

# The Story of My Medical School Colleague

In 1996, as twilight settled over the ancient city of Aleppo, I stood shoulder to shoulder with my friend and classmate, Dr. Muhammed Samer Nasher-Alneam. We had made it—graduates of the University of Aleppo's medical program, young and hopeful beneath mortarboards and desert sky. We had studied together in stone-walled lecture halls and whispered through all-night revision sessions, swapping notes and dreams in equal measure. But after that day, our paths diverged.

I chose internal medicine and psychiatry. Samer took a different road—neurology and pain management. He emigrated to the United States, built a practice, and eventually opened the Neurology & Pain Center, PLLC, in Charleston, West Virginia. His mission was clear: to bring relief to those who lived in constant pain. He believed in his patients. He believed in his work.

We stayed in touch. For a time, he lived in Pennsylvania's Lehigh Valley, not far from me. After a difficult divorce, he remarried. I saw him happy again. Grounded. Rebuilding. But peace in this field is fragile.

In July 2018, everything collapsed. Samer was arrested—federal charges: illegal distribution of controlled substances, healthcare fraud, money laundering. They accused him of running a pill mill. Said he was prescribing opioids—oxycodone, methadone—without medical necessity. Two patients had died, and they laid those deaths at his feet.

The image painted by the prosecution was stark. Profiteer. Danger to the community. A man corrupted by power. But I knew another Samer. A man who had treated pain not as a commodity, but as a duty. A man whose compassion sometimes outpaced his documentation.

His first trial began in April 2019. It ended with a hung jury. No conviction, no acquittal—just a courtroom full of uncertainty. The jury couldn't decide where medicine ended and criminality began.

But the government didn't let go. They prepared for retrial. And Samer, denied bail, waited in a cell. They called him a flight risk, despite his deep roots in the community. Despite his children, his patients, his colleagues. Despite me.

He could have fought again. He almost did. But the weight of a second trial, the looming threat of a life sentence—it was too much. In August 2019, Samer took a plea deal. One count. Methadone without proper documentation. He surrendered his license, his DEA registration, his calling. In June 2020, he was sentenced to 63 months in federal prison. (Justice.GOV)

That sentence was more than a number. It was a reckoning. In prison, Samer confronted everything—the choices, the consequences, the silence that follows disgrace. He lost his career. He lost his place in the only profession he had ever known.

But he didn't lose himself.

When he was released in 2024, he emerged into a world that had moved on. There would be no more clinics. No more white coats. But there was still purpose. He began speaking—quietly, humbly—about what he had endured. About the lines he crossed, and the ones the system had drawn with a heavy hand. He tried, in his way, to make meaning from the ruin.

I think of Samer often. Of Aleppo. Of how far we came and how far we fell. His story is not one of simple guilt or innocence. It is the story of a man caught in the riptide of pain management during a national crisis. It is a story of missteps, yes—but also of a system that punishes imperfection as if it were malice.

As physicians, we live on the edge of judgment—by patients, by insurers, by prosecutors. Samer's life reminds me that good intentions are not always enough. That the rules matter. That documentation matters. But also—that grace matters too.

And that even when medicine ends, humanity doesn't.

# The Husband-and-Wife Duo Who Refused to Surrender

In the punishing world of federal healthcare fraud prosecutions, where the weight of the government can feel like a verdict before trial, there are rare stories of resistance. Of standing ground. Of not surrendering. The story of Drs. Ashis and Jayati Gupta Rakhit is one of them.

Cardiologists. Colleagues. Spouses. They built a life in Moreland Hills, Ohio, devoted to treating hearts and healing lives. And then, one day, they were indicted—87 counts. Fraud. Unnecessary tests. Illegal prescriptions. The government painted them as villains in the opioid crisis. Greedy. Dangerous. A symbol of everything wrong with medicine.

But the Rakhits knew who they were. And they refused to plead guilty to something they hadn't done.

They called in a fighter: José Baez. Famous for big wins, yes—but more importantly, for believing in the people behind the headlines. Baez took the case with the full weight of his reputation and experience, and from the moment he entered the courtroom, the story began to shift.

The trial was brutal. Charts. Testimony. Billing records. The prosecution brought everything. They said the Rakhits ran up insurance bills with needless tests, pumped patients full of opioids, and did it all for profit. But Baez pushed back. He didn't just poke holes in their arguments—he tore at the foundation.

He showed the jury the truth behind the numbers. That what prosecutors called "unnecessary" was, in fact, clinical judgment. That in cardiology, uncertainty is the rule, not the exception. That ruling out a heart attack isn't fraud—it's diligence. He cross-examined key witnesses, exposed contradictions, demanded clarity where there was none.

And when it came to the Controlled Substances Act, Baez went further. He argued that the Rakhits hadn't broken the law—they had practiced medicine. That prescribing opioids in complex cases isn't criminal when done within accepted standards. That what the government had built was a narrative, not a case.

The jury listened.

And then, they spoke.

Not guilty. On all counts.

The Rakhits walked out of that courtroom vindicated—not just free, but cleared. It wasn't just a legal victory. It was a message. That even in a system tilted toward plea bargains and quiet surrenders, truth still has a place. That with the right defense, and the courage to endure, justice *can* be won. (Baez)

Their story matters—not just for doctors, but for anyone who fears the machine of accusation. Because in the worst of it, they stood together. And they won.

## The Ice Cream Salesman and the Medical Executive

In the labyrinth of federal prosecution—where titles mean little and reputations are disposable—the story of Joshua "Josh" Putter is one I carry with reverence. A story that reminds us justice isn't reserved for the innocent. It must also be fought for, endured, reclaimed.

Josh wasn't a doctor, but he moved through medicine with purpose. As Chief Operating Officer of Steward Health Care and formerly president of Health Management Associates' Florida group, he ran vast hospital systems. Thousands of employees. Millions of patients. But he never lost sight of what mattered. He was the kind of executive who walked the halls of the ICU, who knew that healing wasn't just measured in margins—it was measured in trust.

And then, one day, trust turned to suspicion.

In 2013, long after he'd left HMA, federal prosecutors came for him. Obstruction of justice, they said. A conspiracy to cover up alleged Medicare fraud. The claim? That Josh, along with other executives, pressured doctors to admit patients who didn't need it. Not fraud, exactly. Not theft. But a failure to prevent something he may not have even known was happening.

The charges were amorphous. Ominous. They didn't hinge on a specific act, but on the absence of action—on silence interpreted as guilt. It was a charge made of fog. And it nearly unraveled everything.

Most people, when faced with federal indictment, disappear. Josh didn't.

Unable to work in healthcare, unsure what the future held, he opened an ice cream shop. A Cold Stone Creamery. While prosecutors drafted legal briefs to cage him, Josh was behind the counter, scooping vanilla into birthday cones, mixing toppings into frozen resilience. It wasn't just survival—it was defiance. Dignity. A way of saying, I'm still here.

And when the trial came—when the government laid out its narrative, its spreadsheets, its carefully clipped emails—the jury listened. And then they answered.

Not guilty.

Just like that, the government's case crumbled. No evidence. No conspiracy. No crime. Just a man who had been made a symbol and nearly sacrificed on the altar of politics and optics. (The Charlotte Sun)

Our paths crossed later, in 2018 and 2019. I was working with Steward. Josh was already rebuilding. Calm. Steady. You'd never know he'd faced the full weight of the Department of Justice. But when we spoke, I recognized the same weariness in his eyes that I carried in my own. We had both stood at the edge. We had both refused to fall.

His story is one the headlines don't tell. When you're charged, the media comes. When you're acquitted, they're gone. But those of us who've been through it—we remember. We share. Because doctors, executives, anyone who dares to lead—we're all vulnerable in this system.

Federal prosecutors don't just target "bad doctors." They target bold ones. Visible ones. Decisive ones. And sometimes, innocent ones.

Josh Putter's story is a quiet anthem of resistance. It's proof that you can face the machinery of accusation, scoop ice cream to survive, and walk out of the fire whole.

Not guilty.

Two words that gave him back his life.

Two words I wear like armor.

Two words that every physician, every administrator, every person falsely accused must hold close.

Because justice—though scarred, though late—can still arrive.

# A Physician's Burden: The Weight of the Sixth

The Sixth Amendment was meant to be a promise. A protection. A line in the sand that no government could cross: *the right to a speedy and public trial, by an impartial jury.* But in today's federal courtrooms, that promise has curdled. What was written as a safeguard now punishes those it was designed to protect.

The trial penalty is no myth—it is the quiet terror that haunts every physician under indictment. Prosecutors wield it like a weapon. Judges, once the sentinels of fairness, now retreat behind sentencing guidelines, pretending their hands are tied. Downward departures are rare. Mercy, rarer still. And defense attorneys—outnumbered, underfunded, and overwhelmed—look into the eyes of good people and beg them to take the deal.

This is not a justice system. This is a machine. A plea factory. A conveyor belt where nuance is crushed and context discarded. A place where even the innocent calculate risk—not in years of practice, but in decades of prison.

I was lucky.

I had a tribe—family, colleagues, friends who stood by me. I had counsel who believed in my case. I had a jury willing to *listen*, not just nod. But most physicians are not so fortunate. They plead. Not because they're guilty—but because they are afraid. Because they want to protect their children. Because they can't stomach the risk of dying behind bars for the sin of practicing imperfect medicine.

Some are guilty. Yes. But many are not.

And any system that regularly coerces innocent people into false confessions is not broken. It is functioning exactly as it was designed: to intimidate, not to adjudicate. To extract, not to examine. And it is *our* responsibility to name it. To fight it. To fix it.

## Reform and Resistance: What We Must Do

The National Association of Criminal Defense Lawyers has sounded the alarm, and their message is clear: we need more than outrage—we need structural change. Among their urgent recommendations:

- Prohibit the use of acquitted conduct in sentencing. If a jury rejects a charge, it should not haunt the defendant through a back door.

- Require proportionality between plea offers and post-trial sentences. A trial shouldn't carry a penalty twenty times greater than a plea.

- Eliminate mandatory minimums. They are legislative hammers in a system that demands scalpels.

- Mandate full discovery before any plea. Defendants deserve to know what they're facing before surrendering their rights.

- Create independent plea review panels. Oversight matters— especially when the stakes are decades of life.

But policy alone won't save us.

We need courage.

We need physicians to resist—publicly, fiercely. We need juries to be educated, to see through the government's narrative. We need lawyers who understand medicine. And we need defendants who, when the moment comes, are willing to say: *no*.

My trial ended with two words I will never forget: *Not guilty*.

But the trial of the Sixth Amendment continues.

Every physician prosecuted under healthcare fraud statutes becomes a test case—not just for billing compliance, but for the Constitution itself. If we let these prosecutions go unchallenged, if we don't speak, if we don't stand, we aren't just losing individual cases— we're surrendering the very idea of a fair trial.


## The Cost of Silence

There is a saying in medicine: *first, do no harm.*

The law should aspire to the same.

And yet, harm is inflicted daily in federal courtrooms. It is inflicted when prosecutors bury defendants under a mountain of charges, then offer a way out that sounds almost merciful—just plead. Just confess. Just lie. It is inflicted when judges ignore the human behind the case and cling to the cold arithmetic of sentencing tables. It is inflicted when the media parrots press releases instead of asking hard questions.

But the deepest harm is inflicted in silence—when those who know better say nothing.

I could have pled. I could have spared myself the anxiety, the expense, the risk. But I didn't. Because I wasn't just defending my name. I was defending my *profession*.

I was defending the idea that medicine must not be criminalized for complexity. That clinical judgment is not criminal intent. That billing errors are not felonies. That a doctor who dares to care—and falls short on documentation—should not be dragged into court and branded a thief.

The Sixth Amendment is not a relic. It is not symbolic. It is a shield. A living, breathing right that demands our defense.

So let us not lay it down in fear.

Let us, when necessary, *wield it*.

Let us, when we must, go to trial—not because we want to, but because we *must*.

Because the future of medicine, and the soul of justice, may depend on it.

# CHAPTER 13

# Citizens in Judgment — The Federal Jury Selection Process in an Age of Vanishing Trials

*"Trial by jury is part of the bright constellation which leads to peace, liberty, and safety."*

— Thomas Jefferson

## In the Time of Covid

In early 2020, life as we knew it began to unravel. The first murmurs of a virus — one we'd never heard of, but would never forget — rippled across the country. By March, Pennsylvania, like much of the nation, had closed its doors. Offices, schools, restaurants, even medical clinics were shuttered. The roads emptied. The world went still.

But not for me.

Long before "telehealth" became a buzzword, I had already woven it into the fabric of my psychiatric practice. My clinic was agile. Adaptable. And when the call came to serve the public in crisis, I answered — not from obligation, but from instinct. My earlier years in biomedical research, funded by the U.S. Public Health Service, had trained me in the precise handling of biological agents. I never imagined those skills would become vital again, but they did. America had invested in me, and this was my moment to return the favour.

As vaccines moved from theory to production, I reached out to former colleagues at the NIH. It was clear: we needed community physicians to support the rollout — quickly, quietly, competently. But there was a problem. These early vaccines required ultra-cold storage, something few neighbourhood clinics could offer.

No one asked me to step in. I simply did. I sourced a scientific-grade freezer from a nearby facility. Paid for it out of pocket. One grey morning in May, I set out to collect it, driving alone down a highway so empty it felt post-apocalyptic.

That was when the truck tire flew off.

It smashed my car with tremendous force, missing my head by inches. The vehicle was destroyed. I was not. I emerged shaken, breathless, and reminded that life — especially a life lived in service — could be claimed at any time. The near-miss didn't deter me. It solidified my resolve.

When the Pennsylvania Department of Health called for community providers to assist in distributing vaccines, I didn't hesitate. Of the 500 physicians in Northampton County, I was the only one to step forward. My staff — barely twenty people — prepared to do the impossible.

In January 2021, we began administering COVID-19 vaccines to our neighbours. We worked evenings. We worked weekends. We vaccinated over 2,000 people, each requiring two doses. We didn't ask for applause. We asked only: who's next?

We took the vaccine wherever people would gather: a local mosque, a Syrian Catholic church, a synagogue, a Sikh gurdwara. Congregations remembered the effort. Many still do.

Some patients could only come under special circumstances. A 105-year-old neighbour came in on a Sunday morning — the only time his daughter, herself elderly, could bring him safely. We opened the clinic just for him. He survived the pandemic. He's now 107.

Others couldn't come at all. So we went to them. Home visits, coordinated with the help of nursing and medical students, stretched into long nights of planning and reporting. It was exhausting, but it mattered.

We never charged a dime. Not a single dollar. I gave my time, my team, my money, and nearly my life. And yet, today, as I face federal prosecution, the very agencies I served refuse to reimburse any of it. No explanation. No justification.

But I have no regrets.

In my heart, I know what I did. I answered the call. I kept my oath. And even if history forgets me, my patients won't. My country may have turned its back on me — but I did not turn my back on it.

## Twelve, Hopefully Not, Angry Men (And Women!)

Apologies for the mashed-up reference to a great movie.

In the shadowed corridors of federal courthouses across America, a ritual older than the Republic still flickers to life. It begins in silence. It ends in judgment. Twelve strangers—chosen not for brilliance, lineage, or status, but through the quiet lottery of democracy—are seated in solemn duty. This is the federal jury. And this is their story.

Once, this ceremony stood at the center of American justice. Today, it is an artifact—respected in theory, abandoned in practice. In 2022 only 2.3% of federal criminal cases made it to trial. (Gramlich) The rest are absorbed into the machinery of plea bargains and sealed deals, lost to the public eye, invisible to the civic conscience.

But every so often, a trial survives.

In 2024, only 38 criminal trials were conducted in the Eastern District of Pennsylvania. My judge presided over three of them. The Assistant U.S. Attorneys trying my case had barely stepped into a courtroom, their résumés rich with indictments but thin on trial scars. Across the country, there were roughly 1,700 federal criminal trials that year—an average of just 2 to 3 per federal judge, and maybe 20 per U.S. Attorney's Office. There are 93 U.S. Attorneys in America. That's how rare this process has become. (United States Courts), (United States Courts 2)

And yet, when it does happen, it is nothing short of sacred.

# The Democratic Roots: From Master Jury Wheel to Courtroom

Every federal jury trial begins not with lawyers or courtrooms, but with a list—a database known as the Master Jury Wheel. It sounds mechanical, and it is. Yet it embodies the soul of democracy at its most mathematical.

Names are pulled at random from voter registration rolls and driver's license databases, following the mandates of 28 U.S.C. § 1863. (Cornell)) This is justice by algorithm—an attempt to create a jury that mirrors the community, blind to race, gender, income, or ideology. It is imperfect, yes, but sincere in its aim: to build a panel of citizens who, for a brief moment, are asked to weigh the life of another.

From that wheel comes the qualification questionnaire. It looks simple. Bureaucratic. But it filters the civic from the disqualified. Are you a U.S. citizen? Over 18? Have you lived in the district for at least a year? Are you fluent in English? Do you suffer from any condition that would impair your ability to deliberate fairly?

Answer "yes" to all, and the next envelope arrives.

And then it happens.

Ordinary Americans—school teachers, mechanics, students, retirees—open their mail and find the summons: You have been selected for federal jury service.

It lands like a thunderclap in a quiet week. Dread. Curiosity. Resentment. And sometimes—just sometimes—a quiet swell of pride.

# Voir Dire: The Dance of Discovery

In the courtroom, before the trial truly begins, there is a strange ritual—a kind of civic dance, awkward and intimate, known as voir dire. The phrase is French in origin, meaning "to speak the truth." But in this setting, it is not confession. It is not dialogue. It is interrogation.

Voir dire is the moment when strangers, plucked from the quiet rhythms of their lives, are asked to bare just enough of themselves to be judged—not for guilt or innocence, but for fitness to judge.

Judges lead. Sometimes attorneys join. The questions begin simply enough. Where do you work? What do you read? Have you served before? But beneath each query lies a search—for bias, for prejudice, for that hidden sliver of allegiance or suspicion that could tilt the scales of justice. It is one of the few places in our legal system where subjectivity is not only permitted but expected.

Two kinds of challenges emerge in this dance: for cause, and peremptory.

Challenges for cause are boundless. If a juror admits to bias—personal, political, racial, emotional—they can be removed. If they have a conflict of interest or prior knowledge of the case, they're excused. These are the easy cuts. The ones the law embraces.

Then come the peremptory challenges. Each side is allowed only a handful. No reason is required. But that silence—the space between the strike and the explanation—has a long and painful history. These are the challenges that have been misused. Twisted. Weaponized to erase diversity, to shape juries that reflect power more than population. Batson v. Kentucky tried to rein in that abuse, but the shadows remain.

In my own voir dire, those shadows were present.

A prospective juror stood and admitted she had read about my case in the local newspaper. Fair enough. But then she said something I will never forget. She had done the math, she told the court. "One point one million dollars over seven years? That's about $150,000 a year," she said. "If he's a fraudster, he's a loser of one."

The courtroom fell quiet. My lawyer froze. The judge cleared his throat.

She was, of course, dismissed. But her words didn't leave the room.

They lingered.

They echoed.

And I could see them settle into the expressions of others still seated in the jury box. Subtle changes—folded arms, tightened lips, narrowed eyes. Doubt had entered through a side door. It didn't need an invitation. It just needed a moment.

That is the danger of voir dire. It is not just a tool for finding fairness. It can also be a window where bias creeps in and festers.

Where one voice—uninformed, flippant, cruel—can plant seeds in a room that will bear fruit during deliberation.

Voir dire is supposed to purify. But sometimes, it poisons.

And yet, we need it.

Because even with its imperfections, this is the only chance a defendant has to peer into the minds of those who will one day decide whether they walk free or die in prison.

As I sat there watching the process unfold, I felt naked. Powerless. Like a patient under surgical lights, my life splayed open while strangers debated whether they could be "fair."

The woman with the calculator and the casual cruelty was removed.

But her voice remained in the room.

And I knew then that winning a trial isn't just about the law. It's about human perception. About bias unspoken. About the ghosts we invite in, even when the door is closed.

## Batson and J.E.B.: Fighting Bias in the Box

The jury box is sacred ground. Twelve citizens chosen not for their expertise, but for their humanity. It is there that truth is tested—not just by law, but by perception, memory, emotion. And yet, that sacred space has been shadowed by prejudice for generations.

In Batson v. Kentucky (1986), the Supreme Court pulled back the curtain. A Black defendant. Four Black jurors struck from the pool by a white prosecutor. No explanation offered, no cause asserted. Just silence and exclusion.

The Court finally said what should have been obvious: you cannot strike a juror solely because of their race. To do so is to violate the Equal Protection Clause. To do so is to infect the process of justice with the poison of discrimination. (Justia)

Batson was a turning point. A formal acknowledgment that racism doesn't vanish when the jury enters the room. That bias in selection is bias in outcome.

But it wasn't the end.

In J.E.B. v. Alabama (1994), the principle widened. That case involved gender. A prosecutor used every peremptory strike to exclude men from the jury in a paternity case. Again, the Court ruled: discrimination in jury selection—whether based on race or gender—is unconstitutional. The logic was simple: the courtroom must reflect the people. Justice cannot be representative if it is filtered through bias. (Justia)

These two cases, Batson and J.E.B., stand like pillars—attempts to hold the roof of fairness aloft. They are meant to protect not just the defendant, but the public's belief in the verdict. Because when a jury is skewed, so is the outcome. And so is the system.

But even with these rulings, the ground remains uneven.

Peremptory strikes are still used—daily, quietly, expertly—to remove jurors in ways that defy easy scrutiny. The burden lies not with the one making the strike, but with the one challenging it. The party must prove discrimination—must convince a judge that what is silent is sinister. That what is subtle is strategic.

And how do you prove intent?

How do you see into a heart sealed by law school and experience?

I have sat in a courtroom and watched it happen. Watched attorneys look at a potential juror—Black, brown, female, foreign-born—and strike them without blinking. Then offer just enough of a "neutral explanation" to pass muster. "They seemed disengaged." "They hesitated." "They had a scheduling conflict."

And just like that, the box empties of difference.

*Batson* and J.E.B. tried to end exclusion. But they could only build a threshold—not a wall. Bias still gets through. It wears new faces. It speaks the language of professionalism. And it knows that judges, especially in busy courtrooms, are unlikely to push back.

So what do we do?

We name it. We remember that the fight for a fair jury isn't academic—it is existential. Because if you cannot be judged by a cross-section of your community, if your fate is decided by a room shaped by bias, then justice is no longer blind. It is complicit.

## Two Paths: The Jury Box and Struck Method

Federal courts generally use two methods to seat jurors: the jury box method and the struck jury method.

In the jury box method, a fixed number of jurors—typically twelve, plus alternates—are seated in the jury box from the start. Voir dire is conducted, and as jurors are removed through challenges, new individuals are called one by one to replace them until the panel is complete.

In the struck method, a larger pool is questioned all at once. Then, challenges for cause and peremptory strikes are made in bulk. The remaining top names are seated. This method gives attorneys a broader sense of the overall pool before making strategic decisions, while the jury box method allows for more individualized questioning.

In the Eastern District of Pennsylvania, and in my trial, the struck method was used. Approximately 65 potential jurors were called. From them, we ended up with 12 jurors and 3 alternates.

Each court—and sometimes each judge—handles this process differently. Some judges permit attorney-led questioning; others ask all the questions themselves. Some allow written juror questionnaires; others do not. In our case, there was an approved written questionnaire submitted in advance, giving both sides an initial window into the minds of those who would soon be asked to judge.

## The Art of Selection: Profiles, Research, and Strategy

Voir dire is often called an art, and rightly so. With limited time and even less information, attorneys must piece together profiles from fragments—inferring biases, instincts, and inclinations from what little is offered. Some hire professional jury consultants. Others lean on intuition and years of trial experience. Social media is examined. Public records combed. Every detail becomes a clue: profession, age, speech, posture.

We relied on the experience of Paul Hetznecker, but the data is thin. Take, for example, a Medicare fraud case: would you want

Medicare recipients on the jury? Logic offers no clear answer. In my case, we had three—and they turned out to be deeply understanding of what had happened to me.

Is there a juror who works in healthcare? A former police officer? Someone whose family member is in law enforcement—or in prison? Another might rant about politics online. Who is open-minded? Who carries resentment? Who will quietly lead the deliberation? Even posture, clothing, or a single offhand remark can carry weight. A juror who crosses their arms during voir dire may be signaling defensiveness. One who nods in agreement with a prosecutor may already have made up their mind.

## Instructions and Introspection – The Jury Faces the Truth in United States v. Muhamad Aly Rifai

On May 7, 2024, inside the quiet solemnity of the United States District Court for the Eastern District of Pennsylvania, the trial reached its final act. The judge's voice rang out across the room—not forcefully, but with measured gravity—as he read aloud the jury instructions to the twelve citizens who now held my fate in their hands.

I listened as my name, Dr. Muhamad Aly Rifai, was read again. I had heard it many times before during the proceedings. But this time, the courtroom felt different. Quieter. More human. The fluorescent lights reflected off polished wood; the murmur of the gallery had faded. All attention was on the jury.

It had been a long trial—measured not only in days but in the emotional toll it exacted. I had become a character in my own story, described in billing codes and cross-examination. Yet even in that austere space, something deeply human remained. The process—the voir dire, the instructions, the hours of testimony—wasn't just legal machinery. It was moral reckoning.

And now, twelve strangers were asked to weigh not only evidence, but the essence of truth, fairness, and doubt.

The Shield of Voir Dire

Long before the first witness took the stand, the battle had already begun—quietly, strategically—during voir dire. My attorney, Paul Hetznecker, submitted a series of deliberate, pointed questions to the court. They were not designed to provoke, but to reveal—to draw out unconscious bias, to challenge assumption, to safeguard the idea that justice requires neutrality.

The questions were direct:

- Would the fact that Dr. Rifai is Muslim affect your ability to be impartial?
- Have you or anyone close to you been a recipient of Medicare?
- Would you tend to believe or disbelieve a law enforcement agent simply because of their job title?
- Do you understand that the burden of proof lies solely with the government?
- That Dr. Rifai is presumed innocent?

These were not mere formalities. They were shields. Shields against quiet suspicion cloaked in certainty. Against prejudice disguised as patriotism. Against the idea that a Muslim psychiatrist—brown-skinned, foreign-named—must be guilty of something.

Each juror was asked to examine themselves: Had they ever received psychiatric care? Had they been charged with a crime? Did they believe in the rule of law—or only in the people who enforced it? In that moment, the jurors were not just being questioned. They were being asked to confront their own narratives.

# A Constitution in Instruction

When the jury instructions were read aloud, it marked more than a procedural formality—it was the moral fulcrum of the trial. The moment where law, logic, and conscience were fused into duty.

Judge Jeffrey Schmehl, in calm and deliberate cadence, reminded the jury of what was at stake: That their job was to weigh the evidence presented in the courtroom. That speculation, bias, and outside noise had no place in deliberation. That the presumption of innocence was not a courtesy—it was the foundation.

The instructions we proposed, through counsel, followed the Third Circuit's Model Jury Instructions—but they were tailored with intention. They were also, in their way, a message. A request for clarity in a process often clouded by complexity.

Among the key instructions:

- Evidence Defined: Only sworn testimony, admitted documents, and stipulated facts were to be considered. Not the indictment. Not the arguments. Not headlines or whispers.
- Burden of Proof: The government carried the full weight of proof. Dr. Rifai had nothing to prove—because innocence was not a defense. It was his starting point.
- Good Faith Defense: If mistakes were made in good faith, with honest intention, they were not crimes. Medicine is not infallible. Nor is billing.
- Character Evidence: Jurors were to weigh testimony about Dr. Rifai's honesty and integrity with the same gravity as any document or forensic claim.
- Credibility of Government Witnesses: Particularly those with plea deals, financial incentives, or institutional power.

Each instruction was crafted with care, anticipating every possible misunderstanding, every potential slippage in the jury's understanding of its task. It was not only a roadmap. It was a shield.

A plea: judge me by the law, not by fear.

## What the Instructions Did Not Say

Yet the true weight of the instructions lay not in their citations, but in their omissions. Nowhere did they mention that the government's own expert had, under oath, backed away from the central theory of prosecution. They did not note that Agent Stephanie Yeager, the lead investigator, may have compromised his impartiality. Nor did they point out that Medicare—the supposed victim—never testified, never submitted a statement, never even claimed harm.

The instructions held to the sacred neutrality of the law. But beneath that surface, the currents of overreach and imbalance flowed freely.

## The Human Challenge of Credibility

Among the most delicate tasks assigned to jurors is the evaluation of credibility. The court gave them a list:

- Witness demeanor
- Inconsistencies in testimony
- Potential bias or relationships
- Quality of memory and opportunity to observe

These were read plainly, as if fairness could be formulaic. But the deeper question lingered: How do twelve strangers assess a man they've never met, when the government has already called him a liar?

That is the challenge. That is the burden.

And that is the quiet miracle of our system: they must.

And in my case, they did.

## The Final Firewall: Presumption of Innocence

One instruction stood above the rest—repeated, underlined, embedded in every part of the charge:

The presumption of innocence stays with the Defendant unless and until the government has presented evidence that overcomes that presumption.

This was the firewall. The final line of defense. The principle that keeps accusation from becoming automatic conviction.

It is more than a legal standard. It is a moral boundary.

# The Bar Next Door — When the Jury Breaks Down

The night before my verdict, sleep eluded me. I thought not only of myself, but of others—physicians like me who had waited for their fate to be handed down by twelve strangers.

One name echoed through the defense community: Dr. Olarewaju James Oladipo, a Black physician tried in Massachusetts on eleven counts of healthcare fraud. He had called me multiple times, seeking advice, clarity, solidarity.

But what made his case infamous wasn't just the trial—it was what happened behind closed doors in the jury room, and what spilled into the open air afterward.

At a bar. Next door to the courthouse.

## A Trial Fractured by Tension

Dr. Olarewaju James Oladipo had a life built on resilience and achievement. Born in London to Nigerian parents, trained as a surgeon in the U.K., and later a U.S. citizen, he was a Black physician serving a community in need. Like so many of us pulled into this system, he was reduced to a defendant, accused of fraud, stripped of context.

His case went to trial in November 2023 in the District of Massachusetts. The government alleged systematic fraud—billing patterns they claimed were deceptive. The defense countered with expert testimony from Sean Weiss, the same expert who reviewed the evidence in my own case. The argument was familiar: mistakes, not malice. Missteps, not misconduct.

But the jury didn't function as a unified instrument of justice. It splintered.

On December 11, 2023, after three days of deliberation, the jury sent a note to Judge Allison D. Burroughs: "We are not making any progress... people's opinions are not being swayed." It was a warning. A signal that the process had stalled.

When that happens, judges often resort to what's called an Allen charge—the "dynamite charge." It urges jurors to push forward, to reconsider, to resolve their differences and avoid a hung jury. Judge Burroughs issued the charge.

Hours later, the jury returned a mixed verdict: guilty on ten counts, not guilty on one.

But what happened inside the jury room was far more troubling than any verdict.

## *The Lone Juror*

Juror #4—a Black woman, the only juror of color after the prosecution used a peremptory strike to remove the only eligible Black male—was that lone dissenting voice.

The defense had challenged the strike under Batson, but the judge allowed it. That decision would echo into the final hours of deliberation.

After the trial, Juror #4 wrote an unsolicited email to Sean Weiss, the defense expert:

"We almost had a hung jury on Monday. The Judge made us go back in. I was ultimately the only one in favor of Innocence. It was quite a terrible experience. I'm a little bit traumatized by it. There were tears, name-calling… totally like 12 Angry Men in there (11 Angry White Men for right)!"

That line—"I was ultimately the only one in favor of Innocence"—speaks volumes. A solitary juror, isolated in belief, overwhelmed by pressure. Possibly coerced into conformity.

In a public post, she later wrote:

"Some of us entered deliberations believing in total Innocence while others believed in total guilt. We were deadlocked… The judge ordered us back in to figure it out. There were tears & name calling… 'Guilty' won in the end on 10 Counts. Long story short, I was an outlier on so much. I could write a book on what occurred."

And I wish she would.

Because what happened in that jury room, and what followed afterward, raises serious questions—not just about the verdict, but about the integrity of the process itself.

## The Bar on the Corner

On that same Monday—after the jury sent word of their deadlock, received the Allen charge, and were dismissed for the evening—two of Dr. Oladipo's supporters spotted something troubling.

At Zazibar, a bar just steps from the courthouse, they saw two deliberating jurors seated together. One was Juror #4, the known holdout. The other appeared to be Juror #5, who had been seated beside her during trial. It was approximately 3:45 p.m., just minutes after they had left the courthouse.

They weren't passing through. They were seated together at a table, in plain view. The court had been clear: jurors were not to discuss the case outside the deliberation room. And yet here they were—two jurors, including the lone dissenting voice, sharing a social moment during the most critical stage of the trial.

Dr. Oladipo's team acted quickly. They filed a motion for a post-verdict inquiry, supported by an affidavit from a Federal Defender's investigator who confirmed the sighting, complete with photographs. The motion didn't allege misconduct outright—it simply requested a closer look, to determine whether that bar meeting crossed a line.

The court refused.

Judge Allison D. Burroughs ruled that even if the account was true, it didn't meet the threshold for jury misconduct under Rule 606(b) of the Federal Rules of Evidence. The rule bars inquiry into jury deliberations unless there is clear evidence of outside influence. A casual social encounter—even one between a holdout and a fellow juror—was not enough.

And so the matter ended. Dr. Oladipo surrendered to FMC Devens in Ayer, Massachusetts on February 27, 2025. His release date is set for May 15, 2026. (DelMonico)

## The Trauma of Conscience

But Juror #4's voice did not disappear.

Her post-verdict emails and public comments told a story courts rarely acknowledge: the trauma of dissent. "I'm a little bit traumatized by it," she wrote. It wasn't exaggeration. It was the voice of someone who stood alone in defense of innocence and was ultimately pulled under.

Her experience called to mind Peña-Rodriguez v. Colorado, where the Supreme Court carved out a rare exception to jury secrecy: when a verdict is tainted by explicit racial bias. No such slur was spoken in Oladipo's case. But the only Black juror—the only dissenting juror—was isolated and, perhaps, pressured. (VanHofwegen)

Her later statements raise unsettling questions: Was the verdict truly unanimous? Or was it the result of exhaustion, frustration, and emotional attrition?

## The Verdict and Its Legacy

Dr. Oladipo's motion for release pending appeal was denied. The court conceded that his appeal might ultimately succeed—on sufficiency grounds or on the integrity of the jury process. But it concluded that he did not meet the statutory threshold for staying his sentence. So he went to prison, while the doubts surrounding his conviction remain unresolved.

I think often about his case. As a physician, I know that trauma does not disappear when the event ends. It lingers—in the body, in the mind, in memory. What Juror #4 experienced was not just deliberation. It was civic trauma—the kind that occurs when conscience is silenced by consensus.

What if the judge had granted just thirty minutes? A sealed hearing. A pair of simple questions: Did you discuss the case at the bar? Did outside pressure shape your vote? The answers may not have altered the outcome. But they would have honored the principle that justice must be not only lawful—but untainted.

That is the lesson I carry from Dr. Oladipo's story: that even in trials where the process is followed, the outcome can still be unjust. If we want to protect the sanctity of trial by jury, we must not only defend its structure—we must listen for the silences inside it.

Especially when the truth makes us uncomfortable.

## My Thoughts on What I Learned

Having lived through it, I can say this with clarity: jury instructions are not ceremonial. They are moral guideposts—an ethical map handed to twelve citizens asked to weigh truth against power.

The voir dire in my case was not merely a procedural filter. It was an act of resistance. Against bias. Against stereotype. Against the quiet assumptions that follow men like me—Muslim, psychiatrist, immigrant, doctor. Any one of those labels, weaponized in the wrong room, could have meant a conviction.

But my jurors listened. They followed the instructions. They asked questions. They requested readbacks. They debated. They resisted the pull of simplicity.

And they returned with a verdict: Not Guilty.

That verdict didn't just free me. It restored something inside me— faith, however fragile, in a system that nearly destroyed me.

Jury instructions matter. Voir dire matters. These are not boxes to be checked—they are the rails upon which justice must ride.

In that courtroom, I saw the law function. Barely. Precariously. But gloriously.

And I am here to tell the story.

## The Duties of the Jurors and the Trial Process

Once selected, jurors swear an oath to deliver a verdict based solely on the evidence presented and the instructions of the court. They must observe carefully, avoid outside influence, and cannot discuss the case—not even with each other—until formal deliberation begins.

A federal criminal trial unfolds in defined stages: opening statements, presentation of evidence by the prosecution and defense, cross-examination, closing arguments, jury instructions, deliberation, and verdict. Jurors do not decide the sentence. Their role is to determine guilt or innocence—nothing more, nothing less.

## *The Verdict and the Weight of Decision*

After the instructions are read and the evidence is complete, the jurors retire to deliberate. In the privacy of the jury room, they review exhibits, discuss testimony, and strive for a unanimous decision. Their verdict is announced in open court.

And then, just like that, they return to anonymity.

But what they carry—and what they leave behind—can shape lives forever.

# Jury Misconduct: Cracks in the Foundation

The system works best when followed. But it is not infallible. Jury misconduct threatens the core of impartial justice and has become an increasing concern in recent years.

Common forms include:

- Unauthorized discussions
- Exposure to outside information
- Social media activity
- Dishonest answers during voir dire
- Independent research

Each of these can contaminate deliberations and destabilize outcomes.

In Remmer v. United States (1954), the Supreme Court held that any private communication with a juror about the case is presumptively prejudicial. The burden then shifts to the government to prove the interaction was harmless—what's known as the Remmer presumption. (Justia)

In the trial of Martha Stewart, jurors failed to disclose key information on their questionnaires. In Tyco International, juror gestures and later outside contact led to a mistrial. In Scott Peterson's case, post-verdict revelations about juror concealment ignited national debate. (Yin)

Jurors have searched the internet, run personal experiments, and posted on social media during trial. In Dimas-Martinez v. State, a death sentence was reversed because a juror tweeted during deliberations. (Justia)

These cases show how easily digital tools and blurred boundaries can compromise justice—even with repeated warnings.

Some can't resist the glow of a phone screen.

And sometimes, that screen becomes the crack in the foundation.

## Handling Misconduct: Hearings, Standards, and Reversals

When jury misconduct is alleged, courts may hold what's known as a Remmer hearing—a judicial inquiry into whether misconduct occurred, whether it was prejudicial, and whether it warrants a new trial. Rule 606(b) of the Federal Rules of Evidence generally bars juror testimony about deliberations, but makes exceptions for cases involving extraneous information or external influence. (Cornell)

Judges must walk a tightrope—balancing the finality of a verdict with the constitutional right to an impartial jury. The higher the stakes, the more carefully the court must tread. Not every infraction triggers reversal. Courts examine whether outside information reached multiple jurors, whether it introduced factual material not presented at trial, and whether it likely influenced the outcome.

## When the Jury Goes Rogue

I sat in the courtroom each day of my federal fraud trial, watching the jurors enter, twelve strangers whose quiet presence carried the weight of my future. As a physician accused of healthcare fraud, I was fighting not just for my freedom, but for my name. And I couldn't help wondering: Do they understand the evidence? Are they resisting the urge to Google me?

In the early mornings before court, my thoughts drifted to other trials—stories I had heard where juries had gone astray. I imagined the ghosts of those cases lining the back of the courtroom, whispering cautionary tales.

## The Lure of Social Media

One fear loomed larger than the rest: the internet. In our digital age, the judge's routine instruction—"do not research this case or discuss it online"—felt like a relic. I knew how fragile that line was. And I knew the stories.

In one case, a federal judge in Florida declared a mistrial after eight weeks of drug conspiracy testimony. The cause? Several jurors had secretly turned to the internet, researching legal terms and reading news articles. They defied explicit court orders. The media dubbed it the "Google mistrial." Judge William Zloch, visibly stunned, learned the truth as jurors confessed their digital trespasses. Years of preparation—erased by a few clicks. (Schwartz)

That story haunted me. During recess one afternoon, I saw a juror thumbing her phone. My stomach sank. Was she checking texts? Or looking up my case? I'll never know. But the fear was real.

Across the country, courts have been grappling with similar incidents. Jurors tweeting mid-trial. Facebook posts revealing juror opinions. Judges now lecture jurors with increasing urgency, sometimes even making them sign daily affidavits pledging they haven't gone online.

And still, it happens.

In one case, a juror friended the defendant on Facebook. His name was Jacob Jock, and he was dismissed mid-trial. But instead of laying low, he posted: "Score... I got dismissed!! Apparently they frown upon sending a friend request to the defendant... haha." The judge held him in contempt of court and sentenced him to three days in jail. "I cannot think of a more insidious threat to the erosion of democracy than citizens who do not care," she said. (Eckhart)

That statement has never left me.

In the nights before my verdict, I would lie awake, imagining one of my jurors casually tweeting about the "boring fraud case," or worse, polling followers about my guilt. It sounds absurd—until you realize it's happened. Some jurors have posted informal polls online. Others have live-tweeted trials in real time. Even a LinkedIn profile view has raised concerns, suggesting that a juror—or someone close to one—may have quietly researched the defendant's professional history during trial.

Whether intentional or not, these breaches cast shadows. They create doubt. They pierce the supposed sanctity of the jury box.

And as a defendant, it made me feel like the walls of that box were no longer solid. They were glass. And the digital world was seeping in through every crack.

## A Whisper Outside the Court

Juror misconduct isn't always digital. Sometimes, it's old-fashioned—a whisper, a glance, an unguarded comment in a hallway. Courts have struggled with this problem for generations. One case that stayed with me was that of Carl Remmer, tried for tax evasion in the 1950s. During trial, an unknown man approached a juror and implied he could "profit" from returning a favorable verdict. It sounded like a bribe—possibly a joke, but one that struck a nerve.

The juror reported it, and the FBI investigated. But the trial judge, believing the incident harmless, didn't inform the defense. Years later, when Remmer learned of it, he appealed. The Supreme Court weighed in, ruling that any such incident must be treated seriously. A hearing should have been held. Silence was unacceptable. Even the suggestion of outside influence, they said, undermines the very premise of a fair trial. (Eisner Gorin)

That case echoed in my mind every time I passed through the courthouse lobby. I was hyper aware of my proximity to jurors. One morning, I stepped aside, letting jurors and prosecutors take the elevator while I stood still, pretending to study the numbers. Even a "hello" felt dangerous. We all understood: no small talk, no gestures, no contact.

I remembered the case of Parker v. Gladden, where a bailiff whispered to a juror during a murder trial, "Oh, that defendant is guilty, you can bet on it." That whisper led to a conviction being overturned.

A single careless comment, made outside the rules of evidence, had broken the system. (Justia)

Even casual juror conversations—among themselves—can be misconduct if they happen too soon. In one federal trial, the judge discovered that jurors had started discussing the case well before the final evidence was presented. Each juror had to be questioned. Had they formed opinions too early?

I often wondered if, during a break, two of my jurors exchanged glances that meant more than politeness. The thought made my palms sweat.

And then there's the kind of misconduct that blends curiosity with defiance—when a juror brings in outside material. In New York, during a fraud trial, a frustrated juror went home, researched legal precedents, printed out pages, and brought them into the deliberation room the next day.

That wasn't curiosity. It was contamination. It led to a mistrial.

She was held in contempt and reportedly sentenced to community service.

Stories like that circulate among trial lawyers like campfire warnings. They stay with you.

## Prejudice in the Jury Room

Of all the fears I carried, one loomed larger than any Google search or social media slip: bias. Especially racial bias. The kind jurors bring with them—the kind they might not even recognize.

As an immigrant. A doctor. A Muslim. A man with a foreign name. I knew that some part of me would be on trial the moment I walked into that courtroom, even before the first piece of evidence was shown.

We try to root out bigotry during voir dire, but some jurors hide it. Some don't even realize it until deliberations begin.

I remember reading about the case of Michael Allen Smith in Minnesota. He was a Black man on trial for a firearms charge. The evidence against him was weak—no physical connection to the gun, mostly officer testimony. The jury convicted him.

Years later, it came out that, during deliberations, a juror had said aloud: "You know he's just a banger from the hood, so he's got to be guilty."

That racist assumption swayed the jury foreman to change his vote. When the truth surfaced, Judge Susan Richard Nelson ordered a new trial. She cited a 2017 Supreme Court precedent that had finally pierced the veil of jury secrecy in cases of racial bias. Justice Anthony Kennedy wrote, "The jury is to be a criminal defendant's fundamental protection of life and liberty against race or color prejudice." (Justia)

I remember reading those words and feeling both relief and despair—relief that courts might now intervene, and despair that such bias still lives in our most sacred civic space.

The only reason Smith's injustice came to light was because the foreman saw a news story about the Supreme Court ruling and his conscience stirred.

That made me wonder: How many guilty verdicts have been poisoned by hidden prejudice—never to be discovered?

In my own trial, I scanned the faces of every juror during selection. I could feel the weight of my name in the air—Dr. Muhamad Aly Rifai—and wondered what unspoken assumptions it carried.

Bias can wear many faces. A juror might mistrust doctors. Or immigrants. Or psychiatrists. If they lie about that in voir dire, it's misconduct. But proving that is difficult. Courts use the McDonough test to decide if a verdict should be overturned based on a juror's concealed bias. But it's a high bar to clear. (BYU Law Review)

So I placed my faith in my attorney's skill. In the process. And in the hope that we had struck any hidden prejudice at the door.

## The Price of a Verdict

The most shocking form of juror misconduct—though thankfully rare—is outright bribery. It sounds like fiction: envelopes of cash, covert meetings in parking lots, whispered deals. But even in the fortified world of federal justice, it has happened.

When I needed a grim reminder of how far the system could fall, I thought of the infamous case of John Gotti, the New York Mafia boss.

In 1987, Gotti stood trial on federal racketeering charges. To public astonishment, he was acquitted—earning the nickname "Teflon Don."

But it wasn't just his courtroom charm.

Five years later, it was revealed that Juror George Pape had accepted a $60,000 bribe to vote not guilty and influence the outcome. Pape was later convicted in 1992 for this betrayal. By then, the damage was done—justice had been bought, and the 1987 trial became a scar on the credibility of the jury system. (Lubasch)

I imagine those jurors deliberating, unaware that one of their own was a paid agent of the defense. A poison in the room. A shadow at the table.

Even earlier, the case of Jimmy Hoffa showed how deep corruption could run. In one of Hoffa's federal trials in the early 1960s, a hung jury led to a mistrial. But evidence soon emerged: jurors had been offered bribes. Hoffa's own lawyer was caught attempting to pay $10,000 to sway a verdict.

That led to a dramatic follow-up trial in Chattanooga in 1964, where Hoffa and others were charged with jury tampering. Prosecutors called it "one of the greatest assaults on the jury system the country has ever known."

The testimony was stunning: bribes, infiltrators, eavesdroppers—people literally listening at the jury room door. It was more than a trial. It was a war for the soul of American justice. In the end, Hoffa was convicted—not for conspiracy, but for trying to corrupt the system itself. (Justia)

These stories haunted me—not because I feared mob tactics in my own case, but because they show just how fragile the system really is.

As I sat at the defense table, I would sometimes glance at the jurors and wonder: What if?

Every juror in my case had been carefully vetted. There was no hint of impropriety. But once you know how easily it has happened—even in the most secure, high-stakes trials—you realize something sobering:

No trial is ever completely immune.

# Reflections from the Jury's Shadow

Sitting there as a defendant, I felt utterly vulnerable. The courtroom may appear to be a theater with visible actors—the judge, the lawyers, the witnesses—but the real drama unfolds in a room none of us can enter. The jury room might as well have been on the far side of the moon. I had to trust that twelve strangers would follow the judge's instructions, resist outside influence, police one another, and deliberate honestly.

I had to trust that none harbored hidden prejudice. That none would violate the rules out of boredom, curiosity, or impulse. That none would be tempted by anything that had no place in the sacred act of deliberation.

Most jurors, I remind myself, do exactly what is asked of them. That's the quiet faith the system depends on. And even within the horror stories, there is a strange reassurance: often, it is another juror, or a judge, who uncovers the truth. In Smith's case, it was the foreman who later spoke up about the racist remark. In the "Google mistrial," it was the brazenness of the jurors that led the judge to investigate. In Hoffa's trial, a team of investigators peeled back the layers of corruption.

The system is imperfect. But it has mechanisms for self-correction.

Still, I can't help but feel how personal it all becomes when you're the one on trial. These aren't procedural hypotheticals—they are deeply human uncertainties tied to your name, your life, your future. I think back on my trial and feel immense gratitude for my jurors, who—as far as I know—followed the rules and weighed the case with care.

But I also know how easily it could have gone the other way. A different day. A different courthouse. A different juror. In some parallel life, I might be the subject of one of these stories—the defendant whose conviction was overturned years later due to a Facebook post, or a racial slur uttered in deliberation, or, worst of all, never uncovered at all.

We call it a jury "of our peers." But peers are human. They bring into the courtroom everything that society contains: curiosity, decency, prejudice, wisdom, carelessness, integrity, selfishness. The trials I've described reflect the full spectrum—jurors who brag online, jurors who sell verdicts, and jurors who hold firm to conscience under pressure.

These people—ordinary and flawed—decide the extraordinary. And despite everything, we place our bet on them, because the alternative is worse.

So no, these reflections haven't made me lose faith in the jury system. But they have stripped away any illusion. The jury is not a divine oracle. It is twelve human beings in a box. And like every human heart, it carries imperfections.

As a doctor, I understand fragility. I know what it means to depend on systems built from fallible bodies. The jury is the heart of a trial—and it beats with all the uncertainty of human nature.

I emerged from my trial not guilty, and I am profoundly grateful. But I carry with me a sober truth: justice walks a razor's edge. One careless tweet, one whispered slur, one unseen payoff, and the balance tips.

That knowledge now lives alongside the triumph. And it will stay with me—always.

# The Path Forward: Guarding the Sanctity of the Jury

In response to growing concerns about outside influence, courts have begun to strengthen and modernise their safeguards. Jury instructions are being revised to more explicitly underscore the ban on independent research, use of social media, and digital communication related to the case. Judges increasingly remind jurors at the start and end of each day about their obligation to avoid all outside information. In some jurisdictions, jurors are now asked directly—sometimes daily—whether they've encountered any external content or discussions that could compromise their impartiality. These are essential steps toward protecting the integrity of the process—but the risks remain deeply embedded in everyday life.

Smartphones buzz without warning. Notifications arrive without our permission. News alerts flash across screens, sometimes even from locked devices. Algorithms, tuned to our browsing history and location, serve us targeted content—including articles, commentary, or even advertisements that relate, directly or indirectly, to the case at hand. In high-profile or emotionally charged trials, these digital intrusions are not just possible—they're inevitable. Worse, jurors' families or social circles may be approached, questioned, or subtly influenced, turning the courtroom's protective bubble into something more porous than ever before.

Justice in the digital age requires more than updated court protocols. It demands a cultural shift—a reaffirmation of civic ethics and the ancient ideal of citizen duty. Jurors must be reminded that their role is unique: they are not investigators, commentators, or critics. Their job is to listen with care, to weigh evidence with fairness, and to deliberate without distraction. The internet is not a co-juror. The verdict must rise from reason, not from a search bar.

# Chapter 14

# Going to Trial: Should Healthcare Fraud Defendants Fight or Fold?

---

*"The secret to happiness is freedom... And the secret to freedom is courage."*

— Thucydides

## Volunteer Services / Teaching Services

On February 6, 2023, a devastating 7.8 magnitude earthquake struck northern Syria and Turkey, causing widespread destruction and the immediate loss of nearly 100,000 lives. My beloved hometown of Aleppo was among the hardest hit. The scenes of ruin and despair echoed the aftershocks that were already shaking my personal life, having been indicted by federal authorities just months earlier in November 2022. The emotional and psychological weight of those twin catastrophes — one personal, one communal — might have been overwhelming. But instead of retreating, I responded with purpose.

I saw in that tragedy a call to action, not only to stand in solidarity with my people, but to utilise my expertise as a psychiatrist in service of those suffering unimaginable trauma. Through a partnership with the Karam Foundation, I launched a free mental health programme aimed at addressing the acute psychological needs of earthquake survivors. We offered both individual and group counselling sessions, and I took the lead in training other psychiatrists and counsellors in best practices for treating acute anxiety and post-traumatic stress disorder.

Since the programme's inception, we have treated nearly 500 individuals impacted by the earthquake. Many of these survivors were living in makeshift shelters, dealing not only with physical displacement but profound emotional distress. Our initiative became a lifeline. In addition to direct care, I've continued to offer monthly training workshops, biweekly supervision for mental health professionals, and free ongoing psychiatric consultations for individuals battling lingering depression and anxiety.

But my commitment did not stop there. Recognising the importance of long-term capacity building, I volunteered as a faculty member at the Syrian Free University School of Medicine. I taught psychology and psychiatry to medical students, equipping them with the clinical skills and compassion needed to serve communities in crisis. Beyond the classroom, I also served as volunteer faculty for the university's first psychiatry residency programme — guiding residents in providing telehealth services to patients in remote and underserved regions.

These efforts are more than acts of charity. They are acts of resilience — mine and theirs. They are a reminder that even amidst personal and collective crisis, service remains a powerful form of healing.

## Decision Time

There is a moment in the life of every accused physician when the noise falls away.

No more advice from well-meaning friends. No more whispered doubts or stern warnings from attorneys. No more late-night searches for a miracle. Only a raw, private choice remains:

Do I go to trial? Or do I plead guilty and try to salvage what little I have left?

For those of us who have stood at that crossroads, it is not merely a legal decision. It is an existential reckoning. A stripping away of pretense and hope. *Who am I, really?* Am I someone who can wear the label "criminal" even if I know I am not? Or am I someone who will risk everything — freedom, family, future — to say, without apology: I did nothing wrong.

Today, in the United States, the criminal trial — once a hallmark of justice, written in the very bones of the Constitution — is vanishing. It has become an endangered ceremony. Less than two percent of federal criminal cases ever reach a jury. Fewer still end in acquittal. The pressure to plead is relentless, a silent tidal force eroding the bedrock of justice.

And for doctors accused of healthcare fraud or controlled substance violations, the odds are even worse. The government arrives like a hammer. It stacks charges. It threatens decades behind bars. It tells you, plainly: surrender, or be destroyed.

This is what they call the trial penalty. A punishment not for a crime, but for courage. For refusing to confess to something you did not do. And so, many physicians — good men and women — take the deal. They look at their children, their patients, their mounting legal bills, and they fold. Sometimes they are guilty of something. Often they are not. But the system is no longer built to care.

Still, some fight. Not because they are brave. But because they are themselves. Because something inside them refuses to be broken. Because the lie — even a legal one — would be worse than the prison. These rare souls choose to stand.

Dr. Lesly Pompy was one of them.

## The Story of Dr. Lesly Pompy

There are few trials of spirit more brutal than the one Dr. Pompy endured. (Panian) Years before a jury would clear his name, before a courtroom would pulse with the gravity of judgment, he had already begun the fight — not with scalpel or prescription pad, but with silence, endurance, and the quiet knowledge that his life was on trial.

Dr. Pompy was a respected pain physician in Monroe, Michigan. His patients were not numbers. They were veterans, injured workers, and those for whom pain had become a prison. He prescribed boldly, yes — but not blindly. His mission was simple: to treat suffering.

Then came the whispers. Algorithms flagged him. Insurers took note. Blue Cross Blue Shield raised red flags, and soon, the agents arrived. Undercover, posing as patients. Waiting to catch him slipping. He did not. His notes were detailed. His decisions, documented. But the wheels had turned.

In 2017, the U.S. government indicted him on 38 felony counts. They alleged he was running a criminal operation — handing out drugs, gaming the system, poisoning his community. Each charge carried the weight of ruin. He was offered deals. He was offered exits. He said no.

He said no not because he was naïve, but because he knew what he had done. And what he had not.

The government came with everything: spreadsheets, testimony, former staffers who had cut their own deals. They painted him as a pusher in a lab coat. But they misunderstood him. They mistook his silence for fear. His restraint for guilt.

He prepared for trial. He prepared in isolation, as so many of us do — the quiet hours at night, the long walks rehearsing testimony, the haunting recognition that justice, if it came, would arrive slowly and bruised.

And then, just months before jury selection, the U.S. Supreme Court delivered a ruling: *Ruan v. United States*. (Ruan and Kahn) The government, it said, must prove not only that a doctor's prescriptions were outside accepted medical practice — but that the doctor knew it, and intended it. That decision changed everything.

In 2022, Dr. Pompy entered court. The prosecutors came armed with charts, statistics, expert witnesses. The defense came with something else: a life. A story. A reputation earned one patient at a time. They showed a man who had never hidden his work. Who billed properly. Who documented meticulously. They brought in pain specialists. They challenged the assumptions. They reminded the jury that medicine is not a code book — it is a calling.

They told the story of a man who had stayed in his community, who had not packed up and left when the media turned sour. They showed the human cost of treating chronic pain: patients in wheelchairs, patients with degenerative diseases, people whose only alternative was to suffer in silence or turn to the streets.

They spoke of context — of a nation grappling with an opioid epidemic, yes, but also of legitimate pain. They explained that where others saw numbers, he saw names. And each prescription, far from casual, was a decision. A burden. A hope.

They did not tell a story of perfection. They told a story of intent. Of belief. Of medicine practiced in good faith. And it mattered.

And the jury listened.

Not guilty. Not guilty. Not guilty. Thirty-eight times.

The courtroom fell still. Then Dr. Pompy wept.

He had done what few ever dare. He had faced the full weight of the federal government and walked out free. Not untouched — his practice had been gutted, his finances ruined, his name dragged through the dirt. But he had not bowed. He had not lied.

In the aftermath, Dr. Pompy began to speak out. He sued those he believed had wronged him. He vowed to fight for others. And he became something more than a defendant. He became a symbol.

He became a torch-bearer in a system grown dark. He spoke to students. He wrote op-eds. He held workshops for young physicians and told them: document everything. Know your rights. Know your worth. He reminded them that medicine is a human art, and no algorithm will ever understand compassion.

And for every doctor who reads this and wonders whether truth can still survive a courtroom — look to him.

He is proof that it can. He is the reminder that courage, even when bruised and weary, still has power. That justice, though delayed, is not always denied. That if one man can survive the storm, others can too.

His story is not just his own. It is a lifeline — cast backward to those still caught in the undertow.

And it is a warning: that the system, as it stands, asks the innocent to suffer more than the guilty. That without change, it will keep breaking the very people it should protect.

But also this: it is a promise. That if you stand your ground, if you hold your truth, if you remember who you are — then sometimes, even now, the system blinks.

And when it does, it says the words that mean everything:

Not guilty.

# The Story of Dr. Rajendra Bothra

A brilliant surgeon and renowned pain specialist, Dr. Rajendra Bothra was more than a physician. He was a man of healing, of precision, of pride — awarded the Padma Shri by the President of India for his exceptional contributions to medicine. In Michigan, he built a network of clinics that served thousands of patients suffering from relentless, often invisible pain. His name carried weight not just in medical circles but in immigrant communities as a testament to what dedication, education, and service could accomplish. He embodied the American promise — the belief that merit and effort would be enough.

But in America, dreams are fragile things.

It began, as these things often do, with whispers. Complaints. Investigations. Allegations surfaced that he and several colleagues were engaged in a vast conspiracy — defrauding insurance companies through unnecessary procedures and excessive opioid prescriptions. In 2018, the government struck. Federal prosecutors unveiled a sweeping 56-count indictment. It was, they claimed, one of the largest healthcare fraud cases in U.S. history — nearly half a billion dollars. The media pounced. Headlines painted him as the villain in a familiar narrative. A trusted doctor turned profiteer. "Doctors Charged in Massive Opioid Fraud Scheme," the headlines screamed. The nuance was gone. The years of care forgotten. The presumption of innocence? Erased by clickbait and outrage.

But this case carried a cruel twist.

Because of his roots in India and international business ties, prosecutors claimed he was a flight risk. They asked that he be detained pending trial. The court agreed. And so began Dr. Bothra's second sentence — a four-year pretrial incarceration. No conviction. No jury. No opportunity to speak. He waited. Isolated. Silenced. A healer, cut off from his patients, from his family, from his purpose. The pressure mounted. The government's message was unmistakable: plead guilty. Admit defeat. Salvage what little dignity you have left.

He refused.

He knew what he had done. And what he had not. Every procedure had justification. Every prescription came from a place of care. He would not plead to crimes he did not commit.

His trial — delayed by the pandemic and legal wrangling — began in 2022. It would be among the longest healthcare fraud trials Michigan had ever seen. The prosecution laid out an immense case: reams of billing records, testimony from former employees turned government witnesses, expert analyses that painted his surgeries as unnecessary and his prescriptions as reckless. They argued greed. They showed graphs. They brought spreadsheets. They tried to reduce his life's work to codes and claims.

But the defense told a different story.

They brought in pain experts. Specialists who read the same charts and concluded the procedures were within medical norms. They reminded the jury that no insurance provider had denied payment at the time of service. That many of these treatments were commonplace before the opioid crisis became a political talking point. They leaned on science. And on the law — specifically, the Supreme Court's recent ruling in *Ruan v. United States*, which reshaped the standard for physician prosecutions.

In *Ruan*, the Court had raised the bar: the government must prove a doctor not only acted outside of accepted practice but did so knowingly and without medical purpose. It was not enough to make mistakes. It was not enough to disagree with expert opinions. There had to be proof of criminal intent — not clinical divergence.

That was a hurdle the government struggled to clear.

Dr. Bothra did not testify. He sat quietly, respectfully. His lawyers built their case with slow precision. They deconstructed the government's assumptions. They exposed contradictions. They returned again and again to the central truth: medicine is messy. Pain is complex. And healing is not a science of certainties.

The trial dragged on. Jurors waded through months of testimony, insurance claims, and charts. They asked questions. They reviewed evidence. They deliberated for days. They argued, discussed, paused. The responsibility they carried was immense. The fate of a man, a doctor, a reputation — rested in their hands.

And then they returned.

Not guilty.

On every count. Fifty-four times.

Not guilty of fraud.

Not guilty of unlawful distribution.

Not guilty of conspiracy.

In that moment, the courtroom did not erupt in joy. It was quiet. Too stunned for celebration. And yet, something holy had been restored. (Cook)

Later, reflecting on his ordeal, Dr. Bothra spoke softly about what had been taken.

Four years.

His reputation.

His career.

His health.

His peace.

But he also spoke of what he still believed. In justice. In truth. In the jury system. He thanked his legal team. He thanked the jurors. And he vowed to fight — not for vengeance, but for change.

He would speak out. He would write. He would demand that no other doctor endure what he had. He would warn young physicians: document everything. Protect your name. Understand your rights.

Because in today's climate, any doctor who treats complex pain, who works with high-risk patients, who dares to trust their clinical judgment, is a target. The media will not wait for the facts. The system will not ask if you meant to do harm. The machinery moves quickly, and it does not care what it crushes.

The system — bloated, politicised, impatient with nuance — is too eager to prosecute where it should educate. It sees numbers before people. Spreadsheets before suffering. And when the government turns its eyes on you, the weight is staggering.

But Dr. Bothra endured. He survived four years in pretrial detention — one of the longest of any physician charged in a healthcare case. He survived a system designed to crush dissent. And he did so with dignity. He did so with purpose.

His case is a warning: about the awesome power of accusation. About how the presumption of innocence is too often abandoned. About how prosecutors, with limitless resources and media support, can reshape a life with a single press release. About how clinical judgement, in hindsight, can be weaponised.

But it is also a light.

It is proof that truth, when defended with courage and skill, can still prevail. That juries, when allowed to see the whole picture, will not always convict. That sometimes — even now — a man wrongly accused can walk out free.

Dr. Rajendra Bothra is more than a headline.

He is a father. A surgeon. A survivor.

And above all, he is a reminder.

That when the world says confess, when the cell door slams shut, when the system offers only silence and surrender — there remains the power to say:

I am not guilty.

Not because it is easy.

Not because it is safe.

But because it is right.

And in saying so, he does what courts often forget and what the law often fails to ensure — he restores dignity. Not just for himself, but for all who come after him.

Because justice — true justice — demands not only truth, but the courage to speak it when silence would be safer.

That is what Dr. Bothra gave us.

A reason to believe.

# The Story of Dr. Loey Kousa

Long before he found himself standing trial in a federal courtroom, Dr. Loey Kousa had built a life defined by quiet service.

A fellow Syrian immigrant from the Damascus Christian community and a graduate of Damascus University School of Medicine, Dr. Kousa came to America with dreams not of riches or status, but of healing. He settled in Kentucky, far from the towering hospitals of big cities, in towns where ambition often yields to need, where medicine means listening as much as diagnosing. There, among the rolling hills and rural towns scarred by economic hardship and addiction, he opened a small family practice — a modest clinic that quickly became a lifeline.

He treated the forgotten: the elderly, the disabled, the addicted, the uninsured. He welcomed the patients others overlooked — those with chronic pain, mental illness, or simply no other place to turn. He knew their stories. He called them by name. He made house calls, wrote notes by hand, and extended grace where others drew lines. His work was not glamorous, but it was essential. He worked long hours. He saw patients in their homes. He charged what they could pay. And through it all, he kept faith with the ideals that had brought him across oceans: that medicine is a calling, and the patient must come first.

But in an era when the opioid epidemic consumed headlines and algorithms hunted suspects, even compassion could become a crime.

Dr. Kousa prescribed opioids — judiciously, but consistently — to patients in pain. In the numbers tracked by distant analysts, those prescriptions flagged him as a problem. Insurance companies grew suspicious. Federal agencies took notice. In their calculus, there was no room for context. They did not see communities riddled with untreated injuries and poverty. They did not see the scarcity of pain specialists or the desperation of patients. They saw data. They saw outliers. And they moved.

The scrutiny intensified. Audits followed. Data requests turned into subpoenas. His clinic staff grew anxious, then fractured. The unspoken tension of being watched settled like dust over every interaction, every file. And then it happened.

In 2022, Dr. Kousa was indicted on multiple counts, including unlawful distribution of controlled substances and healthcare fraud. The charges were sweeping, the language severe. Prosecutors alleged he had crossed the line into criminality — overprescribing opioids, conducting unnecessary tests, billing improperly. The indictment was a wrecking ball. His medical license was suspended. His clinic shuttered. The man who had devoted his life to healing became a cautionary tale in the national narrative of the opioid crisis.

Friends turned away. Former colleagues hesitated to speak. The press repeated the government's story. Dr. Kousa's name — once associated with care and compassion — now trended online beside words like "fraud" and "pill mill." He was told to plead. Offered a deal. Told to admit guilt and accept a reduced sentence. Told to move on.

But Dr. Kousa refused.

He knew what he had done. And what he had not. He had not profited from addiction. He had not sold prescriptions. He had treated pain in a forgotten place, doing his best with what he had. He would not confess to a crime he had not committed.

And he was not alone. His family stood with him. Former patients wrote letters. Some visited him quietly, reminding him of the lives he had changed. The rural community where he had worked began to stir, not with protest, but with quiet expressions of solidarity. In a world that had rushed to judgment, there were still those who remembered the truth.

The government's case followed a familiar playbook. Data analysts, expert witnesses, and agents testified about charts and outliers. They pointed to high prescription rates and frequent EKGs, calling them red flags. They said his care was outside the bounds of accepted practice.

But the defense — led by attorneys from Chapman Law Group, including Ron Chapman II — fought back with a deeper truth.

They told the jury about rural medicine: about patients with no access to pain specialists, no insurance for expensive procedures, no transportation to hospitals two counties away. They explained that opioids were, for many years, a standard part of chronic pain management. They argued that EKGs were routine for patients on medications that could affect heart rhythms — not scams, but safety protocols.

Most of all, they reminded the jury of what the government had to prove: not just mistakes, not just bad judgment, but intent. Under the standard clarified by the Supreme Court in *Ruan v. United States*, the government had to prove beyond a reasonable doubt that Dr. Kousa knew he was prescribing without a legitimate medical purpose. That he knowingly broke the law.

The defense dismantled the prosecution's assumptions. Experts testified in support of Dr. Kousa's methods. Medical records revealed careful documentation. Patients themselves took the stand. Some testified gratefully, speaking of relief and dignity restored. Others, presented by the prosecution, faltered under cross-examination. Their stories conflicted. Records contradicted their claims. The picture that emerged was not one of a rogue doctor, but of a struggling physician doing his best in an impossible system.

Day after day, the courtroom bore witness to the collision between nuance and accusation. Between medicine and law. Between a man's life and a government's theory.

And then came the verdict.

The jury deliberated. They asked for records. They reviewed testimony. They weighed not just evidence, but implication.

And then — one by one — they spoke.

Not guilty.

On every count.

In the courtroom, there was no celebration. Just silence — the quiet, aching silence that follows a long, hard fight. (R. Johnson)

Dr. Kousa was free.

But like so many who win their legal battles, he emerged into a landscape of loss. His clinic — gone. His reputation — damaged. His savings — drained. The system had not broken him, but it had left its mark. And yet, he chose neither bitterness nor retreat.

He resumed his life slowly. He did not seek headlines. He did not rant or rage. He returned, quietly, to what he had always been: a healer.

He took time to speak to young physicians. He gave quiet advice in private conversations. He reminded those around him that doing the right thing is often lonely — and costly. But it remains right.

His case is more than a courtroom drama. It is a parable — a warning of how fragile justice can be, and how dangerous it is when medicine is judged by metrics alone. It is a lesson in how prosecutorial power, left unchecked, can warp a narrative. And it is a tribute — to a man who stood his ground.

For every physician who treats pain, who bends rules for mercy's sake, who dares to make hard choices in hard places — Dr. Kousa's story is a lifeline. It says: you are not alone. It says: the fight is worth it.

It says: even when the world demands your silence, truth still matters.

And it reminds us — painfully, powerfully — that sometimes the most heroic act is not escape, or compromise, or survival, but simply to stand.

To stand and say: I did nothing wrong.

To believe that justice still listens.

And to hope that next time, it comes sooner.

# The Story of Tom Barrack

In the shadowed corridors of power, where influence and ambition intertwine, few names once carried as much weight as Tom Barrack's. A billionaire real estate investor, founder of the global investment firm Colony Capital, and a close confidant of President Donald Trump, Barrack had achieved what many could only dream of — access, wealth, and political proximity. He built empires, advised presidents, and navigated the volatile waters of business and statecraft with an ease that earned him respect, envy, and suspicion in equal measure. But in modern America, where optics often precede truth, proximity to power can be as dangerous as power itself.

In 2021, federal prosecutors brought sweeping charges against Tom Barrack. He was accused of acting as an unregistered foreign agent for the United Arab Emirates (UAE), lying to federal investigators, and obstructing justice. The indictment painted a picture of betrayal and subterfuge — a wealthy insider secretly serving foreign interests while whispering in the ear of a sitting U.S. president. It was dramatic, cinematic — precisely the kind of high-profile case that federal prosecutors relish. The media pounced. Headlines screamed of treachery. Overnight, Barrack became a symbol not of success, but of suspected disloyalty.

The government's narrative was bold: that Barrack, while acting as an informal advisor to President Trump's 2016 campaign and during his transition into office, used his position to covertly lobby U.S. policy decisions in favour of the UAE. That he concealed these actions from investigators. That he obstructed inquiries into his conduct. Prosecutors built their case on phone records, travel logs, public statements, and associations. They suggested that he had operated in secret, fulfilling the will of a foreign power while camouflaged as a patriotic American businessman.

But like many stories constructed for public consumption, the truth beneath the surface was far more nuanced. Tom Barrack pleaded not guilty to all charges. He did not seek a backroom deal or negotiate a quiet exit. He stood firm. He asserted that he had never acted under the direction or control of any foreign government. His relationships in the Middle East were long-standing and public. He had spent decades building bridges between the U.S. and the Gulf states — through business, diplomacy, and cultural engagement. Those relationships did not begin with Trump, and they were not built in the shadows. They were a matter of record, not concealment.

Still, the stakes were monumental. If convicted, Barrack faced the very real possibility of a lengthy prison sentence, a destroyed fortune, and a legacy rewritten in ink of disgrace. He would be immortalised not as a builder of global alliances, but as a traitor to his country. Few could endure such pressure. Many — even the innocent — would capitulate, plead guilty, and seek mercy.

But Barrack made a different choice. He chose to fight — not only legally, but personally. He chose to testify in his own defence, an extraordinary risk in any criminal trial, particularly one of such magnitude. His lawyers warned of the dangers. Prosecutors would dissect his every word. The press would gleefully analyse every pause and slip. But Barrack believed in the power of truth spoken plainly. And he believed the jury would hear him.

The trial began in Brooklyn in the autumn of 2022. The courtroom was packed. The prosecution opened with a flourish, presenting a tale of influence and deceit. Witnesses were paraded across the stand — FBI agents, communications experts, former officials. Charts were displayed. Text messages analysed. The narrative was rich in drama, light on clarity. The prosecution attempted to show that Barrack's closeness to UAE officials — his public support of UAE policies, his communications with Gulf leaders — amounted to covert lobbying on behalf of a foreign government.

But beneath the spectacle, the evidence wavered. There were no secret payments. No signed directives. No orders received or obeyed. What remained was inference — implication drawn from association, suggestion borne of timing. Much of what prosecutors cast as suspicious behaviour was, in reality, the routine activity of a global businessman — maintaining friendships, advocating for diplomacy, and navigating international interests.

And then came the pivotal moment.

Tom Barrack took the stand.

He spoke with clarity, poise, and conviction. He did not deny his ties to the Middle East. He embraced them. He explained how those relationships were forged through years of dialogue, business ventures, and shared interests. He described meetings that prosecutors called covert as public and transparent. He insisted he had never acted under instruction from the UAE — or from any foreign entity. He had communicated openly, consulted legal experts when necessary, and had never attempted to conceal his work.

The jury listened. They observed his composure, his cadence, the unwavering steadiness of a man who had nothing to hide. They weighed not only his words, but the lack of contradiction from the prosecution. And they deliberated.

After several days, the verdict came.

Not guilty.

On every charge.

Not guilty of acting as an unregistered foreign agent.

Not guilty of obstruction.

Not guilty of lying to federal investigators.

With that verdict, Tom Barrack walked out of the courtroom a free man. Vindicated. Cleared of all accusations. But not unchanged. (Associated Press)

The cost of fighting had been enormous. Financially, emotionally, reputationally. His businesses had suffered. Opportunities vanished. Long-time associates distanced themselves. Even the not-guilty verdict could not un-ring the bell of accusation. In the court of public opinion, scars remain.

Yet, Barrack never lashed out. He did not crow about his victory or attack his prosecutors. Instead, he spoke softly about what had been lost — and what had been preserved. He acknowledged the toll. He thanked his legal team, his family, and the jurors. And he issued a quiet warning about the justice system that had come so close to condemning him without cause.

Tom Barrack's story is a testament — to resilience, to courage, and to the enduring value of a jury that listens. It's also a cautionary tale. It reminds us that accusations, no matter how explosive, are not convictions. That proximity to power, controversial associations, or unpopular views are not crimes. And that the burden of proof remains the government's to bear — not the citizen's to disprove.

In a time when narratives dominate the news cycle and reputations are destroyed in minutes, Barrack's decision to fight — to speak, to stand, to trust the jury — illuminates a path forward for others who face overwhelming odds. Whether physician or politician, teacher or technician, every accused individual deserves the chance to be heard, to be judged not by fear or fiction, but by fact.

Justice, as fragile as it is, survived. And so did Tom Barrack.

## Lessons Learned

You have the right — fragile, precious, hard-won — to stand and demand that your story be heard. And sometimes, against all odds, the truth wins.

The stories of Dr. Lesly Pompy, Dr. Rajendra Bothra, and Dr. Loey Kousa are not merely courtroom dramas. They are mirrors — reflecting the perilous crossroads where medicine, law, and personal conscience converge in today's America. Each man faced the same ruthless machinery:

- Indictment based on suspicion, not evidence.
- Public humiliation without a conviction.
- An offer — spoken or silent — to plead guilty and make it all go away.

Each one heard the siren song of surrender.

And each one said no.

From afar, it is tempting to romanticise that decision. But in truth, it is anything but glamorous. Refusing to plead guilty isn't an act of bravado — it is an act of terrifying vulnerability. It means staring into the abyss, fully aware that no jury is guaranteed to catch you. It means risking not just a verdict, but your freedom, your livelihood, your family's stability, and your life's work.

It means choosing to fight not because you expect to win, but because the alternative — to admit guilt for something you did not do — is unbearable.

For physicians, that fight is uniquely cruel. To practice medicine is to make judgment calls in the face of uncertainty. It is to treat pain and trauma and suffering with incomplete information. It is to balance compassion and caution daily. It is an art as much as a science — and an art that is vulnerable to second-guessing.

When prosecutors descend, they freeze-frame careers. They strip away context. They take split-second clinical decisions and place them under a microscope of suspicion. They criminalise judgment. They demonise compassion. They weaponise honest mistakes.

And they do it knowing that most defendants will fold.

Why? Because of the trial penalty — the punishment, in sentencing and consequence, for those who choose to go to trial. The system is set up not to reward truth, but to reward surrender. Defendants who fight often face sentences three, four, or five times longer than those who plead guilty. Even innocent defendants feel the pressure to admit to crimes they didn't commit — just to stop the bleeding.

It is one of the most tragic ironies in American justice: we do not merely punish criminal conduct — we punish defiance.

And yet, sometimes, someone stands.

- Dr. Pompy stood — alone, battered, but unbowed.
- Dr. Bothra stood — imprisoned, forgotten, but unyielding.
- Dr. Kousa stood — quiet, steady, and defiant.

They chose the harder path because they understood what was at stake. A guilty plea may reduce your sentence, but it rewrites your life. It casts a shadow over everything you've done. It replaces truth with survival. And for them, that cost was too high.

Their victories were not accidents. They were the result of courage — yes — but also of extraordinary legal defence. They were won with cross-examination, with expert testimony, with meticulous documentation. But above all, they were won because juries chose truth over theatre. Because jurors — ordinary people — resisted the government's easy story.

Because the government's greatest weapon is not evidence. It is narrative.

The story that physicians who prescribe opioids are drug dealers. The story that billing disputes are criminal conspiracies. The story that deviation is deception. These are powerful myths — clean, simple, and devastating.

The truth is much messier.

The truth is that medicine is complex. That doctors disagree. That standards evolve. That risk is part of care, and that even the best-intentioned decisions can have unintended consequences. That not every mistake is a crime. That not every outlier is a predator.

The jurors who acquitted Pompy, Bothra, and Kousa did something rare in our current system. They paused. They listened. They questioned the government's assumptions. They looked not just at what happened, but why it happened. They demanded real proof, not insinuation.

Their verdicts did not erase the years stolen, the reputations tarnished, or the anguish endured. But they mattered. They mattered because they reaffirmed something essential:

Innocence is not dead. Truth is not irrelevant. Justice is still possible.

For every physician now standing where Pompy, Bothra, and Kousa once stood — facing indictment, facing ruin, facing the impossible choice — these stories offer more than inspiration. They offer a roadmap. A reason to believe. A guide for what it takes to survive.

But hope alone is not enough.

To endure the storm, you must prepare for war you must:

- hire lawyers who fight like you do — relentlessly.
- learn the law better than your accusers.
- gather your documents, your charts, your records.
- anticipate betrayal.
- brace for isolation.
- fortify your resolve.

And, you must know — deep down — why you fight.

Not for ego. Not for pride. Not for revenge. But because truth matters. Because your name matters. Because your patients, your family, your future deserve more than a lie told for convenience.

Some will not be able to endure. Some will plead guilty — even when innocent. There is no shame in survival. Only those who have stood in the crosshairs can understand the weight of that decision.

But for those who stand, who endure, who walk through the fire — the reward is not just acquittal.

It is something greater.

It is the knowledge that you stayed true. That you did not capitulate. That you faced the full weight of the federal government and did not betray yourself. That you did not trade your integrity for safety.

Yes, you will lose things. Money. Time. Friendships. You may never get them back.

But you will have your soul. You will have your honour. You will have your truth.

And in a system increasingly driven by fear and expedience, that is no small thing.

The real legacy of Dr. Pompy, Dr. Bothra, and Dr. Kousa is not just that they won their cases. It is that they reminded us what winning truly means.

- That justice, though bruised, still breathes.
- That truth, though battered, still speaks.
- That courage, though costly, still counts.

So to every physician, every caregiver, every soul caught in the gears of accusation — hear this:

You are not automatically guilty because you are accused.

You are not powerless before the system.

And if you choose to fight — if you choose to stand — you do not stand alone.

You stand with those who dared. You stand with those who won. You stand with those who proved that even now — in this broken, battered, beautiful justice system — the truth can still prevail.

# CHAPTER 15

# Trial as Theater – The Courtroom Performance and Juror Perception

*"But I suggest Perry Mason endings tend only to happen on late night TV if your station carries reruns."*

— Judge D. Michael Fisher of the Third Circuit Court of Appeals

## The Courtroom as Theatre

The courtroom is not a place for passive storytelling—it is an active stage where human liberty hangs in the balance and where each participant plays their part with the precision and drama of Shakespearean actors. If you were to sit in a federal courtroom, you would notice how even the benches and layout resemble a theatre: the jury box like an audience pit, the judge elevated like a director's chair, and the defendant cast as the tragic lead. The lawyers? They are the playwrights and performers, weaving narratives and invoking emotions—through tone, expression, and choreography.

Having lived this firsthand, I have come to believe that the courtroom is not a sterile place of pure reason. It is a living, breathing space of performance. When I stood trial, I wasn't merely a doctor defending a life's work—I was an involuntary actor in a drama whose script was written by prosecutors, whose lighting was managed by the judge, and whose audience—the jury—held the power to end or resurrect my future. In that crucible, what mattered was not just facts, but how those facts were delivered. And who better understood this than the lawyers?

## The Lawyer as Thespian

Good defence attorneys understand this dynamic intuitively. They move with intention; their pacing is deliberate. A pause before a critical question. A glance toward the jury at just the right moment. The best among them channel elements of Aristotelian tragedy: ethos, logos, and pathos converge not in dry argument, but in embodied persuasion. Their words are both memorised and improvised. Their faces emote carefully calculated sincerity. Their suits are their costumes. Their client—the accused—is a character they must humanise before the curtain falls.

The government, with its formidable team of agents and prosecutors, often casts the defendant in the role of the villain. The person on trial is portrayed not as a physician, a caregiver, a servant of the community—but as a profiteer, a manipulator, a threat to the public. The prosecutor's opening statement becomes an incantation: invoking words like "scheme," "conspiracy," and "fraud" with the ominous certainty of a narrator in a cautionary tale.

But the defence must recast the story. And they do so with a counter-narrative—a deeply human one. They rely on affect. On subtlety. On truth delivered with emotional precision. A gentle clasp of the client's hand. A soft tone in cross-examination. A visible exhale when something difficult is recalled. These are not tricks—they are signals. Cues to the jury that this is not a villain, but a human being. Flawed, perhaps. But real.

The courtroom is theatre, yes. But it is theatre with consequences. And when the performance ends, what remains is not applause or critique—but a verdict that can save or destroy a life.

## Jurors: The Empaneled Audience

Jurors are not mere observers. They are active processors of performance. Their interpretation of facts is deeply influenced by what communication theorists call "expectancy violations." According to Burgoon's Expectancy Violation Theory (EVT), when a courtroom participant deviates from expected behaviour—be it a gesture of warmth or an expression of remorse—jurors assess whether that violation is positive or negative based on the perceived reward value of the actor.

Take, for example, a defendant who weeps while testifying. Some jurors may interpret that as sincere remorse, triggering sympathy and leniency. Others may see it as manipulative, confirming guilt. The difference lies not in the tears themselves, but in the lens through which the jurors view the defendant. If they already perceive him as redeemable, those tears matter. If they see him as a villain, they dismiss the tears as crocodilian.

Empirical research confirms this theatrical reality. A study by Joseph Thomas (2021) demonstrated that defendants who showed nonverbal behaviours associated with remorse—like eye aversion, closed posture, and crying—elicited greater juror sympathy and often received lighter sentence recommendations. But only if their crime was framed as reactive rather than aggressive. In other words, the same behaviour by two different defendants can be received in radically different ways depending on how the jurors perceive their role in the narrative.

## The Power of Presence

In my trial, I was told repeatedly to maintain a neutral expression. Do not smirk. Do not frown. Do not look away when the government presents its accusations. "Sit still, look attentive, and dress modestly," my lawyer whispered.

This advice was not legal—it was theatrical. It was about performance. And indeed, every movement I made was scrutinised. One juror told my attorney after the trial: "He looked like a doctor. He looked like someone who belongs there."

That statement stayed with me. It meant that my presence, my demeanour, my posture—all influenced perception. In a system that claims to be guided by evidence and statute, so much comes down to how you carry yourself.

Nonverbal communication—what scholars call immediacy behaviours—plays a silent but potent role. The smile. The eye contact. The posture. Jurors, consciously or not, respond to these signals. The research shows they associate immediacy with likeability. And likeability correlates inversely with punishment.

## Theatre, Manipulation, and Morality

Critics argue that this theatrical element undermines justice. That trials should be based on evidence, not empathy. But to divorce human perception from legal process is folly. Humans are storytellers by nature. We respond not just to what is said but how it is said.

And the government knows this. They use theatre masterfully. Their agents enter in suits. Their charts are mounted high. Their PowerPoint slides use red to highlight "fraud." Their expert witnesses speak in monotone to feign objectivity. Their closing argument crescendos in righteous indignation.

It is theatre with institutional backing.

So why fault the defence for staging its own play? Why blame a doctor for appearing human?

## United States v. Dr. Ali Shaygan: A Trial of Justice, Theatre, and Retribution

In the annals of federal prosecutions gone awry, few courtroom battles were as dramatic, theatrical, and revealing of prosecutorial overreach as the 2009 case of United States v. Dr. Ali Shaygan. Defended with brilliance and fire by attorney David Oscar Markus, Dr. Shaygan, a soft-spoken pain management physician trained at the Mayo Clinic, faced an astonishing 141 counts of unlawfully prescribing controlled substances. But behind the sterile indictment and procedural language was a tragic story of a man whose life was almost shattered by government theatrics masquerading as justice.

## Setting the Stage: From Accusation to Indictment

Dr. Shaygan's trouble began in 2007 after the death of a young man, James "Brendan" Downey, from a methadone overdose. Among the scattered pill bottles in Downey's room were prescriptions from multiple doctors, including Dr. Shaygan. Federal prosecutors, seizing on the opioid panic and pressure to criminalise prescribing, decided to make Shaygan the face of overprescription.

The U.S. Attorney's Office painted Shaygan not as a physician attempting to treat pain, but as a drug dealer in a white coat. Their opening salvo included allegations that he wrote prescriptions for addicts he met at Starbucks and that he maintained poor medical records. But as defence counsel David Oscar Markus emphasised throughout the trial, medicine is not perfect science—and criminalising imperfection is dangerous.

## David Markus: A Trial Lawyer with a Flair for the Theatrical

Markus, whose courtroom demeanour blends legal precision with theatrical flair, immediately recognised the stakes—not just for his client, but for the practice of medicine itself. During the trial, he invoked the Salem witch trials, stating that the government "wanted to burn Dr. Shaygan like they burned the witches in Salem." The comparison was not hyperbolic. Just as the witches were condemned based on hysteria and hearsay, Dr. Shaygan faced charges rooted in overzealous interpretations and prosecutorial ambition.

From the outset, Markus sensed that the trial was more performance than prosecution. Prosecutors Sean Cronin and Andrea Hoffman arrived at court each day with the aura of authority and righteousness. Their PowerPoint slides splashed with terms like "drug dealer" and "killer doc." But the defence team—Markus, Marc Seitles, and Robin Kaplan—knew that truth lay beneath the government's theatrics. They methodically tore through the allegations, showing the jury that Shaygan used urine toxicology screens, dismissed patients for violations, and prescribed medication in accordance with medical norms.

## *Informants, Recordings, and the Defence Invasion*

As the trial unfolded, the drama intensified with a revelation that stunned the court. Two government witnesses, under direction from the prosecution team, secretly recorded conversations with the defence and its investigator. One of these informants, Trinity Clendening, admitted under oath that he recorded attorney Markus twice without his knowledge. The tapes were not disclosed to the defence before trial, a violation of discovery rules and potentially a breach of attorney-client protections.

The defence was blindsided. Markus argued that these recordings gave prosecutors an illegal window into their strategy, poisoning the fairness of the trial. What made matters worse was the government's failure to build an effective firewall between the trial team and the informants. DEA Agent Wells, for instance, was initially on both sides of what was supposed to be a taint wall. He listened to recordings and had access to the defence's inner workings.

Judge Alan Gold was visibly disturbed. Markus filed a motion for sanctions under the Hyde Amendment, a rare and high-bar remedy for prosecutorial misconduct. The courtroom, once the government's stage, became a forum for its reckoning.

## *The Jury's Verdict: Acquittal and Emotional Release*

Despite the government's attempt to drown Shaygan in a sea of counts—141, to be exact—the jury needed only four hours to reach a decision. Not guilty. On every single count.

The reaction was emotional. Several jurors shook Shaygan's hand. One juror reportedly asked to hug him. The courtroom, previously dominated by the drumbeat of accusation, filled with the catharsis of truth recognised.

"I feel vindicated," Shaygan said, tearfully. "I feel that my life can move forward again."

Jurors expressed sympathy not just for the ordeal Shaygan had endured, but for the broader implications of the government's conduct. "The jury did the right thing," Markus said outside the courtroom. "This sends a message that justice prevails." (Markus)

## A Deeper Injustice: The Prosecution's Misconduct Exposed

Following the acquittal, the defence team continued its pursuit of accountability. In a series of motions and hearings, they exposed the extent of prosecutorial misconduct. The government, under mounting scrutiny, admitted to key violations:

- Initiating a collateral witness tampering investigation without basis.
- Authorising informants to record the defence without proper clearance from the U.S. Attorney.
- Failing to disclose discovery materials and recordings.
- Allowing breaches of the taint wall.

Eventually, Chief AUSA Karen Gilbert stepped down from her role in the Narcotics Section, and AUSA Sean Cronin requested reassignment out of the criminal division. But the damage was done—not just to Shaygan, but to the credibility of the prosecution.

In response to the defence's Hyde Amendment motion, the government agreed to pay for attorneys' fees related to the sanctions litigation. The court later awarded more than $600,000, one of the largest sanctions awards in federal criminal history. Markus, in filings and arguments, emphasised that Shaygan's acquittal was not merely a result of clever lawyering, but of the truth—something the government had tried to obscure.

## Trial as Theatre, Again

Throughout the trial, Markus returned to a recurring theme: this was not just a legal proceeding, but a moral one. He spoke to jurors not as legal technicians, but as human beings. He crafted the defence's closing as a story, not a summation. He invoked the ghosts of Salem and the shadows of McCarthyism. "If we let the government burn people like this," he said, "we lose more than one good doctor—we lose the soul of our system."

This theatrical approach wasn't manipulation—it was strategy grounded in moral clarity. Research confirms that jurors respond powerfully to emotional framing, especially when they feel a defendant is being unfairly maligned. Markus used immediacy behaviours—eye contact, open hand gestures, varied tone—to connect. His client, coached in presence and posture, embodied calm sincerity. The performance, in every sense, was honest.

And jurors responded. In fact, the theatre of trial—the staging, the voice, the presence—became the very mechanism through which justice emerged.

## A Cautionary Tale for Every Physician

For physicians across the country, the Shaygan trial was a chilling reminder: your clinical decisions can be recast as crimes. Your charting errors as conspiracies. Your humanity as guilt.

Dr. Shaygan was lucky. He had the means to hire David Markus. He had a jury that listened. And he had a lawyer unafraid to say, in open court, that the government was wrong—morally, factually, and legally.

But many doctors do not have that luxury. They plead guilty. They disappear. Their stories remain untold.

## Closing Reflection: Theatre with Consequence

The United States v. Dr. Ali Shaygan was not just a courtroom drama—it was a referendum on prosecutorial power and the role of theatre in justice. In this case, the truth triumphed, but only after an epic battle.

Markus's invocation of the Salem witch trials was not metaphorical flourish. It was a historical echo. When fear overrides fairness, when narrative eclipses nuance, when prosecution becomes persecution—then we are all at risk of injustice.

But as long as there are advocates like Markus, jurors who listen, and judges willing to question, there is hope. The courtroom may be a stage, but when truth speaks louder than theatrics, justice can still take a bow.

# The Trial of Dr. Thomas Sachy: A Neuropsychiatrist on Trial

In the theatre of federal prosecution, few stages have been as electric and emotionally charged as the courtroom where Dr. Thomas Sachy stood accused. A neuropsychiatrist with a reputation for compassion and unconventional brilliance, Dr. Sachy found himself entangled in a legal spectacle that threatened to dismantle his career, his life, and the very principles of medical independence. Defended with surgical precision and narrative elegance by attorney Ronald Chapman, Dr. Sachy's case became not only a defence of an individual doctor but a critique of the prosecutorial machine—and a display of courtroom theatrics that ultimately led to a stunning exoneration.

## *From Clinic to Courtroom: The Making of a Target*

Dr. Sachy practised neuropsychiatry in Gray, Georgia, focusing on complex cases of brain injury, seizure disorders, chronic pain, and neurobehavioural dysfunctions. His clinic saw patients that others had abandoned—those whose lives were destroyed not only by illness, but by the silence of a medical system afraid to intervene. He was meticulous in his charting and fearless in his prescribing.

That fearlessness became the very thing federal prosecutors seized upon.

Amid the opioid epidemic's political momentum, Dr. Sachy's controlled substance prescriptions were flagged. The DEA and the U.S. Attorney's Office built a narrative that portrayed him as a rogue physician, a trafficker hiding behind a lab coat. In a sweeping indictment, they claimed his treatment regimens led to patient harm— even death.

But the prosecution's case was built not on medical nuance, but on moral panic.

## *The Government's Narrative: Framing Science as Sin*

During trial, prosecutors displayed photos of pill bottles and patients who had died with multiple substances in their systems. They wielded charts like daggers, with red-highlighted prescription dates. Their expert witnesses spoke in monotones, carefully stripped of clinical context, emphasising milligram doses without mentioning the comorbidities that warranted them.

It was not medicine they presented. It was myth.

And the myth was simple: Dr. Sachy, they claimed, was too liberal with prescriptions, too trusting of patients, and too negligent in monitoring outcomes. They made no effort to parse neuropsychiatric complexity. To them, any deviation from standardised pain management protocols was criminal.

## Enter Ronald W. Chapman: Defender of the Unconventional

Ronald Chapman saw the case for what it was: a witch hunt cloaked in medical terminology.

In the courtroom, Chapman did not merely defend Dr. Sachy. He told his story. He transformed the government's accusation into a referendum on what it means to care for the most vulnerable. He turned the jury's attention not toward pill bottles, but toward lives improved, patients stabilised, families reunited. He began opening statements not with legalese, but with a question: "What happens when a doctor refuses to give up on the patients everyone else has written off?"

It was a powerful frame. Chapman showed that Dr. Sachy did not prescribe recklessly—he prescribed responsibly, within the realm of accepted neuropsychiatric practice. He cross examined the government's experts with a scalpel, revealing their lack of specialisation in neuropsychiatry and their ignorance of the latest research. He didn't yell. He didn't grandstand. But his performance was theatre nonetheless—precise, emotional, and deeply human.

## The Battle of Theatrics: Fear vs. Empathy

The trial became a duel of affect. The prosecution leaned on fear: overdose deaths, addiction, DEA charts. Chapman leaned on empathy: letters from patients, testimony from caregivers, medical literature highlighting the complexities of pain and mental illness. The prosecution showed photos of deceased patients. Chapman introduced video clips of patients testifying about how Dr. Sachy had restored their lives. One woman, who had previously been housebound due to seizures, described how she returned to college after Sachy's treatment. Her tears on the witness stand spoke more than any legal citation ever could. The jury saw two worlds: one of statistical coldness and institutional condemnation, and another of clinical warmth and human salvation. Chapman made sure the jury saw Dr. Sachy not as a defendant but as a lifeline to people who had nowhere else to turn.

## Misconduct and Collapse: The Government's Case Unravels

As the trial advanced, the prosecution's case began to erode.

The patient death at the centre of the indictment was exposed as medically ambiguous. The coroner's report was equivocal, and toxicology showed polypharmacy from several providers—not just Dr. Sachy. The defence showed that the decedent had misused substances outside of any prescribed plan.

But the most damaging blow to the government was its own overreach.

Much like in the Shaygan case, where federal agents secretly recorded defence attorneys and breached discovery obligations, the government in Dr. Sachy's case appeared overeager to criminalise clinical discretion. They ignored exculpatory evidence, relied on witnesses with biases, and failed to consider the full scope of medical records.

Ultimately, the court found that the prosecution had not proven its case. Judge Tilman E. Self III granted a Rule 29 motion to dismiss the death charge, stating unequivocally that the government had failed to provide sufficient evidence for a rational jury to convict. The ruling sent shockwaves through the courtroom. A collective exhale passed through Sachy's family, friends, and patients. The system, at least this time, had not swallowed another doctor whole. (Chapman II)

## Reflections from the Trial: Theatre with Real Consequences

Dr. Sachy's trial was theatre, but unlike the state-sponsored drama staged by the prosecution, the defence's performance was grounded in truth. Every piece of testimony, every exhibit, every cross-examination served a higher goal: to humanise a man the government had dehumanised. In many ways, this was a trial not just of Dr. Sachy, but of the entire justice system. Could a physician still practise complex medicine in America without fear of indictment? Could a neuropsychiatrist treat pain without being labelled a criminal? The jury and the judge answered: Yes. But only barely.

## Aftermath: Vindication and a Warning

After the trial, Dr. Sachy returned to his practice, though the scars of prosecution remained. His reputation, once impugned, slowly began to heal. His patients remained loyal. His colleagues, many of whom had stood at a safe distance during the ordeal, began to reach out. But for every Dr. Sachy who wins, how many doctors plead out? How many families are shattered by fear? How many careers end without the benefit of Chapman's courtroom magic? Ronald Chapman later reflected: "This case shows that science, when defended courageously, can still stand against political theatre. But it takes more than evidence. It takes a story." Indeed, the defence's story—the story of a healer under siege—was what saved Dr. Sachy. And it's the same story that haunts courtrooms across the country, as federal prosecutors continue to cast doctors as villains in a war that ignores nuance.

## The Soul of Doctoring on Trial

Dr. Sachy's case reminds us that the soul of medicine is often what's truly on trial. Not just the lab coats and prescription pads, but the audacity to care beyond algorithms. In my own trial, I felt the same forces: the flattening of complexity into accusation, the moralisation of science into sin. I saw how prosecutors convert healing into harming with the flick of a chart. And I saw, like Dr. Sachy did, how a good lawyer can break through the fog and let the jury see the person behind the indictment. Justice may be blind, but the courtroom sees everything. It sees performance. It sees presence. And, occasionally, it sees truth.

In Dr. Thomas Sachy's trial, it saw truth. And that was enough.

# The Perry Mason Moments – When Truth Pierces the Courtroom Veil

In the grand theatre of American jurisprudence, few phenomena are as electrifying as the "Perry Mason moment." Named after the fictional defence attorney whose courtroom revelations invariably led to dramatic confessions or exonerations, these moments are rare in real-life trials. Yet, when they occur, they have the power to pivot the trajectory of a case, unveiling truths that cut through layers of obfuscation. In my own legal journey, I have witnessed such moments—instances where the courtroom's atmosphere shifts palpably, and justice finds its voice.

## The Essence of a Perry Mason Moment

A "Perry Mason moment" refers to an unexpected revelation during a trial that significantly alters its course. Often arising from a witness's unforeseen testimony or the sudden emergence of critical evidence, these moments can dismantle the prosecution's case or, conversely, bolster it. In an era dominated by meticulous pre-trial discovery, such surprises are uncommon, making their impact all the more profound when they do occur.

## The Cross-Examination of Noreen Thomas, RN

During my trial, one such moment unfolded during the cross-examination of Noreen Thomas, a registered nurse whose testimony was pivotal to the prosecution's narrative. The prosecution painted a picture of negligence, suggesting that I had billed for fraudulent services. Thomas's testimony was intended to corroborate this portrayal.

However, under the incisive questioning of defence attorney Paul Hetznecker, the narrative began to unravel. Hetznecker meticulously dissected Thomas's statements, highlighting inconsistencies and prompting her to acknowledge lapses in her observations. At one point, Thomas admitted that she had not personally reviewed certain patient records that were central to her claims. This admission cast doubt on the reliability of her testimony and, by extension, the prosecution's case.

The courtroom's atmosphere shifted. Jurors exchanged glances, sensing the gravity of the revelation. What was intended to be damning testimony had, through strategic cross-examination, become a linchpin for the defence.

## Confronting the Coroner in Dr. Sachy's Trial

In the trial of Dr. Thomas Sachy, another Perry Mason moment emerged, underscoring the importance of precision in expert testimony. Dr. Sachy, a respected neuropsychiatrist, faced charges alleging that his prescribing practices had led to patient deaths. Central to the prosecution's case was the testimony of a coroner who asserted that pills were found next to the deceased, implying overprescription.

Defence attorney Ronald W. Chapman, however, identified a critical flaw in this assertion. Through rigorous cross-examination, Chapman compelled the coroner to admit that his statement was based on second-hand information rather than direct observation. This concession undermined the credibility of the prosecution's narrative and highlighted the dangers of assumptions in forensic analysis.

The judge, recognising the significance of this revelation, dismissed the charges related to patient deaths. For Dr. Sachy, this moment marked a turning point, transforming a narrative of culpability into one of vindication.

## The Anatomy of a Perry Mason Moment

While each Perry Mason moment is unique, they share common elements:

- **Unanticipated Revelation:** A piece of information emerges that was previously unknown or misunderstood.

- **Credibility Shift:** The revelation challenges the reliability of a key witness or piece of evidence.
- **Narrative Reversal:** The prevailing storyline of the trial is disrupted, prompting jurors to reassess their perceptions.
- **Emotional Impact:** The courtroom experiences a palpable shift in energy, often accompanied by audible reactions or visible expressions of surprise.

These moments are not mere theatrics; they are crucibles where truth is tested and, often, revealed.

### Reflections on the Power of Truth

Experiencing a Perry Mason moment firsthand is a testament to the enduring power of truth in the legal system. Despite the complexities and adversarial nature of trials, these moments reaffirm the principle that justice can prevail when diligence, integrity, and courage converge. For those standing trial, such moments offer a lifeline—a sudden illumination that pierces the darkness of uncertainty. For the legal community, they serve as reminders of the profound responsibility borne by those who seek to uncover the truth.

In the end, Perry Mason moments are not just dramatic plot twists; they are manifestations of justice in action, where the scales are recalibrated, and the path to truth is illuminated.

# Paul Hetznecker's Battle Against the Intelligence Apparatus

In the annals of legal battles for transparency, few stand out as prominently as Paul Hetznecker's confrontation with the U.S. intelligence community. Known for his unwavering commitment to civil liberties, Hetznecker took on the formidable task of challenging the opacity of agencies like the NSA and CIA, seeking to unveil the extent of their surveillance on domestic movements, notably Occupy Philly. (Hetznecker)

## The Genesis of the Legal Battle

The Occupy movement, which began in 2011, quickly became a focal point for discussions on economic inequality and corporate influence in politics. As the movement gained momentum, concerns arose about government surveillance of peaceful protesters. In response, Hetznecker, representing activists and concerned citizens, filed Freedom of Information Act (FOIA) requests to the NSA, CIA, and FBI, seeking records related to surveillance activities targeting Occupy Philly.

The responses were telling. The NSA issued a Glomar response, refusing to confirm or deny the existence of such records, citing national security concerns under Exemption 1 of FOIA. The CIA claimed it had no jurisdiction over domestic surveillance, thus possessing no relevant records. The FBI provided a limited set of heavily redacted documents, invoking various exemptions to justify the redactions.

## Legal Maneuvering and Courtroom Strategy

Undeterred by the agencies' evasive responses, Hetznecker filed a lawsuit in the Eastern District of Pennsylvania in 2016, challenging the adequacy of the searches and the legitimacy of the exemptions claimed. His legal strategy was meticulous, focusing on the agencies' obligations under FOIA to conduct thorough searches and provide justifiable reasons for any withheld information.

In court, Hetznecker employed a combination of legal acumen and compelling rhetoric. He argued that the public had a right to know whether government agencies were surveilling peaceful protesters, emphasising the importance of transparency in a democratic society. His courtroom demeanour was both assertive and respectful, commanding attention and conveying the gravity of the issues at hand.

## Judicial Response and Implications

The court's decision, while acknowledging the agencies' invocation of certain FOIA exemptions, also recognised the necessity of transparency. The judge ordered the intelligence agencies to conduct searches for responsive records and to submit detailed justifications for any withheld information. This ruling underscored the judiciary's role in balancing national security concerns with the public's right to information.

Hetznecker's legal battle highlighted the challenges faced when confronting powerful government entities. It also demonstrated the critical role that determined legal advocacy plays in upholding civil liberties and ensuring governmental accountability.

### Broader Impact on Civil Liberties

Beyond the courtroom, Hetznecker's efforts resonated with activists, legal professionals, and citizens concerned about government overreach. His case became a touchstone for discussions on the limits of surveillance and the importance of safeguarding constitutional rights. By challenging the intelligence community, Hetznecker not only sought justice for his clients but also contributed to a broader movement advocating for transparency and accountability.

## Closing Acts

When my lawyer stood up for the closing argument, I watched his hands. He did not point. He gestured openly. When he addressed the jury, he lowered his voice slightly—almost like a friend confiding a truth. "This man devoted his life to patients," he said. "He believed in what he was doing. You may not agree with every billing code. But this is not a fraudster. This is a healer."

The courtroom was silent.

That was theatre. That was truth.

And it mattered.

# CHAPTER 16

# The Experts

---

*"An expert is an ordinary fellow from another town."*

— Mark Twain

## The Quality of Mercy: The Case of Ummad Rushdi

Few cases have tested the boundaries of my professional commitment like that of Ummad Rushdi. The stakes were harrowingly high: a man accused of murdering his own infant son, facing the death penalty in a state known for its zealous pursuit of capital punishment. I choose to write about this publicly because the case's details were made accessible by the courts. It was not merely the horror of the accusation that set this case apart, but the psychological labyrinth it presented—one that demanded not just expertise, but an unwavering dedication to justice.

In August 2013, the suburb of Upper Darby, Pennsylvania, became the focus of national attention. Ummad Rushdi, a 32-year-old Indian Ahmadi Muslim, was arrested for allegedly abducting and murdering seven-month-old Hamza Ali, his child with his partner. The baby's body was never recovered, despite exhaustive searches. It was, in every sense, a community's worst nightmare. The press wasted no time branding Rushdi a monster. Social media, public opinion, and even those within the justice system seemed eager to close the case with a swift, severe punishment.

But where others saw a villain, I saw a man in torment.

Defence attorney Scott Galloway approached me early in the case. Pennsylvania prosecutors had already announced their intention to pursue the death penalty, and Galloway knew the outcome could rest as much on psychiatric testimony as on forensic evidence. Judge James Nilon recognised the need for thorough examination and allocated a substantial budget—over $30,000—to allow for psychiatric evaluations and expert witness testimony. It was a rare but critical acknowledgement that mental illness, though often invisible, can be as central to a case as DNA.

My initial meeting with Rushdi was revealing. Seated across from me in the drab, cold confines of the detention centre, he appeared more lost than defiant. His responses were vague, his thoughts scattered, and his emotional responses inconsistent. Over the course of several interviews, it became increasingly clear that this was not a case of malice, but of profound psychological dysfunction. Partnering with mitigation specialist Delores Andrews, we dug into years of medical records, behavioural reports, and family interviews. What we unearthed was a man suffering from untreated, severe psychiatric conditions—paranoid delusions, episodes of psychosis, and long-standing cognitive deficits.

Our findings painted a vastly different portrait than that presented by the prosecution. They argued that Rushdi was deliberate, calculating, and fully responsible. We countered with evidence of a man who, in the grip of psychosis, lacked not only rational judgement but the very capacity to understand the nature of his actions.

Presenting this to a courtroom was no small task. The defence of mental illness, particularly in emotionally explosive cases involving children, often meets scepticism and resistance. But the role of the expert witness is not to comfort or to sway with emotion—it is to illuminate, to make visible the mechanisms of the mind that others cannot see.

In my testimony, I stressed that mental illness does not absolve guilt but reframes it. The law must consider the intent behind an action—was it committed with a clear understanding of right and wrong? Could the accused comprehend the consequences? For

Ummad Rushdi, the answer was complicated but ultimately revealing. His illness rendered him incapable of forming the intent necessary to justify a death sentence.

We also pointed to systemic failures: a history of missed diagnoses, inadequate interventions, and insufficient community support. Rushdi's case wasn't an outlier—it was symptomatic of a broader pattern of neglect that afflicts countless individuals living with severe mental health conditions. This case, we argued, was not just about one man but about the society that failed him.

For the jury, the challenge was steep. They had to balance their horror and heartbreak against the sobering reality of mental illness. Our goal was not to ask for pity but for understanding—a nuanced verdict that respected both the gravity of the crime and the complexity of the human mind.

In the end, the case did not go to trial. Rushdi was deemed incompetent to stand trial due to his deteriorating mental state. (Vella) This conclusion, while sparing him from execution, also served as a stark reminder that justice does not always reside in the binary of guilt or innocence. Sometimes, it lies in our capacity to ask the harder question: why?

This case reaffirmed my belief in the role of psychiatric experts in the legal system. We are not just witnesses; we are translators of human behaviour. Our work often requires us to face society's darkest shadows, and to hold space for those whom the world would rather discard. But if justice is to mean anything, it must be rooted in truth— not just about what was done, but about who did it, and why.

"For every expert, there is an equal and opposite expert." — Arthur C. Clarke

But in the end, truth must not be a matter of debate. It must be a mirror held up to the complexities of the human condition, however uncomfortable the reflection might be.

# The Compliance Guy Sean Weiss: Champion of Physician Justice

In the often stormy world of healthcare regulation, where one misstep can lead to career-ending repercussions, Sean M. Weiss stands out as a voice of reason, integrity, and fierce advocacy. His reputation within the medical and compliance communities has been hard-won over decades of unwavering commitment to defending physicians from unjust scrutiny and institutional overreach. More than a compliance officer, Sean Weiss is a crusader for justice in an era when the line between healthcare oversight and overreach has become dangerously blurred.

I first crossed paths with Sean when he was called in to consult on a federal case in which I was involved. From the moment he entered the picture, it was evident that Weiss brought more than just a mastery of regulations. His empathy, strategic clarity, and thoroughness altered the course of our defence. He combined the clinical precision of a surgeon with the impassioned reasoning of a civil liberties advocate. It was this rare duality that made his contributions invaluable, both in our case and in countless others across the United States.

Sean's professional credentials—CPMA, CHC, CMCO—represent more than alphabet soup. They reflect a lifelong devotion to mastering the labyrinth of healthcare compliance. As Chief Compliance Officer at DoctorsManagement, his work bridges the gap between policy interpretation and real-world application. For providers navigating complex regulatory frameworks, Sean is not just a guide; he is a shield.

One of the most powerful examples of his skill and conviction came during the case of Dr. Rajendra Bothra and several of his colleagues, accused in a sweeping federal indictment of operating a so-called "pill mill" in Michigan. Prosecutors alleged nearly $500 million in fraudulent activity tied to opioid prescriptions. The media storm that followed vilified the doctors and destroyed their reputations almost overnight. Practices were shut down. Bank accounts were seized. Lives were upended.

But Sean Weiss wasn't swayed by the narrative. He knew that beneath the headlines, there was another story—a story of prosecutorial zealotry, flawed data interpretation, and a fundamental misunderstanding of clinical judgment. Working tirelessly, Weiss dissected the case against Dr. Bothra with forensic precision. He highlighted investigative inconsistencies, misrepresentations of medical data, and the dangerous misuse of statistical extrapolation to infer guilt.

Sean's approach consistently reinforces one crucial point: compliance must be grounded in clinical context. His defence strategies often focus on the treating physician rule, medical necessity, and the critical role of clinical judgment. These aren't academic theories—they are the real principles that differentiate ethical medicine from bureaucratic box-checking.

The Bothra case, after a six-week trial, culminated in full acquittals. (NAMAS) It was a victory for the physicians involved and a resounding indictment of a system too quick to accuse and too slow to listen. In his article, "Justice Served—Unfortunately, a Bit Late," Sean captured the emotional and professional toll the case exacted on everyone involved. His message resonated with physicians everywhere: the system isn't always just, but with the right defence, justice can still prevail.

When Sean invited me to appear on his widely respected podcast, *The Compliance Guy*, we delved deeper into these themes. It was more than a technical discussion; it was a human one. We talked about the trauma of being investigated, the guilt-by-allegation culture that dominates modern enforcement, and the personal cost borne by physicians unjustly accused. The episode struck a chord with listeners, praised for its raw honesty and clarity.

Sean's impact extends far beyond individual cases. He is a thought leader in the compliance world, educating thousands through webinars, seminars, and written publications. His teachings demystify the tangled web of Medicare regulations, giving practitioners the tools they need to stay compliant—and the confidence to stand their ground when wrongly accused.

His insistence on proactive compliance is perhaps his greatest legacy. Sean doesn't believe in fear-based regulation. For him, compliance should be about empowerment and education. He encourages healthcare providers to understand the "why" behind the rules, so they can avoid violations and, more importantly, deliver care with integrity.

He has also taken a courageous stand against the misuse of statistical modelling in healthcare fraud cases. Weiss argues—correctly—that large-scale extrapolation often lacks the nuance required to judge individual cases. His advocacy pushes back against this trend, urging auditors and courts alike to consider each patient's story and each physician's decision-making process.

Behind all this is a man of deep compassion. Sean Weiss understands that when a physician is accused, it's not just a legal matter—it's a life shattered. Reputations, families, careers—these are often destroyed long before a verdict is rendered. And that's where Sean's empathy shines. He fights not just for legal outcomes but for personal redemption. His work offers hope to those caught in the machinery of a flawed system.

He's also an influential figure at the policy level, consulted regularly by lawyers, healthcare groups, and legislative bodies. His input is shaping reforms that aim to balance accountability with fairness. His goal is clear: a healthcare compliance framework that protects patients without persecuting practitioners.

In today's climate, where distrust of medical professionals can quickly escalate into legal action, Sean Weiss stands as a guardian of the profession's dignity. He reminds us that behind every compliance regulation is a person—one who deserves respect, due process, and the benefit of the doubt.

His work matters because it rehumanises a system that too often reduces people to data points. Sean Weiss teaches us that compliance isn't about avoiding penalties—it's about practising medicine ethically, compassionately, and confidently.

In the battle for physician justice, Sean Weiss is not merely a voice—he is the rallying cry. His influence is felt in courtrooms, boardrooms, and exam rooms across America. And for every doctor who's ever felt the cold grip of accusation tighten without warning, his work is a lifeline. He is, quite simply, one of the most vital allies in the ongoing fight to keep healthcare just.

# The Case of Dr. Brian James August

The legal ordeal of Dr. Brian James August stands as a stark reminder of how quickly a respected medical professional can find themselves ensnared in the unforgiving gears of federal prosecution. Accused under the Controlled Substances Act and federal healthcare fraud statutes, Dr. August faced not only the collapse of his medical career, but the very real possibility of years behind bars. His story might have followed the all-too-familiar arc of many physicians accused in the post-opioid-crisis era, were it not for the timely intervention and expert advocacy of compliance consultant Sean M. Weiss.

In May 2021, a federal grand jury returned an indictment charging Dr. August with fifteen separate offences. Among them were alleged violations of 21 U.S.C. § 841(a)(1), relating to improper prescribing of controlled substances, and 18 U.S.C. § 1347, which concerns healthcare fraud. The prosecution alleged that Dr. August had been issuing prescriptions outside the bounds of acceptable medical practice, and billing for services not rendered or medically unnecessary. The portrait painted by the government was grim: a physician acting more like a drug trafficker than a healer.

Enter again Sean Weiss. As part of Dr. August's defence team, Weiss undertook a deep dive into the medical records, prescription data, and billing codes at the centre of the case. What he discovered was a prosecutorial narrative built on faulty assumptions, regulatory misinterpretations, and an alarming disregard for clinical nuance.

One of the first issues Weiss addressed was the government's tendency to conflate guidance from different regulatory bodies— namely the American Medical Association (AMA) and the Centers for Medicare & Medicaid Services (CMS). Prosecutors often apply these complex and sometimes conflicting standards in an overly simplistic way, assuming any deviation is proof of fraud. Weiss was quick to point out that coding errors, non-standardised billing patterns, or clinical judgment calls do not automatically equate to criminal conduct.

Weiss's review of Dr. August's prescribing history further challenged the narrative that the doctor had acted recklessly or without medical justification. The compliance analysis suggested that

Dr. August had, in many cases, followed reasonable and defensible standards of care, tailored to the individual needs of his patients. Misunderstood dosage levels, rare patient profiles, and administrative coding oversights had been weaponized by the prosecution without full context.

Then came a turning point—one that would reverberate far beyond this single case. In June 2022, the U.S. Supreme Court issued a landmark ruling in *Ruan v. United States*. (Hamm) This decision clarified that, in order to convict a physician under the Controlled Substances Act, the government must prove *beyond a reasonable doubt* that the doctor knowingly and intentionally prescribed medication outside the usual course of medical practice. In other words, honest mistakes or disagreements over clinical judgement were no longer enough to send someone to prison.

The impact on Dr. August's case was immediate and profound. The *Ruan* ruling set a new evidentiary threshold—one the prosecution could not meet. There was no clear proof that Dr. August had the intent to act unlawfully. His records showed a doctor trying to help his patients, not manipulate the system for profit or harm. Within weeks, the prosecution asked the court to vacate the scheduled trial. The case was, for all practical purposes, dead. (Weiss)

Justice, in this case, had not been swift. But it had been served.

Dr. August's exoneration highlights a critical truth: intent matters. In a regulatory environment where medical professionals live under constant threat of investigation, this case reinforces the principle that legal scrutiny must be balanced by clinical understanding. The outcome would likely have been very different without the expert guidance of Sean Weiss, whose clarity of thought and depth of compliance knowledge gave Dr. August's defence the edge it needed.

This case also serves as a warning against the dangers of prosecutorial overreach. Medicine is not a mechanical science; it is an art deeply rooted in patient context. When compliance frameworks are applied without consideration for clinical reality, the results can be devastating.

Weiss's work on the case did more than clear Dr. August's name. It sparked wider discussions within the healthcare community about the need for better education around compliance and the limits of federal enforcement. He continues to advocate for reforms that protect physicians from unjust accusations, promote better training for investigators and auditors, and ensure that clinical judgement remains a protected cornerstone of medical practice.

For Dr. August, the outcome marked the beginning of a long road to rebuilding his professional reputation. But it also marked a victory for all physicians who fear that every patient they treat could be the one that triggers an investigation. It proved that with the right legal strategy and the right compliance advocate, justice can still be achieved.

In an age where doctors must often act with one eye on the exam room and the other on the courtroom, the story of Dr. Brian August offers a rare glimmer of hope. It shows that expert advocacy, sound legal reasoning, and principled resistance can hold the line against injustice. And it proves, once again, that Sean Weiss is among the most formidable defenders of medical ethics and fairness operating today.

The battle for fair treatment in medicine is far from over. But in cases like Dr. August's, we catch a glimpse of what is possible when the truth is properly understood and expertly defended.

## The Vital Role of Medical Experts in Defending Physicians — Navigating the Complexities of Mens Rea

Within the tangled web of healthcare fraud litigation, no concept is more critical, more misunderstood, or more subject to legal debate than *mens rea*—the mental state indicating intentional wrongdoing. In the context of defending physicians accused of fraud, this concept becomes the linchpin between justice and injustice, freedom and incarceration. From personal experience and observation, I know that expert medical testimony can become the most powerful tool in clarifying a physician's intent and defending the practice of medicine itself.

Healthcare fraud allegations—particularly those under the Controlled Substances Act and the False Claims Act—place doctors in a dangerous double bind. On one hand, they face aggressive federal prosecutors, driven by statistics and sweeping narratives of systemic abuse. On the other, their clinical actions, rooted in nuanced medical judgment, must be parsed and defended within the rigid structure of legal standards. The thin line between aggressive care and criminal misconduct can be blurred by misunderstanding, and the decisive factor becomes mens rea—did the physician act knowingly. The 2024 Supreme Court decision in Diaz v. United States further amplified the potential for medical expert testimony to clarify issues of intent. (Golde) Diaz, although originating in a drug trafficking context, broadly impacted expert testimony regarding mens rea. The Court permitted expert testimony that describes typical states of mind within a group, without directly asserting a defendant's specific mental state. The ruling allowed expert testimony to explain typical states of mind in a group—without asserting the individual defendant's exact thoughts. This nuanced ruling is highly significant in the medical arena, as it opens the door for expert witnesses to describe the mindset common among physicians under similar circumstances. This context is crucial in helping juries understand that doctors may act based on accepted clinical models, even if outcomes later become scrutinised.

Sean Weiss exemplifies this bridge between law and medicine. In the defence of Dr. Brian James August, Weiss demonstrated how government misinterpretation of coding and prescribing practices had wrongly cast routine actions as fraudulent. His testimony dismantled the prosecution's case, not with grandstanding but with methodical and authoritative evidence rooted in clinical and regulatory facts. Weiss's approach—integrating knowledge of CMS policies, AMA guidelines, and real-world billing practices—provides a model of how expert witnesses can uphold truth against bureaucratic misunderstanding.

Experts like Weiss serve several critical roles:

- **Necessity:** One of the most misused and misunderstood terms in healthcare fraud prosecutions is "medical necessity." Prosecutors often claim care was unnecessary based on post hoc data or guidelines not applicable at the time of treatment.

Experts help clarify that necessity is a judgment made within context—based on the physician's training, the patient's presentation, and the available evidence.

- **Explaining Coding and Billing Norms:** Federal charges often hinge on perceived irregularities in coding or billing. However, these are frequently clerical, ambiguous, or based on evolving standards. Experts versed in medical billing can explain that deviations from the norm do not equate to intent to defraud.

- **Reframing Prescribing Decisions:** Particularly under the Controlled Substances Act, the intent behind a prescription is everything. Experts help juries understand the difference between dangerous overprescribing and compassionate care under complex circumstances.

- **Illuminating Intent:** Ultimately, jurors must decide what a physician *intended*. Expert testimony, while not asserting direct knowledge of the accused's thoughts, can provide the framework for understanding how and why such decisions were made—often undermining claims of criminality.

Medical expert testimony also serves as a critical check on prosecutorial overreach. In high-profile cases, the temptation to make an example of a physician can eclipse the pursuit of justice. Expert witnesses anchor proceedings in fact, discouraging emotionally driven or overly simplistic arguments. They ensure the complexity of clinical decisions is acknowledged.

Moreover, their role extends beyond the courtroom. The presence of expert advocates pushes back against the chilling effect aggressive litigation can have on medical innovation and patient-centred care. When physicians fear that honest mistakes or novel treatments may land them in prison, the entire healthcare system suffers. Expert testimony defends the space physicians need to practise ethically, creatively, and compassionately.

The broader implications of such work are profound. By helping courts understand that medicine is not black-and-white, that standards evolve, and that intent must be proven—not presumed—experts protect not only individual doctors but the entire practice of medicine. Their insights inform policy reform, encourage more nuanced regulatory enforcement, and offer the public a more balanced perspective on what healthcare fraud truly entails.

Physicians accused of fraud are often treated as criminals before a case even begins. Their reputations are shredded, their careers stalled, their lives overturned. In these moments, medical experts become more than technical witnesses—they become guardians of professional dignity. Their role is not to excuse misconduct but to ensure that the courtroom remains a place of reason, not retribution.

In the end, the most vital contribution of medical experts in healthcare fraud cases is the preservation of justice. By clarifying *mens rea*, explaining clinical norms, and dismantling false narratives, they keep the system honest. They remind jurors, prosecutors, and judges alike that medicine is complex, intention matters, and fairness requires more than assumptions. It demands expertise—and courage.

# The Chinese Surgeon – Dr. Feng Qin and the Weight of Expert Testimony

In the intricate realm of healthcare fraud litigation, the case of Dr. Feng Qin serves as a compelling example of how expert testimony can profoundly influence legal outcomes. Accused of performing unnecessary cardiac procedures on elderly patients, many of whom were immigrants and vulnerable, Dr. Qin faced serious allegations that could have ended his career and led to prison time. Yet through the skillful deployment of expert analysis and the strategic efforts of his legal team, the prosecution's case eventually unraveled.

The story of Dr. Qin is not merely one of personal salvation; it is a cautionary tale of how misunderstandings of medical complexity can lead to near-catastrophic consequences. It also serves as an important reminder that justice in healthcare fraud cases depends not only on courtroom advocacy but on the testimony of those who understand the clinical nuance of medical practice.

In 2015, Dr. Qin, a well-respected vascular surgeon in New York City, found himself under intense federal scrutiny. Authorities alleged that he had conducted numerous medically unnecessary cardiac procedures—such as fistulagrams and angioplasties—on elderly patients covered by Medicare and Medicaid. These accusations were compounded by the demographic vulnerabilities of his patients, many of whom were elderly immigrants with limited English proficiency. Initially, the matter was resolved through a civil settlement. Dr. Qin paid $150,000 to the government without admitting wrongdoing, retained his medical licence, and continued to practise medicine.

However, the case did not end there. A registered nurse working in Dr. Qin's office raised internal concerns about the appropriateness of the procedures being conducted. Acting as a whistleblower, she brought her complaints to federal authorities. This led to a federal indictment in 2018, with Dr. Qin now facing criminal charges, including healthcare fraud and violations under the False Claims Act. The stakes escalated dramatically: the charges carried the potential for up to ten years in prison.

Dr. Qin's legal team, composed of experienced former federal prosecutors, understood that to contest the allegations successfully, they needed more than procedural arguments. They needed medical experts who could challenge the core of the government's claims: that the procedures were unnecessary and thus fraudulent. These experts would be called upon to dissect the clinical decisions made by Dr. Qin and present them in a way that a jury—and the court—could understand.

Expert witnesses evaluated the same procedures that the prosecution claimed were unnecessary and presented evidence that the medical decisions in question were consistent with recognised clinical standards at the time. They explained the justifications for each procedure based on the specific symptoms and conditions of the patients. These experts emphasised the subjective nature of medical necessity—an often-contested term in fraud cases—and argued that the procedures were defensible as good-faith clinical judgments.

The defence's expert testimony created a critical turning point. By challenging the government's narrative and highlighting the gaps in its understanding of clinical decision-making, the experts raised significant doubts about Dr. Qin's intent. The case was no longer a simple matter of whether the procedures were needed but became a deeper exploration of the physician's mindset and medical rationale. The government, recognising that the bar for proving *mens rea*—intentional fraud—could not be met convincingly, chose not to proceed to trial.

In 2021, prosecutors dropped the criminal charges. Instead, the case was once again resolved through a civil settlement. Dr. Qin agreed to pay $800,000 and accepted a temporary ban from billing public health programmes until February 2025. (Fiore) Importantly, he avoided criminal conviction and retained his ability to practise medicine in the future.

This resolution would not have been possible without the intervention of medical experts. Their testimonies did not merely provide technical opinions—they offered context, clarity, and credibility. They demonstrated that medical practice is not always black and white, that physicians must make decisions in real time with imperfect information, and that deviations from standard procedures do not automatically equate to criminal intent.

Dr. Qin's case highlights the immense responsibility borne by medical experts in legal settings. These professionals must balance objectivity with clarity, ensuring that complex medical decisions are fairly presented to those with little clinical background. Their role becomes even more vital when the legal system risks punishing clinical ambiguity as criminal fraud.

Furthermore, this case underscores a troubling trend in healthcare enforcement: the increasing reliance on whistleblowers and post hoc medical reviews to build fraud cases. While whistleblowing is an essential tool for uncovering genuine abuse, it also presents risks when subjective disagreements about care are elevated into federal indictments. This is where expert review is vital—to filter legitimate concern from prosecutorial overreach.

For Dr. Qin, the outcome represented relief but not vindication. His reputation suffered, his finances were drained, and the emotional toll was immense. Nonetheless, the case stands as a powerful argument for the inclusion of expert voices in fraud litigation. Without their input, prosecutors might have misrepresented complex medical judgments as outright fraud—and secured a conviction that could have irreparably harmed a capable and compassionate physician.

In conclusion, the case of Dr. Feng Qin demonstrates the indispensable value of expert testimony in safeguarding physicians' rights and reputations. These experts play a critical role in distinguishing between clinical judgment and criminal conduct, ensuring that the justice system recognises the realities of medical practice. In a climate of increasing regulatory scrutiny, the role of these expert witnesses will only grow more essential in defending the integrity of medicine—and the humanity of those who practise it.

# Dr. Kenneth DiNella – The Accidental Expert

In the often-bleak arena of healthcare fraud litigation, victory sometimes hinges not on flashy arguments or dramatic courtroom tactics, but on calm, credible, and utterly human testimony. For me, in the case of *United States v. Muhamad Aly Rifai*, that steadying force came in the form of Dr. Kenneth DiNella—a physician whose journey into the courtroom was as unplanned as it was essential. I have long referred to him, affectionately and gratefully, as "The Accidental Expert."

Dr. DiNella was not a seasoned legal consultant or professional witness. His expertise wasn't shaped by courtroom battles but by decades of compassionate, hands-on patient care and leadership in clinical settings. As the medical director of the Perry Wellness Center, his approach to healing was rooted in a philosophy that wove mental wellness into the fabric of everyday living. An avid cyclist and advocate for proactive health, he led by example—both in his community and in his practice.

It was this background of integrity, clarity, and deep clinical experience that made his courtroom testimony so transformative. When Dr. DiNella agreed to serve as an expert witness in my defence, he brought no theatrical bravado—only the power of truth. He was calm, thoughtful, and unshakably committed to explaining what real medicine looks like to a room of jurors with no medical training and a federal prosecutor intent on painting me as a criminal.

From the moment he took the stand, Dr. DiNella commanded attention not with volume, but with credibility. He explained psychiatric care as it truly unfolds: a discipline guided by trust, patient nuance, and the art of interpretation as much as science. He reminded the court that psychiatry is not a procedural conveyor belt, but a patient-centred discipline where therapeutic conversations are inseparable from medical treatment. His words reshaped the narrative.

At the heart of the prosecution's case were claims about billing fraud—specifically, that I had billed for psychotherapy during times that seemed, to the government, "impossible." But as DiNella pointed out, their conclusions were based on a fundamental misunderstanding of clinical workflow. He explained how patient care in psychiatry rarely fits into rigid time slots. Conversations in corridors, brief yet significant interactions, and integrated care sessions were all valid components of therapeutic engagement.

He further addressed the role of supervisory oversight. The prosecution suggested that my supervision of other providers was cursory or disingenuous. Dr. DiNella disagreed. He explained the clinical and administrative importance of such oversight, noting that proper supervision often includes real-time consultations, chart reviews, and support for treatment decisions. In many cases, it is the cornerstone of safe and ethical care.

Perhaps most importantly, he addressed the concept of *mens rea* — the physician's intent. With clarity and passion, he explained that while documentation may be imperfect, and care practices can vary widely, the presence or absence of criminal intent cannot be divined from billing records alone. "What you see as errors," he said, "are more often reflections of medical complexity and clinical judgment, not signs of deceit."

He also deconstructed the government's portrayal of my days as impossibly full. The idea that I could not have treated the number of patients shown in records was, in DiNella's words, based on an unrealistic and overly simplistic model of patient care. "The government has mistaken fluid clinical practice for fraud," he testified.

He went on to describe how multidisciplinary teams, electronic documentation, and efficient care delivery make seemingly packed schedules not only possible but common.

His testimony gave voice not just to me, but to countless other physicians whose work is similarly misunderstood. It reframed the conversation around clinical complexity and cast serious doubt on the prosecution's entire theory.

And yet, for all his clinical insights, it was perhaps Dr. DiNella's integrity that made the deepest impression. He was not there to defend me blindly. He was there to explain. To clarify. To tell the truth. Under cross-examination, when the prosecution tried to twist his words or question his neutrality, he remained composed and consistent. Each answer was measured, grounded in reality, and delivered with the quiet force of someone who knows what it means to be responsible for real lives.

Beyond the confines of the courtroom, Dr. DiNella's presence became symbolic. His cycling stories, once just endearing tales, came to represent endurance, focus, and the long, hard road toward healing—whether personal, professional, or legal. He embodied a vision of medicine as both science and humanity, one that prosecutors and auditors often overlook in their hunt for misdeeds.

Looking back, I realise how rare it is to encounter such a witness. Expert testimony often aims to impress or overwhelm; DiNella's aim was different. He sought only to illuminate. His impact extended well beyond the verdict. He restored faith—in me, in the process, and in the belief that truth can, in fact, prevail.

His journey to the witness stand may have been accidental, but its effect was anything but. He reminded the courtroom that behind every chart, every code, and every bill is a human story—one that deserves to be heard in full, not filtered through the lens of suspicion or bureaucratic rigidity.

Dr. Kenneth DiNella's legacy as "The Accidental Expert" will endure. Not because he saved me, though he did. But because he reminded everyone watching that medicine is not fraud. That care is not crime. That truth, told clearly and compassionately, can still matter in a courtroom. And that sometimes, the most powerful advocates are those who never intended to be.

In an age of increasing scrutiny, his example will inspire not just those of us who defend, but those who practise. He is a reminder that integrity matters—and that sometimes, it shows up on two wheels, ready to speak truth to power.

CHAPTER 17

# Presenting Your Evidence – Litigation Support Services

―――――

*"Those judges who clearly recognize the voice of their own conscience, usually recognize also the voice of justice; because conscience is the chamber of Justice."*

— Judge Mohammad Sergie (1915–1975), Chief Appellate Judge, Aleppo, Syria, from A Dream in Arafat, 1969

## Words of Life: Negotiation Amidst Desperation

"Doctor, this is the Easton Police Department SWAT Team."

In July 2022, while I waited beneath the dark cloud of an impending federal indictment, my identity as a psychiatrist and healer was summoned into action in a way I could never have anticipated. At 2 a.m., I answered a call expecting arrest; instead, the officer on the line said, "No, Doctor, we need your help with a suicidal patient who asked for you."

Just blocks away from my home, a desperate man teetered on the edge of self-destruction. Despite the allegations swirling around me, the police chose to see not the accused, but the doctor. They recognised in me the skills essential to de-escalate crisis and connect with a human soul in agony.

The streets of Easton were thick with tension. Emergency vehicles flanked the scene; flashing lights painted the night sky in rhythmic pulses. The man inside the modest home was overwhelmed by despair, threatening to end his life. It was a moment of profound human crisis—and I had been asked to step in.

Driving to the scene, my heart thudded beneath the calm exterior honed over decades of emergency psychiatry. This was a real-time test of everything I had written about, practised, and taught as a member of the Project BETA De-escalation Workgroup for the American Association for Emergency Psychiatry. Those guidelines, the *Ten Domains of De-escalation*, had become gospel in crisis intervention circles—and now I would put them to their ultimate test. (University of Rochester Medical Centre)

Arriving on-site, I was quickly briefed by officers. The man, armed and volatile, was isolated and vocalising suicidal thoughts. The perimeter was secure, but resolution seemed precariously distant. I approached slowly, deliberately, my hands open, my posture non-threatening.

"I'm Doctor Rifai," I said, my voice steady but warm. "I'm here to listen, to understand, and to help."

Silence.

Then the soft rasp of crying. A broken voice emerged. He began to speak—about unbearable pressure, grief, financial ruin. His pain poured out, unfiltered. My response was consistent, compassionate. "I hear your pain. You are not alone in this."

What he didn't know—what no one knew—was that I was facing a darkness of my own. Awaiting indictment, fighting for my professional life, I stood with him as a peer in despair. In his voice, I heard my own struggle.

I applied the Project BETA principles in real time: active listening, respecting personal space, maintaining neutral body language, avoiding confrontation. I validated his emotions, reflected back his distress, and patiently offered alternatives. (Roppolo et al.)

"Would you feel safer if we stepped outside together?" I asked.

He hesitated.

Minutes passed like lifetimes. Each word from me was carefully chosen. Each gesture mattered. Gradually, he edged closer to trust. I reinforced his agency. "You are in control. We can do this together."

Eventually, he agreed.

He stepped outside, slowly, shakily, and was safely secured by officers. No violence. No trauma. Just a man saved by the power of connection and the insistence of empathy.

## Reflections on Purpose and Proof

Later that night, alone in my home, I felt something stir within me: not triumph, not relief, but clarity. Even as the full force of the federal government bore down on me, I had been asked to do what I do best. I had reminded myself—through action—who I truly am.

That night was more than an anecdote; it was a metaphor. Amidst my own legal crisis, I continued to fulfil my vocation. Even the same authorities prosecuting me recognised the value of my skills when life was on the line. They didn't see an indictment—they saw a healer.

And yet, in the court of law, facts often need amplification. Good intentions alone are not enough. That's where litigation support services come in—where psychiatry meets legal advocacy.

## The Need for Litigation Support Services

Litigation support services for physicians facing federal charges are indispensable. They provide the scaffolding upon which truth can be displayed. These services extend beyond legal counsel to include clinical expertise, expert witness preparation, evidence interpretation, and strategic communications with jurors and judges.

In cases involving allegations of healthcare fraud, overbilling, or improper documentation, context is everything. The prosecution may present cold data: billing codes, time logs, charting patterns. But litigation support services enable the defendant to present *meaning*: clinical decisions, therapeutic nuances, and medical realities.

This includes:

- Medical Record Analysis: Skilled reviewers can explain why certain documentation patterns exist and show how these align with legitimate medical practice.

- Expert Witness Coordination: Matching the defendant with the right expert—someone who understands both the specialty and the courtroom.
- Trial Strategy Consultation: Understanding how to communicate medical complexity in a way juries can grasp.
- Ethical Framing: Demonstrating how the accused's actions were motivated by care, not criminality.

Litigation support doesn't fabricate defence—it clarifies it. It ensures that juries and judges don't mistake deviation for deception, or clinical adaptation for corruption.

My own story, with its ironies and reversals, reinforces this point. Even as the government moved against me, they asked me to help save a life. They trusted my training. The same skills used to protect one man in crisis could also defend me in court—through the diligent application of those skills in presenting my evidence.

The power of story, supported by fact, clarified by expert testimony, framed within legal strategy—this is the art of presenting your evidence.

## Closing Reflections

In the Gospel of Matthew, it is written: *"Blessed are the peacemakers, for they shall be called children of God."* On that July night, I remembered what it meant to be a peacemaker—not only in the spiritual sense but in the most tangible, earthly way.

I stood between despair and hope—not only for that man, but for myself. I realised that presenting one's evidence is not merely about documents or legal arguments. It is about demonstrating character, proving intention, and telling the story behind the facts.

As my grandfather, Judge Mohammad Sergie, once wrote: *"My priest and pastor are you all, my readers... please ask God for my forgiveness, because the more that people pray for my forgiveness, it may be a cause for the forgiveness of large sins."*

And so, to those who read this: I ask not only for your understanding, but for your prayers—for me, for the man whose life I helped save, and for all those caught in the maelstrom of litigation who still seek to serve, to heal, and to do good in a complicated world.

# Cornerstone Discovery – The Digital Lifeline That Saved My Life

In the crucible of a federal courtroom, where the full weight of the government's accusations bore down with relentless force, I was not merely defending my license or my reputation—I was fighting for my very survival. The charges were severe, the evidence overwhelming in volume and complexity, and the stakes impossibly high. Amidst this maelstrom, two allies emerged as lifelines: Cornerstone Discovery, and their revolutionary AI-powered platform, Junto.

## *The Architects of Defense: Cornerstone Discovery*

From the very beginning, Cornerstone Discovery proved to be more than just a litigation support company—they were the architects of a robust, technologically-driven defense. Their full-service model was not just rhetoric; it manifested in a seamless integration of digital forensics, trial graphics, data analytics, e-discovery, and strategic support that breathed life into our case. They took the mountain of raw, chaotic data facing us—millions of lines of billing entries, emails, medical records, time logs—and crafted a coherent and compelling narrative.

What truly set Cornerstone apart, however, was their human approach. Each interaction felt personal. Their team didn't just provide services; they provided presence, clarity, and belief. Chief among them was Kevin Segal.

## *Kevin Segal: The Technological Maestro*

Kevin Segal, a Litigation Support Project Manager at Cornerstone Discovery, brought a unique blend of technical mastery, courtroom fluency, and human insight. With a background in music business, entrepreneurship, and technology from the University of the Arts, Kevin's brain was wired for patterns—and the courtroom became his concert hall.

Segal's contributions to high-profile cases—including his early work in the Led Zeppelin "Stairway to Heaven" copyright trial—had already established his credibility. But in my case, his impact was transformational.

He led the charge in analyzing a vast digital record of my practice. Every interaction, every billing code, every timestamp was evaluated, contextualized, and organized into a story that humanized the clinical decisions I had made. He created demonstratives that turned indecipherable billing data into accessible visuals. He sat through strategy sessions like a second-chair litigator, anticipating how digital evidence would be perceived by a jury.

When chaos reigned, Kevin brought structure. When anxiety crept in, he brought calm. When the government painted me as a numbers manipulator, Kevin showed the truth: a clinician immersed in complexity, not corruption.

## *Junto AI: The Silent Defender*

Junto, the AI-powered platform developed by Cornerstone Discovery, became the silent guardian of my defense. It processed data with a precision and speed beyond human capacity. Thousands of documents were indexed, analyzed, and cross-referenced. Subtle discrepancies in the prosecution's interpretation of my billing patterns were flagged. Redundant or cherry-picked evidence was exposed.

What set Junto apart was its usability. Unlike many data platforms, Junto wasn't locked behind a wall of complexity. It had an intuitive interface that allowed everyone—lawyers, expert witnesses, and even myself—to explore the evidence, trace links, and test theories in real-time. This transparency was empowering.

Through Junto, we uncovered patterns that reinforced my innocence. The AI flagged inconsistencies that helped us rebut the notion of "impossible days." It clarified time blocks, established the legitimacy of supervisory practices, and revealed overlooked contextual data that aligned with routine psychiatric care.

## The Synergy: Human and Machine

The true strength of my defense lay in the synergy between human expertise and artificial intelligence. Kevin and Junto operated in concert: he understood how to wield the platform, and it responded by giving him the ammunition he needed. Together, they dismantled the prosecution's case.

Patterns that prosecutors deemed fraudulent were revealed to be misinterpretations—flawed readings of a complex clinical schedule. Charts meant to show deceit were replaced with visuals showing care coordination. Emails painted as conspiratorial were recontextualized as documentation of collaboration.

## Legal Strategy and Collaboration

Paul Hetznecker, my lead attorney, recognized the vital edge Cornerstone provided. He worked closely with Kevin to craft a story not just of data, but of purpose. The collaboration between Paul and Kevin transformed digital noise into a legal narrative. It allowed us to humanize complex arguments, counter distorted assumptions, and demonstrate the operational reality of psychiatric practice.

Kevin's input even helped shape cross-examination strategies— providing rebuttals before the prosecution could mount their arguments. It was like playing a game of chess three moves ahead, with AI and human intelligence working in perfect sync.

## The Verdict: Truth Prevails

The jury saw through the haze. They saw, not a rogue practitioner, but a doctor navigating the real-life chaos of patient care. They saw, not fraudulent intent, but a tapestry of service, supervision, and ethical adaptation to clinical demand. This was possible because of how well our evidence had been organized, understood, and presented.

When the verdict of acquittal came, I knew it wasn't just a legal win—it was a triumph of innovation, clarity, and justice.

## *A New Standard for Legal Defense*

This experience made one truth clear: the future of legal defense lies in the fusion of expert strategy and cutting-edge technology. Cornerstone Discovery and Junto didn't just support my defense—they enabled it. In an era where prosecutors are armed with powerful investigative tools, defense teams must be equally equipped. Juries need stories they can understand. Judges need evidence they can trust. Defendants need allies who can turn mountains of data into bridges of truth.

To anyone facing federal prosecution—especially healthcare professionals navigating the grey zones of documentation and billing—my message is simple: do not walk into that arena without digital warriors by your side. Cornerstone Discovery and Junto were mine, and they saved my life.

In the end, it was not just about proving innocence—it was about restoring narrative, revealing intention, and reclaiming the truth that had been buried beneath fear and complexity. In Cornerstone and Junto, I found justice—not just in the verdict, but in the very process of being heard and understood.

# The Case of Dr. William Daniel "Nick" Nicholson

In the annals of American healthcare jurisprudence, few cases have resonated as profoundly as the Forest Park Medical Center trial. Among the 21 individuals indicted in a sweeping federal investigation into alleged bribery and kickbacks, only one—Dr. William Daniel "Nick" Nicholson—emerged entirely acquitted. This outcome was not merely a legal victory, but a testament to the power of foresight, ethical compliance, and the strategic brilliance of his legal team at Winston & Strawn LLP, led by attorney Thomas M. Melsheimer. (Melsheimer and Thomas)

The government's allegations stemmed from what they claimed was a pay-to-play scheme orchestrated by Forest Park Medical Center in Dallas, Texas. Prosecutors argued that physicians were receiving kickbacks, masked as marketing payments, in exchange for steering surgical cases to the physician-owned hospital. These accusations fell under the purview of the Anti-Kickback Statute and the Stark Law, two powerful federal tools used to investigate and prosecute potential healthcare fraud. Many defendants in the case were convicted and sentenced to prison. But Dr. Nicholson's story diverged.

What set Dr. Nicholson apart was his early and consistent commitment to legal transparency. Long before any government inquiry began, he had retained independent counsel to evaluate the legality of his contracts with Forest Park. His concern wasn't theoretical—he understood the gravity of anti-kickback regulations and wanted to ensure he was not inadvertently violating the law. That preemptive diligence turned out to be a critical element in his defense.

Equally important was the data. The prosecution's theory relied on the assumption that physicians who received marketing payments from Forest Park were incentivized to increase their surgical referrals. But Dr. Nicholson's surgical volume at the hospital told a different story. In fact, data showed that his volume of procedures increased after the marketing payments stopped—a trend that completely undermined the idea that he was being "bought." His practice's growth was attributable to patient care, not profiteering.

Melsheimer's team masterfully wove these facts into a narrative centered on integrity. Rather than argue technicalities, they painted a picture of a physician who prioritized compliance, ethics, and patient outcomes. Dr. Nicholson was not just defending himself; he was holding up a mirror to a healthcare system where honest practitioners must navigate a minefield of overlapping regulations.

One of the most compelling elements of the defense was the absence of any smoking gun. No damning emails. No covert conversations. No veiled language suggesting quid pro quo. The government, while rich in theory, was poor in evidence. And Melsheimer knew it. Instead of reacting to the prosecution's tactics, he forced them to prove their case—an approach that ultimately left the jury unconvinced.

In post-trial interviews, Melsheimer emphasized that individualized defense strategies are essential in multi-defendant cases. "What might be true for one doctor is not necessarily true for another," he explained.

"You can't paint everyone with the same brush. Nick Nicholson was unique—not just because he was the only one acquitted, but because he did things the right way from the beginning."

This sentiment reverberates within the medical community. Physicians, particularly surgeons with private practices or ownership in medical facilities, operate in a climate of extreme scrutiny. While financial arrangements are common and often necessary to sustain private institutions, the line between legitimate compensation and prohibited remuneration is razor-thin. The Nicholson case highlights that this line, though narrow, can be respected—if navigated with transparency, documentation, and legal guidance.

Moreover, the trial cast a spotlight on a broader issue: the criminalization of complex healthcare business arrangements. Critics argue that vague regulatory language combined with aggressive federal prosecution strategies has created an environment of fear and uncertainty. Physicians often feel they must choose between growth and safety. Dr. Nicholson chose both—and his victory shows it is possible.

Yet, this case also raises a profound question: How many ethical physicians have been unfairly swept into federal investigations simply because they lacked the resources or knowledge to preemptively guard against risk? Dr. Nicholson's defense team had the skill, experience, and resources to mount an aggressive and nuanced defense. Many do not.

Another major issue interwoven with Nicholson's trial was the rise of digital discovery and forensic analysis. As in other recent healthcare cases, the ability to mine vast amounts of digital records proved critical. Nicholson's legal team used billing data, referral patterns, internal communications, and contract timelines to construct a timeline that made logical and ethical sense. They didn't just tell a story—they showed it, graph by graph, chart by chart, grounded in objective reality. The visual component was powerful in court.

At the heart of this case was also a fundamental misunderstanding about marketing in the healthcare space. The prosecution assumed that any financial relationship between a hospital and a physician was inherently suspicious. But in reality, marketing is a standard, accepted practice. Physicians promote their practices, hire public relations firms, engage in brand-building, and maintain websites. Forest Park's marketing program wasn't inherently illegal—what mattered was whether payments were tied directly to referrals. For Dr. Nicholson, the evidence said no.

The acquittal also reverberated within legal circles. At conferences and symposiums, the Forest Park trial is now frequently cited as a cautionary tale about the risks of prosecutorial overreach and the necessity of tailored, evidence-driven defenses. It underscores how critical it is for defendants to retain attorneys who understand the nuances of healthcare law—not just general criminal defense. Healthcare fraud cases are fundamentally different: they require knowledge of coding, billing, medical necessity, peer review, Stark law, safe harbors, and more. Melsheimer's firm had all these tools in their arsenal.

In reflecting on his journey, Dr. Nicholson reportedly expressed profound relief—but also a sense of solemnity. His name had been dragged through the mud. His patients questioned him. His peers doubted him. Though the jury saw the truth, the damage to his reputation took time to heal. This highlights another truth: even when physicians win, they often lose.

Still, Dr. Nicholson's case remains a blueprint. It illustrates how doctors can protect themselves—not just reactively, but proactively. It shows that engaging legal counsel, maintaining compliance documentation, and avoiding even the appearance of impropriety are not just good practices—they are survival strategies. In today's hyper-regulated healthcare environment, the Hippocratic Oath must be paired with a legal playbook.

Dr. Nicholson's vindication also serves as a message to federal prosecutors: medicine is not commerce. Outcomes cannot be measured solely in dollars, and intent cannot be inferred solely from spreadsheets. At its best, the law can protect the innocent. But when misapplied, it can ensnare them.

Ultimately, the Forest Park case, and Dr. Nicholson's acquittal in particular, calls for a recalibration in how we view healthcare fraud enforcement. Zealous prosecution must be tempered with fairness, evidence must outweigh assumptions, and defendants must be judged individually—not collectively.

For medical professionals facing similar scrutiny, the case of Dr. William Daniel "Nick" Nicholson stands as both a warning and a guidepost. It is a reminder that vigilance, documentation, and legal foresight are as vital as any scalpel or suture. And for the legal community, it's a masterclass in the power of patient, fact-driven advocacy.

Because sometimes, doing the right thing—quietly, diligently, and consistently—is the most powerful defense of all.

# The Rise of the Machines – AI and the Criminal Prosecution of Physicians

In 2001, Steven Spielberg gave us the cinematic dream of artificial intelligence in the form of a childlike android who longed for love. It was hopeful, endearing—even tender. But just a year later, he released a far darker vision in *Minority Report*, where future crimes were punished before they were committed, thanks to psychic "Precogs." In that film, preemptive punishment blurred the line between justice and tyranny. I've mentioned this before in a previous chapter. However, given the rapid development of AI tools it is worth revisiting this.

Fast forward to 2024, and the U.S. Department of Justice has cast its lot not with the dreamy child android, but with the dystopia of pre-crime. And they've found their precogs—not in a tank of amniotic fluid—but in artificial intelligence algorithms humming away inside data centers owned by federal contractors. This isn't science fiction anymore. This is healthcare enforcement today.

AI is no longer a futuristic tool used to identify disease, track drug interactions, or detect early-stage cancer. It is a weapon of compliance. It is a sword—not a scalpel. It is being used by Medicare auditors, federal prosecutors, and insurance recovery contractors to find, target, and punish physicians for what is often nothing more than clinical judgment wrapped in paperwork. And the consequences are devastating.

Let's begin with the basics: In 2015, the Centers for Medicare and Medicaid Services (CMS) awarded a contract to Safeguard Services LLC (SGS), designating them as a Unified Program Integrity Contractor (UPIC). Their job? To audit and recover funds using predictive analytics and AI. Yes, the machines were unleashed on us not to help us—but to find patterns, anomalies, and deviations that *must* be fraud, even when it's merely a doctor doing their job.

SGS's parent company is Peraton, one of the largest government defense contractors, with clients that include the CIA, FBI, and NSA. Their slogan? "Solving the toughest national security challenges fearlessly." In other words, the same folks responsible for intelligence surveillance and military-grade cyber ops are now in charge of auditing your patient notes.

If that doesn't raise your blood pressure, consider this: CMS has since expanded SGS's reach to more than half of the U.S. Medicare jurisdiction. If you're billing Medicare, odds are high that Peraton's AI will review your records—not for better care, but for better recoupment. These aren't clinicians reviewing your notes. They are engineers feeding algorithms that look for statistical anomalies and flag them as red-alert fraud.

In essence, every physician is now practicing under the gaze of a digital overseer. We are being watched not by a human eye, but by pattern recognition tools that can't tell the difference between a coding error and criminal intent.

What's worse is that this AI-driven enforcement isn't theoretical. It's already been weaponized.

Physicians across the country are being investigated, indicted, and in some cases imprisoned because AI flagged their billing patterns as suspicious. Maybe they coded level 4 instead of 3. Maybe they saw 32 patients in a day instead of 27. Maybe their usage of modifier 25 was above average. It doesn't matter that each of those cases may have had a sound clinical basis. The precogs have spoken.

Even my own experience in federal court gave me a front-row seat to this terrifying new reality. The government doesn't come in asking why. They come in showing you a graph, a chart, an Excel spreadsheet produced by an algorithm—and then demand that you prove your innocence. It's not law. It's actuarial combat.

And yet, here's the tragic irony: these same AI tools have failed spectacularly at protecting patients when it really counts. Just ask the 191 million Americans whose private health information was exposed in 2024's Change Healthcare cyberattack. (Whittaker) Or the patients who never received medications because AI denied prior authorizations based on flawed predictive models. Or the disabled child whose wheelchair was denied because the algorithm said no.

What we have created is a system in which AI is judge, jury, and executioner—only it doesn't know medicine. It doesn't know nuance. It doesn't know care. And it doesn't care.

Consider the implications. The DOJ has hinted that AI may be used to preemptively detect fraud. Meaning: it will identify physicians who appear likely to commit fraud in the future. Not because they've done anything illegal, but because they have patterns that "match" known cases. That's *Minority Report*. That's predictive policing. And in medicine, it is a dangerous perversion of justice.

Let's pause here.

I'm not against AI. In fact, I believe that when used ethically, AI can revolutionize patient care. We're already seeing it in radiology, where pattern recognition can flag early-stage cancers. In dermatology, where it can track suspicious moles. In psychiatry, where it can help personalize treatment. But there's a vast difference between augmenting care and automating prosecution.

The danger isn't the technology. It's the intention.

AI reflects the data it is given. If we feed it biased data, it will produce biased outcomes. If we use it to criminalize every outlier, it will criminalize innovation. If we train it on the assumption that more care equals more fraud, then it will punish the best among us—the ones who spend extra time with patients, who code accurately, who go above and beyond.

And yes, AI will be wrong. It will hallucinate. It will misclassify. It will learn from flawed assumptions. It already does.

What happens when a physician is flagged by AI and a federal agent acts on that flag? Who's accountable if the case falls apart? Not the algorithm. Not the contractor. It's the physician who pays the price—financially, professionally, emotionally.

We must demand transparency. If AI is used in healthcare enforcement, it must be auditable. Physicians should have the right to know how decisions were made. The models should be publicly vetted. The logic should be explainable—not hidden in black-box proprietary code.

We also need a Bill of Rights for physicians in the age of AI. A right to human review. A right to context. A right to challenge AI-based findings. Because the burden of defending oneself from an automated accusation should not fall on the shoulders of a doctor fighting to keep their practice alive.

I know many of you will read this and think: *This can't happen. This sounds paranoid.* But it already has. It happened to me. It's happening to others. The era of AI-assisted criminal prosecution is not coming— it's here.

Let us not wait until more good physicians are lost to an algorithm's misfire. Let us act now. Let us protect the sacred space of medical judgment from the cold indifference of machine logic. And let us do so with the urgency of those who know what it feels like to be wrongly accused by something that doesn't bleed, doesn't think, and doesn't care.

Because the machines are here. And we must decide whether they serve medicine—or devour it.

# The Illusion of Data Integrity – A Physician's Warning From the Front Lines

We live in an era intoxicated by data. It pulses through every fiber of the healthcare system—coursing through electronic health records, feeding machine learning models, informing diagnostics, shaping policy, and, increasingly, fueling the prosecutions of physicians. But what if the data we rely on isn't just flawed, but misleading? What if the integrity of this data—the fidelity and accuracy upon which our reputations and freedom rest—is more illusion than reality?

In my own case, the data illusion nearly destroyed me.

Let's begin with definitions. Data fidelity refers to how faithfully information reflects its source. High-fidelity data should act like a mirror—precise, undistorted, trustworthy. Accuracy, on the other hand, reflects whether the data is true, not just consistent. A monitor may display blood pressure readings every second with remarkable fidelity, but if the cuff is miscalibrated, the data is useless—if not dangerous.

This distinction between fidelity and accuracy matters deeply. It matters in diagnosis, in documentation, in policymaking. And it matters most in the courtroom, where data is now weaponized against physicians.

I learned this firsthand during my prosecution. Among the government's many accusations: that I had billed for services rendered to Medicare beneficiaries who were already deceased. A ghastly charge. A data-driven gotcha. But when examined closely at trial, the house of cards collapsed. The government's own expert stumbled under cross-examination, unable to explain how 90% of the so-called dead patients had died before I was even born—or while I was in kindergarten. One beneficiary, supposedly defrauded by me, was listed as being over 360 years old.

Let that sink in.

This wasn't an isolated clerical error. This was systemic decay in the very data repositories that healthcare prosecutors now rely upon. The Social Security Administration's master file, long considered the gold standard of mortality data, is riddled with inaccuracies. In 2011, a government audit found that Medicare paid on behalf of numerous "deceased" beneficiaries—because the death file itself was flawed. The watchdogs couldn't distinguish data error from fraud, and so, they defaulted to assumption: if it looks like fraud, prosecute first. Ask questions later.

This flawed assumption doesn't just end careers. It endangers lives.

In my case, the jury saw through it. But many aren't so lucky. Dr. Richard Paulus, an interventional cardiologist from Kentucky, endured two federal trials and served prison time before the charges against him were dropped. (Walter) Why? Because the government's data—purportedly proving that he had inserted unnecessary cardiac stents—was based on degraded digital images. Their resolution had been reduced by 70%. The anatomy was pixelated, the measurements distorted. The precision of the heart's blood flow had been sacrificed to fit a narrative.

Yet, prosecutors persisted. They cherry-picked 70 cases out of 1100, ignoring the 1030 procedures that were medically appropriate. They didn't want truth. They wanted conviction. And the data—stripped of context, degraded in fidelity—became a blunt instrument.

This is what I call data nihilism: the belief that data, by virtue of being digital, is somehow infallible.

But data is not divine. It is created by humans, coded by humans, and interpreted by humans. And all of us—yes, even the best-intentioned among us—are fallible.

The use of artificial intelligence only exacerbates this problem. Algorithms now scan physician billing patterns, flagging outliers as suspects. Did you code more level 4 visits than your peers? The algorithm thinks you're a fraud. Did you spend longer with patients than average? Clearly, you're upcoding. Never mind that your patients are sicker, or that your clinical setting is different, or that your notes reflect medical necessity. The data doesn't understand context. The algorithm doesn't care.

AI is only as good as the data we feed it. Garbage in, garbage out. But when it comes to federal enforcement, the garbage is dressed in the robes of authority. Prosecutors present charts, timelines, and bar graphs—produced by software—as if they were sacred scripture. The physician becomes a statistic. The medical chart becomes an indictment.

And somewhere in the shuffle, care dies.

Consider the very real fear this creates. Doctors stop writing what they see. They avoid sensitive terms. They undercode. They second-guess their treatment plans. They refuse to take on complex patients. They spend more time managing electronic impressions than human conditions. Because the real illness they fear is not malpractice—it is data misinterpretation.

This environment is not one of healing. It is one of paranoia.

The COVID-19 pandemic taught us just how dependent we are on high-quality data. Case rates. Hospitalizations. Mortality. We watched in real-time how data dashboards shaped policy, funding, and public perception. But we also saw how inconsistent definitions, flawed input systems, and outdated software distorted that data. People died because the data was wrong. Others died because the data said they didn't exist.

And now, we're building enforcement regimes atop that same rickety infrastructure.

Cognitive dissonance runs deep in this space. Prosecutors cling to flawed data because it affirms their assumptions. Defense teams must then overcome not just the evidence, but the narrative. And narratives, especially data-driven ones, are seductive. They offer the illusion of objectivity. But that illusion, once cracked, reveals a terrifying truth: that our healthcare system is increasingly governed not by care, but by code.

What do we do?

First, we must demand transparency. Government agencies must disclose the limitations of their data sources. If the Social Security death master file is flawed, it must not be treated as gospel. If imaging data is degraded, it must be excluded. If AI is involved, its logic must be explained—not hidden in black-box contracts with defense contractors.

Second, we need a new ethic of data stewardship. Medical data is not just information. It is the story of human vulnerability. It deserves respect. Those who manage it—coders, analysts, auditors—must understand its weight. Lives depend on it.

Third, we must protect physicians from data-based persecution. Yes, fraud exists. Yes, it must be rooted out. But we must distinguish between intentional deception and human imperfection. Not every outlier is a criminal. Not every deviation is a scheme.

Finally, we must educate the next generation of doctors, lawyers, and regulators on the perils of data overreach. Data is a tool, not a truth. And when misused, it becomes not a scalpel—but a weapon.

I write these words not just as a physician who has faced federal prosecution, but as a father, a healer, and a believer in the promise of data. I still believe that data can help us. That it can guide us to better treatments, better equity, and better systems. But only if we treat it as the fragile, context-bound, human-made artifact that it is.

Because the illusion of data integrity—when used to condemn the innocent—becomes not just a legal error. It becomes a moral crime.

## CHAPTER 18

# More Than Truth – The Weight of Being Believed

───────

*"The only difference between reality and fiction is that fiction needs to be credible."*

**– Mark Twain**

## Working with Hepatitis C

"Doctor Rifai, this is Gretchen Cook from the New York Times. Can we talk?"

In the early 2000s, as I navigated the corridors of medicine and psychiatry, I found myself drawn to a niche yet profoundly human intersection: infectious disease and mental health. My work with hepatitis C patients illuminated an overlooked reality—these individuals were battling more than a virus. They were also fighting stigma, isolation, and the heavy psychological toll of chronic illness.

Many of my patients had histories of substance use, compounding their social marginalization. The treatments we offered at the time—interferon-based regimens—came with their own burden: neuropsychiatric side effects that often exacerbated pre-existing mental health issues. I began researching these interwoven struggles, aiming to promote a more integrated model of care. Our findings emphasized what many in medicine still miss: treating hepatitis C effectively requires addressing not just liver enzymes, but human suffering.

That research led to a turning point: in 2005, The New York Times featured me in a story titled "In a Judgmental World, She Was Ashamed of Getting Sick." (G. Cook) It highlighted the emotional cost borne by hepatitis C patients and gave voice to stories that typically remained invisible. I was struck by the response—from patients, families, and even policymakers—who found validation and empathy in those paragraphs. It was my first glimpse of what it meant not just to speak truth, but to be *believed*.

## Credibility and Challenging Credibility

In federal court, belief is currency. Credibility can make or break a defense. The accused physician may have the evidence, the data, and the facts—but if the jury doesn't believe them, none of it matters. Nowhere is this truer than when law enforcement officers take the stand.

Police and federal agents arrive in court cloaked in institutional credibility. They are presumed truthful before they even speak. For defense attorneys, challenging that credibility without antagonizing the jury is like walking a tightrope over a canyon of doubt.

The National Association of Criminal Defense Lawyers (NACDL) notes that "breaking down the credibility of a police officer before a lone judge at a motion hearing is one of the most difficult tasks defense lawyers face." It's not just the challenge of facts—it's the cultural weight of the badge. Add to this the "blue wall of silence," an informal pact of mutual protection among officers, and the defense faces an uphill climb.

Discrediting a government witness requires more than contradiction. It demands surgical precision. Attorneys must comb through police reports, cross-reference bodycam footage, and identify even the smallest inconsistencies. But it also requires psychological insight. Witnesses under pressure may be suggestible or defensive. Questioning must be calculated—disarming yet assertive.

Take, for instance, a moment in my own trial where the prosecution's key witness, a federal agent, testified that I had knowingly submitted fraudulent Medicare claims. But on cross-examination, my attorney calmly presented email records, billing guidelines, and training manuals that contradicted the agent's assumptions. The agent stumbled. The jury noticed. And just like that, the spell of presumed credibility began to crack.

Credibility is not just a matter of truth. It's a matter of narrative coherence. The defense must build an alternative story that feels not just plausible, but human—flawed, complicated, and true.

## Scientific Credibility: My Interview with NPR

In September 2016, I was invited onto WDIY's *Take Charge of Your Life* to discuss the mental health needs of older adults. The host, Eleanor Bobrow, was deeply informed and deeply empathetic—a rare combination. We spoke about aging not as a medical inevitability, but as a social and psychological transition.

As Director of the Older Adults Behavioral Health Unit at Easton Hospital, I had come to understand how invisible older adults could become—especially when their mental health needs were misinterpreted as "normal aging." Depression, anxiety, and even psychosis often go undiagnosed in seniors. Caregivers dismiss symptoms as senility; physicians overlook them in favor of more "tangible" problems.

On air, I emphasized that while some memory decline is natural, confusion, paranoia, or mood shifts are red flags. Families must be willing to ask hard questions. Physicians must be trained to listen. And most importantly, older adults must be given space to speak for themselves.

We also touched on social isolation. As mobility decreases and social circles shrink, many seniors experience crushing loneliness. I advocated for community engagement—programs that bring elders together, build friendships, and detect early signs of distress.

Eleanor asked me, "What's the biggest myth about aging and mental health?" I replied, "That suffering is inevitable." Aging doesn't have to mean surrendering to despair. But that requires medical systems to treat seniors with the same psychological nuance as younger patients.

We also discussed caregivers—the silent second victims. Caring for a spouse or parent with declining mental health is exhausting. Many burn out. I argued for policy reforms to fund respite care, caregiver education, and mental health screening for caregivers themselves.

The interview taught me something I'd sensed for years but never articulated: credibility in medicine isn't just about credentials. It's about communication. When physicians speak in ways that acknowledge lived experience, they earn trust. Not because of the letters after their names—but because they see the whole person.

## *When the Stakes Are Your Life*

In federal court, the credibility you've built over a lifetime can evaporate in minutes. The prosecutor need only cast one shadow of doubt. A single misinterpreted phrase, a minor billing error, a statistical anomaly—it can all become fodder for a narrative of criminality.

But here's the paradox: the more honest you are, the more vulnerable you become. Truth, especially in medicine, is rarely simple. A physician who explains context—why a note was phrased a certain way, why a code was used based on evolving guidelines—is doing the right thing. But in the courtroom, nuance is risk. Precision is punished.

And so, many defendants opt for silence or soundbites. Credibility is no longer about who you are. It's about who you appear to be under cross-examination.

That's why, for me, storytelling became a survival skill. I worked with my legal team to present not just my defense, but *myself*. My research, my interviews, my patient care—all became pieces of a mosaic that jurors could relate to. We didn't just argue innocence. We argued humanity.

Credibility, I realized, is not a credential. It's an emotional resonance. It's the reason a juror leans forward instead of looking away. It's the echo between what you say and what they believe. And in the fight of your life, it may be the only thing that stands between freedom and a cell.

## Conclusion: Credibility as a Lifeline

Whether in a medical interview, a courtroom, or a national broadcast, credibility is more than truth—it's the weight of being believed. It's built through consistency, context, and compassion. It can't be rushed. It can't be faked. And once lost, it's nearly impossible to rebuild.

But when earned—when fought for—it can change lives.

In my own case, it did more than that. It saved one.

# When the Judge Speaks Last: The Case of Dr. Ron Elfenbein and the Anatomy of a Judicial Acquittal

There are few moments in American jurisprudence more sobering than when a federal judge overturns a jury's guilty verdict. It's a legal thunderclap—rare, deliberate, and deeply unsettling to the status quo. In the case of Dr. Ron Elfenbein, it was also profoundly necessary. The system had moved too fast, too simplistically. The judge, in the end, chose reason over rhetoric. He upheld the law, not the momentum of prosecution.

Dr. Ron Elfenbein, an emergency medicine physician based in Maryland, was indicted in 2022 on five counts of healthcare fraud. The charges stemmed from billing codes submitted during the height of the COVID-19 pandemic—specifically, the use of level 4 Evaluation and Management (E/M) codes. The government accused him of upcoding: billing for complex services (CPT codes 99204 and 99214) while providing what it claimed were brief, straightforward encounters, often in drive-through testing settings.

To the prosecution, the case was clear. Dr. Elfenbein was depicted as someone who exploited the chaos of the pandemic to line his pockets. They painted him as a profiteer, a physician turned opportunist. And it worked—at first. On August 4, 2023, a jury convicted him on all five counts. He faced up to 50 years in prison. The headlines were immediate. Commentators, unaware of the nuances, nodded along. Another doctor, caught in the act.

But then, in December 2023, something extraordinary happened.

Senior U.S. District Judge James K. Bredar issued a 93-page opinion overturning the conviction in full. He found that the government had not met its burden of proof—that no reasonable jury could conclude beyond a reasonable doubt that Dr. Elfenbein had knowingly and falsely submitted the codes in question. (Porter)

"The Government failed to present sufficient evidence from which a reasonable jury could conclude beyond a reasonable doubt that the Defendant's use of the level 4 code was objectively unreasonable and therefore false," Judge Bredar wrote. "Judgment of acquittal is mandated on all five counts."

Let that sink in.

The crux of the case wasn't fraud in the classic sense. It was disagreement over coding interpretations. At the heart of it all was the CPT Manual—an arcane document revised in 2021 by the American Medical Association (AMA). That year, the AMA updated its guidance to allow providers to select E/M billing levels based on total time spent or the complexity of medical decision-making. COVID-19 added further chaos: doctors were encouraged to offer detailed counseling, interpret rapidly changing guidance, and provide emotional reassurance to panicked patients.

Dr. Elfenbein, operating several COVID testing centers, saw hundreds of patients a day. He relied on the updated guidelines and billed accordingly. To the prosecution, the speed of these visits indicated fraud. But Judge Bredar saw the bigger picture. He saw evolving rules, ambiguities in coding language, and—most importantly—evidence that did not prove criminal intent.

One of the prosecution's own expert witnesses admitted under cross-examination that he had not reviewed critical CMS memos issued during the pandemic. These memos clarified that level 4 codes could be used when providers reviewed test results, educated patients, and made complex risk-based decisions—even if those interactions were brief.

The AMA itself filed an amicus brief warning that disagreements in CPT interpretation are common, and not indicative of fraud. Billing disputes, they argued, are often grounded in good-faith differences, not criminal deception. Judge Bredar agreed. In his analysis, the government had failed to distinguish error from intent, disagreement from deception.

That distinction matters.

Because what happened to Dr. Elfenbein is more than a cautionary tale—it is an indictment of how we criminalize ambiguity in healthcare. Coding errors are inevitable. The CPT system is dense, confusing, and often self-contradictory. When criminal intent is inferred from complexity, every physician becomes a potential defendant.

The implications are enormous. If using a CPT code differently than a prosecutor expects can lead to federal indictment, the risk to doctors—and to healthcare itself—is staggering. Fear of prosecution can discourage providers from offering care during emergencies. It can deter physicians from engaging in innovative delivery models. It can chill every clinical decision made under pressure.

The real threat is not fraud. It's overreach.

What saved Dr. Elfenbein wasn't just his defense team or expert testimony. It was a judge willing to examine the case with rigor, honesty, and clarity. Judge Bredar didn't just evaluate whether procedures had been followed. He questioned whether justice had truly been served. In doing so, he reminded us all that the courtroom is not merely a stage for punishment—it is a place for truth.

This case should be required reading in law schools, medical schools, and compliance offices across the country. It's a study in nuance, in the importance of context, and in the limits of data divorced from understanding. It shows how quickly a narrative—once formed—can steamroll the facts, and how hard it is to undo that damage.

I know this world. I've lived it. I've felt the weight of assumption, the chill of misinterpretation, the suffocating burden of having to prove your integrity with every word and document. I understand what it means to be on trial not just for your actions, but for your profession.

Dr. Elfenbein's acquittal is not just his vindication—it's a lighthouse. A beacon signaling that fairness still matters. That nuance still counts. That sometimes, the system—if nudged hard enough—can still correct itself.

But the price he paid—years of stress, legal fees, reputational damage—cannot be refunded. And that is the tragedy beneath the victory.

His case must serve as a warning: that we cannot afford to conflate complexity with conspiracy. That we must not let prosecutors treat ambiguity as evidence of guilt. And that judges must continue to exercise their rare but essential power to say: enough.

Because in the end, it was not data or dogma that saved Dr. Elfenbein.

It was discernment.

And in that discernment, justice found its voice.

# The Chelation Therapy – The Case of Dr. Gary Spangler

In the annals of American jurisprudence, few cases underscore the delicate balance between medical innovation and regulatory scrutiny as poignantly as the trial of Dr. Gary Spangler. Accused of healthcare fraud and money laundering, Dr. Spangler's journey through the legal system reveals the precarious terrain physicians navigate when pioneering treatments intersect with the hard lines of federal oversight.

## *The Genesis of the Case*

Dr. Spangler, a family medicine physician based in Texas, found himself at the center of a federal investigation in March 2018. The indictment charged him with 25 counts: 18 counts of healthcare fraud and seven of money laundering. At the heart of the government's case was the claim that Dr. Spangler knowingly submitted false claims to Medicare for chelation therapy—treatments that allegedly lacked medical necessity. In total, more than $65 million in services were billed, according to prosecutors.

Federal authorities also alleged that Dr. Spangler failed to provide proper supervision over non-physician staff who administered the treatments, violating CMS regulations requiring physician oversight. The narrative was familiar: a physician, allegedly chasing profit, disregarding rules, and manipulating the system. But as with many cases brought under the banner of healthcare fraud, the truth was not so easily distilled.

## Chelation Therapy: A Contested Medical Frontier

Chelation therapy is a well-established treatment for acute heavy metal poisoning. It involves the administration of chelating agents that bind to metals in the bloodstream, facilitating their removal from the body. However, its use has been controversial in other contexts, particularly for chronic exposure to lead or for broader, less well-defined medical complaints.

The prosecution's toxicology expert testified that chelation was inappropriate outside of acute poisoning scenarios. They framed the therapy as a fringe treatment, unsupported by modern science. But the defense saw things differently.

Dr. Spangler's legal team brought in an expert epidemiologist with experience responding to environmental crises, including the Flint, Michigan water disaster. He testified that while chelation is not mainstream for low-level lead exposure, it is not categorically unreasonable—particularly in regions like Galveston, Texas, where historical environmental contamination is well-documented. Physicians, he argued, have discretion in treating complex, poorly understood conditions when supported by legitimate clinical concern.

## Legal Nuances: Intent and Medical Judgment

As in many healthcare fraud trials, the linchpin of the case was not just whether the treatments were advisable—but whether Dr. Spangler *intended* to deceive Medicare. Under federal law, fraud requires not just factual error, but "mens rea"—a knowing and willful intent to defraud.

The defense emphasized this point, arguing that disputes over medical necessity are not equivalent to criminal deception. Disagreement over evolving or unconventional therapies must remain within the bounds of clinical discretion. Judge Lee Rosenthal, Chief Judge of the Southern District of Texas, agreed.

In her ruling, Judge Rosenthal highlighted that the government failed to provide evidence that Dr. Spangler knowingly submitted false claims. While experts may debate the merits of chelation for certain patients, the court concluded that such disputes are not criminal acts. They are medical decisions.

## *The Verdict and Its Implications*

Following a nine-day bench trial, Judge Rosenthal delivered her verdict: full acquittal on all counts. In her decision, she affirmed that while the government may question the prudence of Dr. Spangler's treatments, it had not proven fraudulent intent beyond a reasonable doubt. (B Hobson)

This outcome carries significant implications for the medical and legal communities alike. It reinforces the principle that clinical judgment, even when unconventional, is not criminal by default. Physicians must retain the latitude to tailor treatments to individual patients—particularly when dealing with novel or poorly understood conditions.

Moreover, the case sends a strong message to regulators and prosecutors: oversight must be exercised with precision, not overreach. The courtroom is not the place to resolve every debate in medical science. To criminalize every divergence from standard practice is to risk paralyzing innovation and discouraging physician autonomy.

Dr. Spangler's acquittal stands as a beacon for due process in the age of data-driven enforcement. It reminds us that medicine is not algorithmic—it is human, contextual, and often messy. It evolves. And in that evolution, the law must remain measured.

In the end, Dr. Spangler was not just vindicated—he was vindicated by the very principle at the heart of medicine: *primum non nocere*—first, do no harm. His case teaches us that good faith, properly examined, still matters. And that when judges understand the full story, justice can prevail.

# When a Hospital is Indicted – The Corporate Death Penalty

In a rare and striking moment in American jurisprudence, Chesapeake Regional Medical Center (CRMC) in Virginia was indicted on federal charges of healthcare fraud and conspiracy to defraud the United States. This case marks a significant pivot in healthcare enforcement: the attempt to hold an entire hospital criminally responsible for its alleged role in a physician's decade-long fraud scheme. While healthcare fraud prosecutions have typically focused on individual wrongdoers—doctors, executives, billers—this case signals an emerging frontier: institutional accountability that goes beyond civil penalties and into the realm of criminal law.

## The Background: Dr. Javaid Perwaiz and the Pattern of Abuse

At the center of the CRMC indictment is Dr. Javaid Perwaiz, an obstetrician-gynecologist who had surgical privileges at the hospital from 1984 until his arrest in 2019. In 2020, Perwaiz was convicted on 52 counts of healthcare fraud and false statements, after prosecutors presented evidence that he performed unnecessary surgeries—including hysterectomies and sterilizations—on hundreds of women. His conviction resulted in a 59-year prison sentence. (Mettler)

But the story did not end there.

In 2023, federal prosecutors turned their attention to CRMC itself. The indictment alleges that the hospital was not merely a passive venue where the surgeries occurred, but an active enabler of Perwaiz's scheme. From 2010 to 2019, the hospital received approximately $18.5 million in reimbursements for procedures performed by Perwaiz—procedures the government now asserts were fraudulent. (Zachary A et al.)

## Institutional Failures and Alleged Complicity

The indictment paints a damning portrait of corporate neglect and willful blindness. Despite knowing that Dr. Perwaiz had his privileges revoked by another hospital in 1983 for unnecessary surgeries—and that he had been convicted of felony tax fraud—CRMC continued to grant and renew his credentials every two years for decades.

Hospital staff repeatedly raised red flags. Concerns about the volume and necessity of Perwaiz's procedures, irregularities in consent forms, and suspicious billing practices were reportedly ignored. The government alleges that CRMC allowed Perwaiz to classify inpatient-only surgeries as outpatient, thereby facilitating improper billing and maximizing reimbursement.

These allegations amount to a claim not of mere negligence, but of systemic compliance failure and profit-driven complicity.

## Legal Defense and Constitutional Questions

CRMC has pleaded not guilty. One of its primary defenses is rooted in constitutional law: the hospital argues that, as an arm of the Commonwealth of Virginia, it enjoys sovereign immunity from federal criminal prosecution. It also contends that it lacked the specific intent required to sustain charges of fraud or conspiracy.

Whether these defenses will prevail remains to be seen. But the very fact that a hospital is facing felony charges—charges typically reserved for individuals—is a seismic development in the landscape of healthcare law.

## Implications for the Healthcare System

The indictment of CRMC sends an unmistakable signal to hospitals and healthcare systems across the country. No longer can institutions rely on plausible deniability or hide behind credentialing boards when bad actors flourish under their watch. This case has the potential to redefine institutional accountability and incentivize more aggressive internal oversight, whistleblower protections, and proactive compliance strategies.

Healthcare organizations must recognize that their risk profile now includes not just civil fines or reputational harm—but criminal indictment. This could result in more conservative credentialing, robust internal audits, and a culture that prioritizes ethical conduct over revenue.

The case is also a sobering reminder that the consequences of institutional failure are not abstract. They are measured in the lives of patients who were subjected to unnecessary surgeries, emotional trauma, and permanent bodily harm. When oversight breaks down, it is the most vulnerable who suffer most.

### The Broader Trend: Prosecuting the Institution

The CRMC indictment fits within a growing pattern of attempts to prosecute corporations and institutions for systemic wrongdoing. Whether it's banks laundering money or pharmaceutical companies fueling the opioid crisis, prosecutors are increasingly applying criminal theories of liability to entire entities. The healthcare sector, once thought immune due to its essential public service function, is no longer exempt.

While critics may argue that indicting a hospital is a form of judicial overreach, others see it as long overdue. Civil settlements and deferred prosecution agreements have often allowed bad actors to escape meaningful accountability. A criminal trial forces institutions to confront the full weight of their decisions—or lack thereof.

# A Parallel Cautionary Tale: The Death of a Guitarist and the Physician Who Stood Trial

The case of Dr. Richard Snellgrove, an Alabama physician charged in the overdose death of Matt Roberts, former guitarist of the band 3 Doors Down, offers a contrasting but equally important perspective. In 2016, Roberts died from a lethal combination of fentanyl, hydrocodone, and alprazolam in a Wisconsin hotel room. The media narrative quickly turned to his doctor, and Dr. Snellgrove was indicted on 13 federal counts, including healthcare fraud and unlawful distribution of controlled substances.

But in May 2018, a jury acquitted Dr. Snellgrove on all counts. His defense demonstrated that Roberts had obtained drugs from multiple sources, including illicit dealers, and that the physician's prescribing patterns were consistent with the medical record. Text messages showed that Roberts actively deceived his physician to fuel his addiction. (Specker)

The verdict served as a vindication not just for Dr. Snellgrove, but for the broader principle that physicians must be judged by their intent, not just outcomes. Like the CRMC case, it underscored the need to differentiate between negligence and willful misconduct.

### Concluding Reflections: From Compliance to Conscience

The juxtaposition of CRMC and Dr. Snellgrove's cases offers a profound meditation on where responsibility lies in healthcare. Institutions must not be allowed to abdicate their oversight duties while profiting from fraud. At the same time, physicians must be protected from criminal liability when they act in good faith under complex and ambiguous circumstances.

We are entering a new era of healthcare enforcement—one that demands clarity, accountability, and, above all, integrity. If the law is to serve both justice and medicine, it must evolve to hold the right people—and the right entities—accountable.

CRMC's fate will be determined in court. But its indictment alone may be a turning point. Because sometimes, the threat of the corporate death penalty is the only force strong enough to change a broken system.

# Cheaper Botox from Canada – The Acquittal of Dr. Gregory Connor and the Perils of Medical Coding

In a federal courtroom in Tulsa, Oklahoma, a quiet neurologist stood accused of being a criminal. His crime? Trying to stretch a dollar in a broken system. Dr. Gregory Connor, a solo practitioner treating patients with movement disorders, tremors, and spasticity, found himself battling the full force of the U.S. government over his choice to import a cheaper version of Botox—not counterfeit, not unsafe, just less expensive and sourced from Canada.

The government charged him with 36 counts of healthcare fraud, one count of receiving a misbranded drug with intent to defraud, and four counts of aggravated identity theft. All of it hinged not on patient harm, nor on deception in the traditional sense, but on whether a vial bore the precise American label demanded by the FDA. It was bureaucracy in its most prosecutorial form.

## The Decision to Care, Not Profit

Dr. Connor did what many physicians have quietly considered in a system that often reimburses less than the cost for vital medications. He purchased FDA-approved Botox from Canadian suppliers to treat his Medicare patients. The drug—Onabotulinumtoxin A—was the same compound, manufactured by the same company, Allergan. The only difference? The label.

Dr. Connor's patients desperately needed this treatment. Without it, their quality of life would plummet. But the government insisted that unless the Botox came with the precise American label and National Drug Code (NDC), it was "misbranded" and non-reimbursable. The irony? The medication was safe, effective, and medically necessary. The only thing that was "counterfeit" was the narrative constructed to turn this into a crime.

Prosecutors leaned on labeling violations, claiming that Connor's imported Botox lacked FDA-required elements. They said his use of Medicare patient data to bill for these treatments—the very patients who came to him for help—constituted aggravated identity theft. Because the label was wrong, the billing was fraudulent. Dr. Connor, in their telling, stole from the very people he was treating.

## A Jury That Understood Context

After a four-day trial, the jury rejected this theory. They acquitted Dr. Connor on all counts. (Morelaw) Vindication came not because the law made sense, but because jurors applied common sense. The court later ruled that Dr. Connor was not entitled to attorney's fees under the Hyde Amendment; the government's case, while weak, was not "vexatious, frivolous, or in bad faith," according to the judge. But the damage was done. A good doctor had been put through hell.

## When Labeling Becomes a Weapon

The broader implications are sobering. If a physician—acting without malice, prescribing authentic medication, billing honestly—can be prosecuted over administrative details, then no one is safe. This is where the complexity of medical coding becomes a matter of liberty, not just compliance.

The AMA has long acknowledged that coding is both science and art. Mistakes are common and often innocent. "Medical coding errors can cost physicians significant revenue, and even worse, increase compliance risk," their guidance states. Most coding errors stem from interpretation, not deceit. But Dr. Connor's case shows how even a well-meaning interpretation can be twisted into a felony.

The government's position was that using a J-code for a vial not bearing the FDA label amounted to fraud. By billing Medicare for a treatment that lacked a matching U.S. NDC number, Dr. Connor—despite delivering the actual service—was accused of theft. The logic was chilling: a doctor was guilty of fraud because the pharmacy sticker was Canadian.

## A Chilling Effect on Care

Dr. Connor cooperated fully. He gave investigators access to his office, his records, even his refrigerators. He explained everything. In fact, he had kept a vial of U.S.-labeled Botox for a particular insurer that required it. The government later used this against him, arguing it was part of a deceptive cover-up. The court, however, called this theory "strained."

This was no pill mill. Dr. Connor did not profit excessively. He treated his patients with compassion and professionalism. And for that, he was nearly destroyed.

## The Kafkaesque Reality of Healthcare Enforcement

Dr. Connor's story is a modern parable about how regulatory enforcement has lost its way. What should be a matter for clarification or administrative correction became a federal indictment. The use of Medicare patient information for legitimate billing became aggravated identity theft. The failure to match an NDC code became health care fraud. This is Kafka with a stethoscope.

The Department of Justice, CMS, and the OIG must take heed. Fraud is real and must be pursued. But fraud must be based on intent, not imperfection. We need legal reforms that provide safe harbors for honest coding errors, clearer definitions of misbranding, and a more balanced approach to enforcement.

## A Call for Clarity and Compassion

Medical professionals should not need legal counsel to interpret every CPT code or verify every barcode. The American healthcare system is already strained. Prosecuting well-intentioned doctors like Dr. Connor further endangers patients by discouraging innovation, frugality, and clinical compassion.

The labeling on a vial should never carry more weight than the care given at the bedside. The code on a claim form should never outweigh the trust between doctor and patient. Dr. Connor was acquitted, but not before his reputation, his practice, and his peace of mind were put on trial.

His case must be a turning point. It is a clarion call to distinguish criminal intent from administrative error, to restore reason to prosecution, and to protect physicians who act in good faith. Until we do, every doctor is just one code away from catastrophe.

# CHAPTER 19

# Beyond the Verdict – Healing After Battle

*For your Lord has decreed that you worship none but Him. And honor your parents. If one or both of them reach old age in your care, never say to them 'even' 'ugh,' nor yell at them. Rather, address them respectfully.*

— Quran 17:23

## Combined to Compromise

"Can you apply to a combined program? Just humor us—I know it's very, very competitive, but you'll get in."

Those were the gentle yet resolute words from my parents in 1997, as I stood on the cusp of a medical career in a country far from my birthplace. I had just completed medical school in Syria and was honored to receive the prestigious National Research Service Award from the National Institute of Mental Health. With top-tier USMLE scores, impressive research credentials, and strong clinical experience in the U.S., I had my pick of residency programs. One institution stood out: the University of Texas Southwestern in Dallas. They courted me actively, and for good reason.

At the time, I was conducting research on small G proteins—specifically the RAS family—and their pivotal role in signal transduction. My focus was how neurotransmitters like serotonin, norepinephrine, and dopamine communicate with the internal architecture of cells. This was cutting-edge science. Alfred Gilman, a recent Nobel laureate for his discovery of G proteins, was affiliated with UT Southwestern and had expressed keen interest in my work. I visited the campus in December 1997, captivated by its intellectual energy and state-of-the-art facilities. My parents, proud of my achievements, were nevertheless uneasy.

The stigma surrounding psychiatry within the Middle Eastern community cast a long shadow. My father, always pragmatic, feared the social implications. And so, he proposed a compromise: apply to a combined internal medicine and psychiatry program. The University of Virginia's program in Roanoke and Salem surfaced as a promising alternative. It offered rigorous dual training and, importantly, social legitimacy.

When Dr. John Joseph Yazel, the program's director, personally picked me up from the airport during my visit, his warmth and sincerity made a lasting impression. I liked him instantly. The program was less prestigious than Dallas but had a soul, a sense of belonging. Still, after my visit, there was an unsettling silence. No follow-up, no confirmation. The days ticked down to the submission deadline for the residency match.

In February 1998, I made the agonizing decision to rank Dallas first, with UVA second. I was torn—between ambition and family, between prestige and filial duty. I asked my parents to pray. My father assured me, with complete faith, that a parent's prayers never go unanswered.

Then came Tuesday, February 10, 1998—a day I will never forget. My father called that morning, his voice heavy with emotion. He had dreamt of his father, my grandfather Aref Rifai, who told him that good things were ahead for me. It was a moment of divine reassurance. Still, I didn't have the heart to tell him that my choices had already been submitted, with Dallas ranked first.

Just hours later, at exactly 11:00 a.m., the phone rang. It was Dr. Yazel from UVA. "Aly, where have you been? We've been trying to reach you. We want you now. Forget the match. I'm sending your acceptance letter tomorrow." I was stunned. Disbelief gave way to tears—tears of gratitude, of divine alignment.

When I told my parents, they too wept. They saw in this moment not just an answer to their prayers but a validation of faith, of the deep and often mysterious interplay between intention, surrender, and grace. That moment, and one many years later—when we stood together in a courtroom and heard the jury declare me not guilty—are bound in my heart by the same force: belief. Belief in something higher than ourselves.

I spent five transformative years at UVA's combined residency program. It was rigorous, humbling, and deeply formative. In 2002, Dr. Yazel wrote to the National Institute of Mental Health to recommend me for a federal appointment. His words still echo in my soul:

"In my 25 years as a residency program director, Muhamad Aly Rifai is one of the best—if not the best—resident that I have ever trained. I strongly recommend him."

Two months later, I joined the NIMH as a federal employee. That journey—from a boy in Syria to a scientist in Texas, from a conflicted son to a respected physician—was not a straight line. It was a spiral of faith, perseverance, and grace.

Beyond the courtroom, beyond the acquittal, lies the deeper work: healing. Healing the wounds of accusation. Healing the fractures in reputation. Healing the inner self. But also, giving thanks—for parents who prayed, for mentors who believed, and for a system, however flawed, that still made room for redemption.

This chapter is not just a reflection. It is a tribute. To all who stood by me. To all who doubted me and gave me the chance to prove them wrong. And most of all, to my parents—whose dreams and prayers carved the road I walk today.

# Not Everyone Survives Prosecution – The Story of Charles Szyman

Dr. Charles Szyman was not merely a doctor; he was a healer, a veteran, and, above all, a man deeply committed to alleviating the profound pain of others. His journey through the labyrinthine corridors of American healthcare would ultimately become emblematic of the crushing toll that unchecked prosecutorial power and sensationalized media scrutiny can exact upon the noble calling of medicine.

Born into humble beginnings, Charles Szyman carried within him a resolute drive to serve—a drive that first led him into the disciplined ranks of the United States Air Force. It was here, amid the structured chaos and camaraderie of military life, that Szyman developed the quiet fortitude that would sustain him in the turbulent years to come. After his honorable service, driven by a persistent passion for healing, he earned his medical degree, dedicating himself entirely to the art and science of pain management.

At a time when chronic pain was emerging as a misunderstood epidemic, Dr. Szyman found his calling. His compassion was boundless, evident in his tireless care for those forgotten by conventional medicine—patients suffering from intractable, soul-crushing pain. He became their advocate, their last hope. His clinic in Manitowoc, Wisconsin, soon became a haven where the desperate and abandoned could find relief and dignity.

However, his noble efforts would soon place him in the crosshairs of a government fervently fighting an ill-conceived war against opioids—a war that often blurred the lines between legitimate medical practice and criminality. In an instant, Dr. Szyman, a decorated veteran and dedicated physician, was transformed from healer to accused, a man relentlessly pursued by prosecutors eager to showcase victories in their war against opioid abuse.

The government accused Dr. Szyman of recklessly prescribing opioids, alleging his practices had contributed to the overdose deaths of several patients. Suddenly, his reputation—carefully built over decades of impeccable medical practice—was reduced to ruinous headlines. The media, hungry for sensational stories, painted him as a villain, a rogue physician driven by greed rather than compassion.

Yet the truth was starkly different. Those who truly knew Dr. Szyman recognized his unwavering integrity. He was meticulous in documenting every decision, thoughtful in every prescription he issued, always mindful of the thin line between relief and risk. His patients stood by him, testifying passionately about how his careful management had restored their lives, dignity, and hope.

After a grueling legal battle, during which Dr. Szyman endured endless accusations, humiliations, and exhausting scrutiny, a jury saw through the government's overreach. On a cold November day in 2017, they declared him unequivocally "Not Guilty." The courtroom erupted in relief and vindication, yet the damage inflicted upon his spirit was profound and lasting. (Schafer)

Though vindicated legally, Dr. Szyman soon discovered that the stigma of accusation lingered insidiously. In the court of public opinion, fueled by unrelenting media reports, his acquittal mattered little. His reputation remained tainted. He faced wrongful death lawsuits—civil battles that would prolong the agony and drain his spirit further. These actions kept his name perpetually tied to tragedy, making any semblance of a normal life impossible.

As months passed, the profound emotional and psychological wounds became increasingly evident. Dr. Szyman, once vibrant and filled with purpose, began to withdraw into himself. Friends noticed a shadow overtaking him, a weight too heavy to bear alone. Despite their earnest support, his resilience had been eroded by the relentless persecution, the ongoing civil suits, and the ceaseless whispers that echoed long after the legal gavel had fallen silent. Ultimately, the burden became unbearable. On February 20, 2018, in the tragic solitude of his own anguish, Dr. Charles Szyman took his life. His suicide shocked those who loved him but hardly surprised those who witnessed firsthand the devastating psychological toll exacted by wrongful prosecution and merciless public shaming.

Even in death, the media could not let him rest. Newspapers continued to invoke his name, rehashing accusations he had already overcome in a court of law. His legacy, once defined by compassion and sacrifice, became unfairly overshadowed by controversy perpetuated for sensationalist appeal. His obituary tells a very different story—one that captures his true essence. It celebrates his military service, his medical expertise, and his unwavering dedication to his patients. It describes him not merely as a victim of circumstance, but as a man who, despite insurmountable odds, strived every day to ease the suffering of others.

The story of Dr. Charles Szyman is not merely a cautionary tale but a call to action. It highlights the urgent need to protect the very individuals society entrusts with our health and well-being from reckless prosecution and sensationalist journalism. Physicians who are unfairly targeted suffer not only professional ruin but profound emotional trauma that too often proves irreversible.

In honoring the memory of Dr. Charles Szyman, we must advocate for a system that respects due process, acknowledges the complexity of medical care, and protects those who dedicate their lives to healing. Only then can we ensure that no other healer, committed to alleviating human suffering, will ever again feel the crushing despair that tragically ended Dr. Szyman's life. Let the narrative of Dr. Charles Szyman serve as both tribute and warning—a powerful reminder that justice delayed or denied is not only a moral failing but a devastating human tragedy.

## Reprise – The Bothra Story and the Unmentioned Co-Defendants

Dr. Ganiu Edu's story is not merely one of professional resilience; it is a profound testament to the indomitable spirit of a physician whose life embodies compassion, integrity, and an unwavering commitment to patient care. In the quiet corridors of medicine, away from the glare of media sensationalism and the clamor of legal battles, Dr. Edu's dedication has always spoken louder than words. His journey, from passionate physician to unjustly accused, and ultimately back to his cherished calling, is an emblematic narrative of redemption and fortitude in the face of overwhelming adversity.

Originally from Nigeria, Dr. Edu pursued medicine with an earnest passion to heal, uplift, and restore dignity to the suffering. His gentle demeanor and steadfast ethical principles quickly earned him respect within the medical community, as well as heartfelt gratitude from countless patients whose lives he touched profoundly. Colleagues often described him as meticulous, compassionate, and above all, profoundly humane in his approach. Each patient encounter was a sacred responsibility for Dr. Edu, a commitment he approached with reverence, care, and a sincere desire to alleviate suffering.

Yet, despite his profound dedication and impeccable professional integrity, Dr. Edu found himself thrust into a harrowing nightmare, caught in the devastatingly wide net cast during the aggressive governmental crackdown on opioid prescriptions. It was this misguided crusade that led to the prosecution of several physicians at The Pain Center USA in Warren, Michigan, including Dr. Rajendra Bothra, Dr. Christopher Russo, Dr. David Lewis, and Dr. Edu himself.

The case was a spectacle that captivated media attention, transforming dedicated physicians overnight into perceived villains in the public eye. For Dr. Edu, a physician whose life's work had always been about alleviating pain, to be accused of contributing to a national opioid crisis was not merely professionally devastating; it was personally excruciating. The indictment alleged healthcare fraud and improper opioid prescriptions, accusations that fundamentally misconstrued the nature of the compassionate care he provided.

Throughout the protracted legal battle, Dr. Edu maintained his quiet dignity, bolstered by unwavering support from patients and colleagues who knew the truth about his character and practice. Testimonies poured forth, filled with genuine gratitude from patients whose lives had dramatically improved under his attentive and empathetic care. They spoke fervently of how Dr. Edu meticulously balanced compassionate treatment with strict adherence to medical guidelines, always putting their well-being first.

The trial itself was an exhausting ordeal, both emotionally and professionally. The prosecution painted with a broad brush, attempting to frame the practice of pain management as inherently suspicious. Yet, Dr. Edu's legal team fought tirelessly to present the truth, revealing that the government's narrative was based on misunderstandings, selective interpretations, and dangerously generalized accusations. With quiet resolve, Dr. Edu stood firm, trusting that justice would eventually illuminate the truth of his compassionate practice.

After weeks of testimony, exhaustive scrutiny, and a relentless onslaught of accusatory rhetoric, the jury ultimately saw beyond the superficial sensationalism. In June 2022, Dr. Ganiu Edu was fully acquitted, his innocence unequivocally affirmed. (Baldas) The vindication was more than a legal victory; it was a restoration of his professional honor, an acknowledgment of his integrity, and a poignant affirmation of the compassionate physician he had always been.

Despite the overwhelming relief of acquittal, returning to the life he once knew was not simple or immediate. The scars of such an ordeal run deep, marking both professional and personal spheres of life. Yet, remarkably, Dr. Edu found within himself a profound resilience. He was driven by an undiminished passion to continue healing, a calling far too compelling to abandon despite the shadows of trauma and injustice.

With characteristic grace, Dr. Edu resumed his medical practice, steadfastly returning to his patients and community. His return was not simply a personal triumph but a profound testament to his commitment to service. The community that had witnessed his unjust persecution now rallied around him with renewed respect and deeper appreciation for the strength and dedication he embodied. Patients who had endured significant suffering during his forced absence welcomed his return with heartfelt relief and deep emotional gratitude.

Today, Dr. Edu continues to practice medicine with the same unwavering dedication that defined his career long before the turmoil. On platforms like Doximity, his profile now quietly but powerfully reaffirms his ongoing commitment to healing, a symbol of enduring dedication and compassionate care that transcends even the harshest of injustices.

The broader narrative of Dr. Edu's ordeal reveals significant lessons about the intersection of medicine, law, and societal perception. It underscores the urgent necessity for a more nuanced understanding of pain management and compassionate care. Dr. Edu's acquittal symbolizes a critical victory for ethical medical practice, yet the trauma and disruption caused by aggressive prosecution remain cautionary reminders of vulnerabilities within our system.

Dr. Ganiu Edu's story, at its core, is profoundly human. It speaks powerfully about resilience in the face of grave injustice, the enduring strength derived from an unwavering sense of purpose, and the deep healing that comes from serving others, even in the shadow of personal adversity. His journey serves not only as a compelling narrative of personal redemption but as a beacon of hope and inspiration for all physicians who may unjustly find themselves navigating the treacherous intersection of medicine and the legal system.

Honoring Dr. Edu is not merely about recognizing a single individual's triumph over adversity; it is an acknowledgment of every physician who silently bears the burdens of their sacred profession amidst misunderstanding and misrepresentation. His story implores us to protect those whose lives are dedicated to caring for others and to champion a system that safeguards rather than endangers these healers.

Ultimately, Dr. Ganiu Edu's narrative is a testament to the indestructible spirit of healing—a powerful reminder that compassion, truth, and integrity can withstand even the most daunting trials, returning stronger and more impactful than ever before.

## Reprise – The Bothra Story and the Doctor in the Hood

Dr. David Lewis was not merely the youngest physician among those accused in the notorious Bothra case—he was a beacon of hope, youth, and promise whose ordeal underscores the profound vulnerabilities physicians face within a justice system that often misunderstands and mischaracterizes their noble intent. His journey is a stark reminder of the personal and professional devastation that ensues when overzealous prosecution intersects with compassionate medical practice.

From an early age, David Lewis embodied an intense passion for healing. Drawn irresistibly toward medicine, he pursued his studies with remarkable vigor, driven by a heartfelt desire to relieve human suffering. Colleagues and mentors alike recognized in him a rare combination of intellectual brilliance and empathetic depth, qualities that made him a standout even among highly accomplished peers.

After rigorous training, Dr. Lewis joined The Pain Center USA in Warren, Michigan, guided by an unwavering commitment to delivering compassionate, evidence-based care to patients struggling with debilitating chronic pain. Despite his youth, Dr. Lewis rapidly developed a reputation for meticulous patient care, exhibiting a maturity and clinical wisdom far beyond his years. Patients revered him not merely for his clinical expertise but also for his deeply humane approach—each patient encounter characterized by genuine empathy, attentiveness, and respect.

Yet, abruptly, Dr. Lewis's promising trajectory was derailed. In December 2018, he found himself thrust into an unimaginable nightmare when federal prosecutors targeted The Pain Center and its physicians in an aggressive crackdown linked to the broader national opioid crisis. For Dr. Lewis, the accusations were deeply personal and professionally shattering. He had entered medicine solely to help, to heal, and to provide solace to those in desperate need. To be portrayed instead as a negligent contributor to patient harm was devastating. At the heart of these accusations lay a fundamental misunderstanding, a distortion of the careful, ethical care he provided daily.

As the youngest defendant, Dr. Lewis faced unique pressures. Amid the relentless media scrutiny and the painful public spectacle of a high-profile trial, he confronted not only the immediate threats to his freedom and career but also the profound sense of disillusionment and betrayal that accompanied such unjust accusations. Yet, rather than succumbing to despair, Dr. Lewis channeled his inner strength into resilience. His defense, rooted in integrity and unwavering truth, would illuminate the courtroom, shining a light on the injustice of his prosecution.

During the grueling seven-week trial in May 2022, Dr. Lewis emerged not only as a defendant but as a powerful advocate for truth. His testimony resonated deeply within the courtroom, piercing the fog of misconceptions propagated by prosecutors. Calm yet passionate, Dr. Lewis articulated his clinical decisions clearly, emphasizing his adherence to established medical standards and protocols. His voice, though youthful, carried undeniable authority and authenticity, speaking powerfully to jurors about the complexities and nuances inherent in pain management.

Witness after witness affirmed Dr. Lewis's integrity, painting a vivid portrait of a physician deeply dedicated to his patients' well-being. Patient testimonies highlighted the profound impact he had on their lives, narrating stories of renewed hope, reclaimed independence, and restored dignity. Medical experts systematically dismantled prosecutorial claims, underscoring the legitimacy and meticulous nature of Dr. Lewis's practice.

In the face of intense prosecutorial aggression, Dr. Lewis maintained remarkable composure, anchored by his profound belief in the righteousness of his practice and the strength of his ethics. He confronted misleading accusations head-on, demonstrating with absolute clarity how each clinical decision was thoughtfully reasoned and medically justified. His confidence was not born of arrogance but of steadfast truth—a physician unwavering in the conviction that his calling was pure and his actions justified.

The culmination of Dr. Lewis's steadfast testimony arrived on June 29, 2022. The jury delivered a unanimous verdict: Dr. Lewis, along with his colleagues, was declared unequivocally "Not Guilty." It was more than a judicial victory—it was a profound vindication, an affirmation of Dr. Lewis's character, clinical judgment, and unwavering dedication to ethical patient care.

Though cleared legally, the toll of the ordeal was significant. The scars of public accusation and intense scrutiny do not fade overnight, particularly for a young physician at the outset of a promising career. Yet, Dr. Lewis's resilience became a beacon of inspiration. Rather than allowing bitterness to take root, he recommitted himself passionately to medicine, determined that the injustice he faced would fuel rather than diminish his dedication to patient care.

In the aftermath, Dr. Lewis returned to his vocation with renewed purpose, stronger and more profoundly empathetic than ever before. His experience, while deeply painful, had imparted critical lessons about compassion, vulnerability, and resilience. Today, Dr. Lewis continues practicing medicine with unblemished integrity, his ordeal having strengthened rather than broken his commitment to healing.

Dr. David Lewis's journey stands as an urgent call for reform within a system prone to misunderstanding the nuanced practice of medicine, particularly in fields as complex as pain management. His story implores society to pause before making assumptions, to recognize the inherent dignity and commitment of physicians, and to approach accusations against healers with careful deliberation rather than reckless zeal.

Ultimately, Dr. Lewis's triumph is not merely a personal victory—it is a broader affirmation of justice, truth, and the essential dignity of compassionate medical practice. His narrative powerfully reminds us of the potential consequences of unchecked prosecutorial fervor and the imperative to protect and honor those who dedicate their lives to healing humanity.

## Reprise – The Bothra Story and the Master Memologist

Dr. Christopher Russo's story is not merely a tale of survival—it is a profound narrative of defiance, wit, resilience, and relentless courage in the face of overwhelming adversity. His journey through the painful maze of injustice and wrongful prosecution is a gripping testament to the indomitable human spirit, passionately illustrating the power of truth wielded bravely, even humorously, against the oppressive machinery of misguided authority.

Born into a family deeply rooted in the healing professions—his parents were dedicated medical professionals—Christopher Russo inherited a profound sense of purpose, integrity, and service. Medicine was not merely his chosen career; it was a sacred calling, instilled in him from his earliest years. Growing up in a household where patient care was the everyday language at the dinner table, Russo developed an earnest passion for healing, coupled with an incisive wit that would later become both a weapon and a refuge during his darkest times.

Christopher Russo established himself as a thoughtful, meticulous pain management physician at The Pain Center USA in Warren, Michigan, earning the deep respect of both colleagues and patients alike. Known for his clinical precision and unwavering commitment to ethical practice, Dr. Russo dedicated himself to alleviating chronic pain, significantly improving the quality of life for countless patients suffering in quiet despair.

Yet, in December 2018, Dr. Russo's life was abruptly and irrevocably shattered. In the aggressive wave of opioid-related prosecutions sweeping across America, he found himself unjustly accused alongside his colleagues—Dr. Rajendra Bothra, Dr. Ganiu Edu, and Dr. David Lewis—of prescribing opioids excessively and fraudulently billing insurers. Overnight, Russo went from respected physician to perceived villain, trapped within the Kafkaesque nightmare of federal prosecution.

The indictment was more than just a legal document—it was a crushing betrayal of the trust he had earned through years of dedicated practice. The accusations painted Russo not as the meticulous healer he was, but as a reckless and unethical profiteer exploiting human suffering. The media eagerly consumed and disseminated this narrative, compounding his humiliation and deepening the profound sense of injustice.

Amidst this turmoil, Russo faced the unimaginable—imprisonment. For over two years, he endured confinement, denied the basic freedoms and human dignity he had always worked tirelessly to uphold for others. The stark walls of his cell became a grim reminder of the devastating consequences when justice fails, when healers become convenient scapegoats for broader societal issues.

Yet, even within the cold confines of incarceration, Russo's indomitable spirit refused to yield. Stripped of his professional practice, his home, and the comforting embrace of normalcy, he turned to an unexpected outlet for defiance—social media. Dr. Russo embraced the moniker "Master Memologist" on platforms like X (formerly Twitter), wielding humor, irony, and pointed satire as powerful tools against prosecutorial overreach and bureaucratic absurdity. His memes, sharp and incisive, cleverly mocked the irrationality and injustice of his predicament, garnering widespread attention and support from peers, advocates, and the public.

Russo's social media presence was not merely cathartic humor; it became a significant force for advocacy, highlighting the broader implications of his case and similar injustices nationwide. His posts were bold, fearless, and unrelenting, spotlighting the human cost of misguided government policies and zealous prosecution. Through the masterful artistry of his memes and unfiltered commentary, Russo transformed his personal suffering into a rallying cry for reform, transparency, and compassion.

The trial itself was a grueling seven-week ordeal beginning in May 2022, where Dr. Russo stood firmly alongside his colleagues in the defense of their innocence. He was defended by his childhood friend, Attorney Laurence Margolis. Ultimately, justice emerged from the chaos. On June 29, 2022, Dr. Christopher Russo was fully acquitted, alongside his colleagues, affirming his unwavering ethical standards and professional integrity.

However, the emotional and financial devastation was severe. Russo had indeed "lost everything"—his practice, financial security, and years of his life were irretrievably stolen by unjust imprisonment and relentless scrutiny. Yet, in freedom, Russo found renewed vigor, channeling his harrowing experiences into continued advocacy and education. His presence on social media did not wane but rather intensified. The "Master Memologist" grew louder, more passionate, his voice amplified by the authenticity born of painful lived experience. His humorous yet piercing critiques became a powerful platform not just for his redemption but for systemic change, shedding light on the wrongful persecution of physicians across America.

Dr. Russo's story underscores critical lessons about the dangers of unchecked prosecutorial zeal and the essential need for a balanced, informed understanding of medical practice, particularly within pain management. It vividly illustrates the profound personal and professional costs borne by dedicated physicians when falsely accused, spotlighting the urgent need for reform in prosecutorial practices.

Today, Dr. Christopher Russo continues his passionate fight not only for his own restoration but for every physician who finds themselves unjustly targeted. His resilience serves as a beacon of hope and defiance, his story a powerful narrative that demands society re-examine its perceptions and judgments about medical practice and justice.

Ultimately, Russo's journey is more than just a narrative of suffering—it is an epic testament to the strength of humor, truth, and humanity in confronting injustice. His courage in embracing humor and satire in the face of overwhelming adversity demonstrates the profound strength of the human spirit. Through memes, advocacy, and relentless truth-telling, Dr. Christopher Russo has forever etched his name as not merely a survivor but a transformative advocate, reclaiming dignity, justice, and the true meaning of compassionate healing.

## The Not So Lucky Ones – The Bothra Case

Within the dramatic and harrowing saga known as the Bothra Case, two poignant stories stand as stark and heartbreaking contrasts to the narratives of vindication and triumph. Dr. Eric Backos and Dr. Ronald Kufner represent the tragic and deeply unsettling outcomes that arise when physicians, facing overwhelming pressure, uncertainty, and fear, decide not to fight but instead to surrender—pleading guilty to charges that their peers ultimately overcame.

Dr. Eric Backos was a respected figure in pain management, a physician who had devoted his life to compassionately addressing chronic pain. His practice, characterized by empathy, clinical diligence, and meticulous attention to patient needs, was similar in every essential way to his colleagues who would later stand trial. Yet, confronted by the immense weight of federal indictment, media scrutiny, and the looming prospect of years imprisoned, Dr. Backos faced an agonizing crossroads. The overwhelming pressures exerted by prosecutors who wielded the threat of devastating consequences pushed him toward a tragic decision: pleading guilty, even to allegations he fundamentally believed were unfounded.

The decision Dr. Backos made was not one born lightly. It was a painful surrender, a stark acknowledgment of the realities many physicians face when entangled within the often merciless gears of federal prosecution. The calculus was agonizingly simple: plead guilty, accept reduced consequences, and attempt to salvage some fragments of his shattered life—or risk everything by fighting charges that were misunderstood, misrepresented, and sensationalized by the prosecution. In his choice, he sought some measure of certainty, a way to mitigate the catastrophic toll on his family, his reputation, and his future. Tragically, it was a decision that would forever haunt him, becoming a poignant symbol of the crushing pressure innocent physicians can face.

Equally heart-wrenching was the narrative of Dr. Ronald Kufner, whose story carried an additional, deeper dimension of personal tragedy and moral compromise. Faced with similar daunting pressures, Dr. Kufner's decision to plead guilty came with an even heavier burden—he testified against his colleagues, those very peers whose practices he once deeply respected and shared. The choice to cooperate with prosecutors was devastating, driven perhaps by desperation, fear, and the terrifying uncertainty that gripped his life amid the chaos of legal entanglement.

Dr. Kufner's testimony, given under immense duress, underscored the complexities inherent within such prosecutions. In agreeing to cooperate, he traded his integrity, his honor, and the bonds of professional solidarity in a desperate attempt to secure personal relief. It was a tragic calculation, reflecting the stark reality faced by defendants ensnared within aggressive prosecutions. Yet, even as he testified, the true tragedy emerged clearly—the anguish etched unmistakably on his face, revealing the profound inner turmoil of a man forced to turn against his colleagues, against himself, in a desperate bid for survival.

What makes the fates of Dr. Backos and Dr. Kufner especially heartrending is that their colleagues—Dr. Rajendra Bothra, Dr. Ganiu Edu, Dr. David Lewis, and Dr. Christopher Russo—faced the same accusations, endured similar emotional and professional devastation, yet emerged acquitted and vindicated. The acquittal of their peers profoundly underscores the tragedy of Drs. Backos and Kufner's decisions, illustrating that the charges they pleaded guilty to were fundamentally questionable, easily dismantled when placed under rigorous scrutiny and fair judicial review.

Dr. Backos's and Dr. Kufner's stories vividly demonstrate the profound vulnerability of physicians caught within the grasp of a legal system more inclined toward accusation than understanding, more focused on prosecution than on nuanced investigation. Their pleas represent not a validation of prosecutorial claims, but rather a painful and cautionary tale about the tragic choices physicians may feel compelled to make when faced with seemingly insurmountable odds.

For Dr. Backos, the consequences extended far beyond his professional career; they permeated deeply into his personal life, casting long shadows of regret, loss, and unanswered questions. For Dr. Kufner, the emotional toll was even more devastating, permanently altering the very fabric of his identity and relationships. The decision to testify against colleagues introduced a profound rupture, a moral injury that would linger, unhealed, long after the trial concluded.

In reflecting upon their stories, society must confront difficult questions about justice, compassion, and the ethical imperatives that must guide prosecutorial decisions. Their narratives challenge us to reconsider how accusations are levied against professionals whose very lives revolve around alleviating suffering. The tragedy of Dr. Backos and Dr. Kufner implores us to reform a system that too often pushes the innocent toward false admissions of guilt, driven by fear rather than truth.

Ultimately, these two physicians embody the tragic cost of prosecutorial aggression and the immense human suffering wrought by a legal system that can, at times, lose sight of the essential humanity at its core. Their stories compel a profound reevaluation of how we treat those entrusted with healing, underscoring the urgent need for reform, compassion, and fairness within medical jurisprudence. Their fates remind us that justice is not merely about verdicts or pleas—it is fundamentally about safeguarding human dignity, protecting ethical integrity, and ensuring that those who dedicate their lives to healing others are themselves shielded from undue harm.

Let the deeply tragic choices of Dr. Eric Backos and Dr. Ronald Kufner serve as a poignant, unforgettable lesson and a clarion call for systemic change, ensuring no physician ever again faces the unbearable decision between false admission and catastrophic ruin. Their stories, filled with pathos and stark moral complexity, remind us that behind every case number and indictment lies a human being whose life, career, and spirit deserve respect, understanding, and, above all, true justice.

# CHAPTER 20

# The Summation

———

*"The future has several names. For the weak, it is impossible. For the fainthearted, it is unknown. For the thoughtful and valiant, it is ideal."*

**—Victor Hugo**

My life has always been a battle—a battle for truth, dignity, and the sacred principle of healing. Born amidst the haunting echoes of violence in war-torn Aleppo, I learned resilience long before I donned my white coat. Childhood trauma etched itself deeply into my consciousness, teaching me early that survival was not just a matter of strength, but of defiance and hope. As a child witnessing unspeakable atrocities, my heart learned compassion, and my mind learned to seek truth relentlessly. These early experiences became the crucible that shaped me not merely as a physician but as a fervent advocate for justice and healing.

My medical journey, filled with academic rigor and pioneering research, was driven by an intense desire to understand human suffering deeply. My groundbreaking work at the National Institute of Mental Health was not just about unraveling scientific mysteries—it was about alleviating human pain. Awarded the prestigious National Research Service Award, my career trajectory seemed destined for research excellence. Yet, life had different plans, steering me toward the intricate tapestry of psychiatry and internal medicine, compelled by my parents' prayers and wisdom.

In those formative residency years, my mentor Dr. John Joseph Yazel recognized a zeal within me, a fervor for patient care that transcended routine practice. His profound recommendation echoed through my subsequent career, a constant reminder of my duty to embody both skill and compassion. My journey from a highly promising researcher at UT Memphis to a committed healer at UVA Roanoke embodied my life's recurring theme—the pursuit of meaningful service over personal glory.

However, this noble path, built upon empathy and integrity, became perilous when my practice faced relentless scrutiny by federal authorities. The painful irony was clear: the same system entrusted to protect public health turned aggressively against healers like myself. My prosecution was not merely a personal ordeal but symbolic of a broader systemic tragedy—where physicians, in their diligent pursuit of patient well-being, became easy scapegoats for the failures of complex societal and healthcare systems.

Throughout my ordeal, I found myself at the mercy of misinterpretations and overzealous prosecutors who blurred the line between legitimate medical decisions and criminal acts. Like many colleagues, I faced an unjustified accusation of healthcare fraud, and yet my resolve never wavered. I recognized this not just as a fight for my freedom, but as a battle for every physician practicing medicine honestly and compassionately. In the cold, sterile environment of courtrooms, my clinical judgments—made meticulously to serve my patients—were scrutinized mercilessly by those unfamiliar with the nuanced realities of patient care.

My eventual acquittal was more than a personal triumph; it was a vindication of the very essence of ethical medical practice. Yet, the victory was tempered by the recognition of the ongoing, silent tragedy afflicting the medical profession: talented, dedicated doctors like Charles Szyman, driven to despair and ultimately suicide by relentless prosecutorial pressures and public vilification. Dr. Szyman's heartbreaking story remains a haunting testament to the devastating toll these misguided prosecutions exact upon those whose life's work is healing.

My advocacy did not end with my own acquittal; rather, it intensified. Physicians such as Dr. Ganiu Edu, Dr. David Lewis, and Dr. Christopher Russo from the Bothra case exemplify the resilience required to withstand such assaults on their character and practice. Dr. Edu's graceful return to his community, Dr. Lewis's unwavering advocacy for ethical patient care, and Dr. Russo's clever use of social media humor to expose prosecutorial absurdities—all demonstrate the profound courage and commitment these healers embody.

However, the tragic decisions by Dr. Eric Backos and Dr. Ronald Kufner, who felt compelled to plead guilty under immense pressure, underscore a devastating truth: the immense power imbalance between prosecutors and physicians. Their pleas reflect not guilt, but rather the brutal reality many face—choosing survival over justice, acceptance of a lesser punishment to avoid total ruin.

Throughout my trial, invaluable support from experts such as Sean Weiss provided clarity amid complexity, offering an impassioned defense grounded in nuanced clinical realities. Weiss's advocacy exemplifies the necessity of informed, precise defense strategies in healthcare litigation, safeguarding both patient care and physician dignity. The impact of these unjust prosecutions extends far beyond individual lives. Society suffers when fear of prosecution chills medical innovation and compassionate patient care. The erosion of trust between physician and patient, driven by fear of legal repercussions, undermines the very foundation of healing professions. My experience illuminated this broader societal consequence, reinforcing my commitment to advocate vigorously for reforms that protect medical autonomy, encourage compassionate care, and uphold the essential dignity of physicians.

Ultimately, the journey detailed in *Doctor Not Guilty* is more than a narrative of personal survival—it is a call to action. It demands systemic change within the judiciary and regulatory frameworks that govern healthcare. It insists upon a society that differentiates genuine criminality from complex clinical judgments, advocating relentlessly for fairness, empathy, and true justice.

My life, punctuated by resilience amidst adversity, has continually reminded me of the profound power of healing—of minds, bodies, and broken systems. My advocacy for reform is unyielding, driven by the conviction that we must protect those who dedicate their lives to healing. Only then can we ensure a healthcare system truly rooted in compassion and justice, ensuring that no physician is forced to choose between their integrity and their freedom.

The fight continues, emboldened by every triumph, tempered by every tragedy. My story, deeply personal yet universally resonant, remains a testament to the indomitable spirit of those committed to healing—a passionate plea for a justice system that truly understands and respects the sacred practice of medicine.

# Conclusion

## Final Thought: The War is Not Over

I have faced war, terror, trauma, and now injustice. I have stood on the precipice of death as a child, addiction as a family member, and prison as a physician. Through it all, I have refused to break.

Physicians across America are being hunted, prosecuted, and imprisoned—not for crimes, but for falling into the crosshairs of an overzealous system. This book is my weapon. Let it be yours too.

There is a poem written by a follower of the Rifai Doctrine and chanted by Rifai family members throughout the Arab world. My traumatic experience of the dreadful and often irresistible legal forces that bear down on doctors has led me to find more personal meaning in its words.

> *O! Son of Rifai !*
>
> *All people depend on you.*
>
> *You are a sea of virtues,*
>
> *Responder to our calls.*
>
> *Support to the oppressed!*
>
> *Focus of existence.*
>
> *O! Son of Rifai!*

Perhaps it is those words, words I heard repeated at family gatherings throughout my youth, words that I have taken to heart, that has led me to write this book as *support to the oppressed.*

# References

ACLU. "Abdullah Al-Kidd v. United States, et Al." *American Civil Liberties Union*, 2015, www.aclu.org/cases/abdullah-al-kidd-v-united-states-et-al.

Aloe, B., and C. R. Weinberg. "The Real Annie Lee Moss." *OAH Magazine of History*, vol. 24, no. 4, 1 Oct. 2010, pp. 16–16, https://doi.org/10.1093/maghis/24.4.16. Accessed 26 Jan. 2020.

americanbar.org. "Plea Bargain Task Force Report." *Americanbar.org*, 2023, www.americanbar.org/content/dam/aba/administrative/criminal_justice/reports/plea-bargain-tf-report.pdf.

Associated Press. ""Kids for Cash" Judge Gets 28 Years in Pennsylvania Bribery Case." *The Guardian*, 11 Aug. 2011, www.theguardian.com/world/2011/aug/11/kids-for-cash-judge-pennsylvania.

---. "Trump Ally Tom Barrack Acquitted of Foreign Agent Charges." *POLITICO*, Politico, 4 Nov. 2022, www.politico.com/news/2022/11/04/trump-chair-tom-barrack-acquitted-uae-00065186. Accessed 24 May 2025.

B Hobson. "Press Release - Houston Doctor Found Not Guilty of Healthcare Fraud." *Wendell Odom*, 3 Dec. 2024, www.wendellodom.com/houston-area-doctor-found-not-guilty-on-eighteen-counts-of-healthcare-fraud/. Accessed 5 June 2025.

Baez. "The Baez Law Firm." *Baez Law Firm*, 2024, www.baezlawfirm.com/media/cardiologists-acquitted-of-50-counts-related-to-health-care-fraud/. Accessed 21 May 2025.

Baldas, Tresa. "How 4 Doctors Beat the Feds in Botched $500 Million Pill Mill Case." *Detroit Free Press*, 30 June 2022, eu.freep. com/story/news/local/michigan/macomb/2022/06/30/ doctors-opioid-scheme-birmingham-bothra/7778004001/. Accessed 6 June 2025.

Basil, Biju, et al. "Is There Evidence for Effectiveness of Transcranial Magnetic Stimulation in the Treatment of Psychiatric Disorders?" *Psychiatry (Edgmont)*, vol. 2, no. 11, Nov. 2005, p. 64, pmc.ncbi.nlm. nih.gov/articles/PMC2993526/.

Bentley, Quinlan. ""Knew What Doctors Should Do": NKY Physician Sentenced for Prescriptions at Pain Clinic." *The Enquirer*, Cincinnati Enquirer, 8 May 2025, eu.cincinnati.com/ story/news/crime/2025/05/08/northern-kentucky-doctor-sentenced-for-prescriptions-at-pain-patients/83519374007/. Accessed 21 May 2025.

Blake, Richard. "McDonald Hopkins Government Compliance, Investigations, and White Collar Defense Team Secures Acquittals for Cleveland-Area Client." *@Mcdonaldhopkins*, 29 Oct. 2021, www.mcdonaldhopkins.com/insights/news/government-compliance-investigations-acquittal. Accessed 2 May 2025.

Busner, Joan, and Steven D Targum. "The Clinical Global Impressions Scale: Applying a Research Tool in Clinical Practice." *Psychiatry (Edgmont)*, vol. 4, no. 7, July 2007, p. 28, pmc.ncbi.nlm. nih.gov/articles/PMC2880930/.

BYU Law Review. *State v. Thomas and the McDonough Test: A Safety Net Proposal to Cure the Square Peg-Round Hole Dilemma* . 1993. https://digitalcommons.law.byu.edu/cgi/viewcontent. cgi?article=1944&context=lawreview.

Cary, Robert M. *Not Guilty : The Unlawful Prosecution of U.S. Senator Ted Stevens*. Washington, D.C., Nacdl Press, 2014.

CBC. "Judge Upholds Dismissal of Alec Baldwin's Involuntary Manslaughter Charge." *CBC*, 25 Oct. 2024, www.cbc.ca/news/ entertainment/alec-baldwin-verdict-upheld-1.7363643. Accessed 4 Apr. 2025.

Chapman. "CCG Healthcare Compliance." *CCG Healthcare Compliance*, 31 May 2023, www.ccghealthcare.com/resource-library/ccg-leads-charge-in-physician-manslaughter-acquittal. Accessed 21 May 2025.

Chapman II, Ronald. "Federal Judge Dismisses Patient Death Charges in Opioid Trial of Dr. Thomas Sachy." *Ronald W. Chapman II*, 11 May 2023, ronaldwchapman.com/blog/sachy-dismissal. Accessed 24 May 2025.

---. "Kentucky Interventional Pain Physician Acquitted of Federal Charges." *Ronaldwchapman.com*, 2025, ronaldwchapman.com/blog/ kendallhansenacquitted. Accessed 21 May 2025.

Congress.GOV. "H.R.5773 - 98th Congress (1983-1984): Sentencing Reform Act of 1984." *Congress.gov*, 1984, www.congress.gov/ bill/98th-congress/house-bill/5773.

Congress.gov. "Ted Stevens." *Congress.gov*, 2025, www.congress. gov/member/theodore-stevens/S000888?page=11. Accessed 2 May 2025.

Constitutional Accountability Center. "Timbs v. Indiana | Constitutional Accountability Center." *Constitutional Accountability Center*, 2018, www.theusconstitution.org/litigation/timbs-v-indiana/.

Cook, Gretchen. "In a Judgmental World, She Was Ashamed of Getting Sick." *The New York Times*, 12 Apr. 2005, www.nytimes. com/2005/04/12/health/psychology/in-a-judgmental-world-she-was-ashamed-of-getting-sick.html.

Cook, Jameson. "Pain Doctor Acquitted of Criminal Charges Agrees to Pay $6.5 Million to Feds." *Macomb Daily*, 25 Aug. 2023, www.macombdaily.com/2023/08/25/pain-doctor-acquitted-of-criminal-charges-agrees-to-pay-6-5-million-to-feds/. Accessed 24 May 2025.

Cornell. "28 U.S. Code § 1863 - Plan for Random Jury Selection." *LII / Legal Information Institute*, www.law.cornell.edu/uscode/text/28/1863.

---. "Rule 606. Juror's Competency as a Witness." *LII / Legal Information Institute*, 2011, www.law.cornell.edu/rules/fre/rule_606.

---. "UNITED STATES v. BANKS." *Cornell.edu*, 2022, www.law.cornell.edu/supct/html/02-473.ZS.html.

Cornell Law School. "18 U.S. Code § 1347 - Health Care Fraud." *LII / Legal Information Institute*, 2016, www.law.cornell.edu/uscode/text/18/1347.

---. "18 U.S. Code § 1349 - Attempt and Conspiracy." *LII / Legal Information Institute*, www.law.cornell.edu/uscode/text/18/1349.

DelMonico, Kim. "Ortho Surgeon Receives 16 Month Prison Sentence." *Orthopedics This Week*, 7 June 2024, ryortho.com/2024/06/ortho-surgeon-receives-16-month-prison-sentence/. Accessed 22 May 2025.

Dror, Itiel E., et al. "Contextual Information Renders Experts Vulnerable to Making Erroneous Identifications." *Forensic Science International*, vol. 156, no. 1, Jan. 2006, pp. 74–78, www.sciencedirect.com/science/article/pii/S0379073805005876, https://doi.org/10.1016/j.forsciint.2005.10.017.

EBSCO. "Martha Stewart Is Convicted in Insider-Trading Scandal | EBSCO." *EBSCO Information Services, Inc. | Www.ebsco.com*, 2022, www.ebsco.com/research-starters/law/martha-stewart-convicted-insider-trading-scandal.

ECKHART, ROBERT. "Juror Jailed over Facebook Friend Request." *Sarasota Herald-Tribune*, 16 Feb. 2012, eu.heraldtribune.com/story/news/2012/02/16/juror-jailed-over-facebook-friend-request/29082355007/. Accessed 22 May 2025.

Edwards, Breanna. "Ron Paul: "Thankful" for Snowden." *POLITICO*, Politico, 10 June 2013, www.politico.com/story/2013/06/ron-paul-thankful-for-edward-snowden-092524. Accessed 4 Apr. 2025.

Eisner Gorin. "Eisner Gorin LLP." *Thefederalcriminalattorneys.com*, 2025, www.thefederalcriminalattorneys.com/juror-misconduct.

Explorable.com. "Confirmation Bias and the Wason Rule Discovery Test." *Explorable.com*, 2019, explorable.com/confirmation-bias.

FBI. "Former Pennsylvania County President Judge Michael Conahan Sentenced." *FBI*, 23 Sept. 2011, archives.fbi.gov/archives/philadelphia/press-releases/2011/former-pennsylvania-county-president-judge-michael-conahan-sentenced.

federalrulesofcriminalprocedure.org. "Rule 41. Search and Seizure - Federal Rules of Criminal Procedure." *Federal Rules of Criminal Procedure*, 2019, www.federalrulesofcriminalprocedure.org/title-viii/rule-41-search-and-seizure/.

Fiore, Kristina. "Vascular Surgeon Admits Doing Unnecessary Procedures." *Medpagetoday.com*, MedpageToday, 11 Mar. 2021, www.medpagetoday.com/special-reports/exclusives/91586. Accessed 5 June 2025.

Golde, Kalvis. "Diaz v. United States." *SCOTUSblog*, 20 July 2023, www.scotusblog.com/cases/case-files/diaz-v-united-states/.

Gramlich, John. "Fewer than 1% of Defendants in Federal Criminal Cases Were Acquitted in 2022." *Pew Research Center*, 14 June 2023, www.pewresearch.org/short-reads/2023/06/14/fewer-than-1-of-defendants-in-federal-criminal-cases-were-acquitted-in-2022/.

guiltypleaproblem.org. "Why Innocent People Are Pleading Guilty." *Let's Fix America's Guilty Plea Problem*, 2018, guiltypleaproblem. org/.

Hamm, Andrew. "Ruan v. United States." *SCOTUSblog*, 12 Apr. 2021, www.scotusblog.com/cases/case-files/ruan-v-united-states/. Accessed 21 May 2025.

Hetznecker, Paul J. "Paul Hetznecker Attorney at Law." *Pauljhetznecker. com*, 2024, www.pauljhetznecker.com/news/. Accessed 25 May 2025.

---. "Pre-Crime and the Danger of Risk Assessments." *Pauljhetznecker. com*, 2016, www.pauljhetznecker.com/blog//2016/09/12/Pre-Crime-and-the-Dangers-of-Risk-Assesments.html. Accessed 4 Apr. 2025.

Inbau, Fred E, et al. *Criminal Interrogation and Confessions*. Burlington, Ma, Jones & Bartlett Learning, 2001.

Innocence Project. "DNA Exonerations in the United States." *Innocence Project*, 2020, innocenceproject.org/dna-exonerations-in-the-united-states/.

John D. Rogers. "Law Offices of John D. Rogers." *Law Offices of John D. Rogers*, 20 June 2024, johndrogerslaw.com/the-scooter-libby-trial-a-comprehensive-overview/.

Johnson, Carrie. "Report: Prosecutors Hid Evidence in Ted Stevens Case." *NPR.org*, 12 Mar. 2012, www.npr.org/2012/03/15/148687717/report-prosecutors-hid-evidence-in-ted-stevens-case.

---. "The Vast Majority of Criminal Cases End in Plea Bargains, a New Report Finds." *NPR*, 22 Feb. 2023, www.npr.org/2023/02/22/1158356619/plea-bargains-criminal-cases-justice.

Johnson, Renardo. "EKY Doctor Found Not Guilty in Federal Court." *Https://Www.wymt.com*, WYMT, 21 Aug. 2023, www.wymt.com/2023/08/21/eky-doctor-found-not-guilty-federal-court/. Accessed 24 May 2025.

Justia. "Batson v. Kentucky, 476 U.S. 79 (1986)." *Justia Law*, 1986, supreme.justia.com/cases/federal/us/476/79/.

---. "Dimas-Martinez v. State." *Justia Law*, 2011, law.justia.com/cases/arkansas/supreme-court/2011/cr11-5.html.

---. "Hoffa v. United States, 385 U.S. 293 (1966)." *Justia Law*, 1966, supreme.justia.com/cases/federal/us/385/293/.

---. "J. E. B. V. Alabama Ex Rel. T. B., 511 U.S. 127 (1994)." *Justia Law*, 1994, supreme.justia.com/cases/federal/us/511/127/.

---. "Parker v. Gladden, 385 U.S. 363 (1966)." *Justia Law*, 1966, supreme.justia.com/cases/federal/us/385/363/.

---. "Remmer v. United States, 347 U.S. 227 (1954)." *Justia Law*, 2024, supreme.justia.com/cases/federal/us/347/227/.

---. "United States v. Michael Allen Smith, No. 13-2105 (8th Cir. 2014)." *Justia.com*, 2014, law.justia.com/cases/federal/appellate-courts/ca8/13-2105/13-2105-2014-07-25.html. Accessed 22 May 2025.

Justice.GOV. "Charleston Doctor Sentenced to over Five Years in Federal Prison for Illegal Distribution of Methadone." *Justice.gov*, 29 June 2020, www.justice.gov/usao-sdwv/pr/charleston-doctor-sentenced-over-five-years-federal-prison-illegal-distribution. Accessed 21 May 2025.

Justice.Gov. "Moreland Hills Physicians Indicted on Charges of Performing Unnecessary Medical Tests and Procedures, Overbilling Insurance Providers and Illegally Distributing Opioids and Other Drugs." *Justice.gov*, 24 Jan. 2018, www.justice.gov/usaondoh/pr/moreland-hills-physicians-indicted-charges-performing-unnecessary-medical-tests-and. Accessed 2 May 2025.

Juvenile Law Center. "Juvenile Law Center Responds to Sentencing of "Kids-For-Cash" Judge | Juvenile Law Center." *Juvenile Law Center*, 11 Aug. 2011, jlc.org/news/juvenile-law-center-responds-sentencing-kids-cash-judge. Accessed 2 May 2025.

Kumaraswamy, Nishamathi , et al. "Healthcare Fraud Data Mining Methods: A Look Back and Look Ahead." *Perspectives in Health Information Management*, vol. 19, no. 1, 2022, p. 1i, pmc.ncbi.nlm.nih.gov/articles/PMC9013219/.

Legal Information Institute. "SALINAS v. TEXAS." *LII / Legal Information Institute*, 2013, www.law.cornell.edu/supremecourt/text/12-246.

Levinson, Daniel. *Department of Health and Human Services OFFICE of INSPECTOR GENERAL MEDICAID DRUG PRICING in STATE MAXIMUM ALLOWABLE COST PROGRAMS*. 2013.

---. *Department of Health and Human Services OFFICE of INSPECTOR GENERAL UPDATE: MEDICARE PAYMENTS for END STAGE RENAL DISEASE DRUGS*. 2014.

Lubasch, Arnold H. "Juror Is Convicted of Selling Vote to Gotti." *The New York Times*, 7 Nov. 1992, www.nytimes.com/1992/11/07/nyregion/juror-is-convicted-of-selling-vote-to-gotti.html.

Marcus, Ruth. "THE DISTRESSING CASE of JUDGE HASTINGS." *The Washington Post*, 6 Aug. 1989, www.washingtonpost.com/archive/politics/1989/08/06/the-distressing-case-of-judge-hastings/2cbe5884-7962-4ab8-a941-6e04bd181f4d/. Accessed 2 May 2025.

Markus. "United States v. Dr. Ali Shaygan (Alleged Pill Mill Case)." *Markuslaw.com*, 2010, markuslaw.com/united-states-v-dr-ali-shaygan/.

Marten, J. Thomas. "United States v. Henson, No. 16-10018-01-JTM | D. Kan., Judgment, Law, Casemine.com." *Https:// Www.casemine.com*, 2019, www.casemine.com/judgement/us/5c7fba6a342cca0e57b9e55b. Accessed 21 May 2025.

McCormick, Rob. "The Halo Effect - the Power of First Impressions." *Www.idealrole.com*, 20 July 2021, www.idealrole.com/blog/halo-effect.html.

Melsheimer, Thomas M, and Scott Thomas. "Nine Defendants, One Acquittal: Aggressive Federal Prosecution Puts Medical Marketing in the Crosshairs." *Winston & Strawn - Nine Defendants, One Acquittal: Aggressive Federal Prosecution Puts Medical Marketing in the Crosshairs*, Winston & Strawn LLP, 2021, www.winston.com/en/insights-news/nine-defendants-one-acquittal-aggressive-federal-prosecution-puts-medical-marketing-in-the-crosshairs.

Meterko, Vanessa, and Glinda Cooper. "Cognitive Biases in Criminal Case Evaluation: A Review of the Research." *Journal of Police and Criminal Psychology*, vol. 37, no. 37, 23 June 2021, pp. 101–122, link.springer.com/article/10.1007/s11896-020-09425-8, https://doi.org/10.1007/s11896-020-09425-8.

Mettler, Katie. "Virginia OB/GYN Sentenced to 59 Years in Prison for Performing Unnecessary Surgeries." *Washington Post*, 2021, www.washingtonpost.com/local/public-safety/perwaiz-virginia-doctor-unnecessary-surgeries/2021/05/18/2e4d7ff4-b7f2-11eb-96b9-e949d5397de9_story.html.

Morelaw. "United States of America v. Dr. Gregory Sinclair Connor." *Morelaw.com*, 2019, www.morelaw.com/verdicts/case.asp?s=OK&d=135772.

Murrin, Suzanne. *Department of Health and Human Services OFFICE of INSPECTOR GENERAL MACS CONTINUE to USE DIFFERENT METHODS to DETERMINE DRUG COVERAGE.* 2016.

NACDL. "NACDL - the Trial Penalty: The Sixth Amendment Right to Trial on the Verge of Extinction and How to Save It." *NACDL - National Association of Criminal Defense Lawyers*, 10 July 2018, www.nacdl.org/Document/TrialPenaltySixthAmendmentRighttoTrialNearExtinct.

NAMAS. "Justice Served - NAMAS." *NAMAS*, 28 July 2022, namas.co/justice-served-unfortunately-a-bit-late/. Accessed 5 June 2025.

Nickerson, Raymond S. "Confirmation Bias: A Ubiquitous Phenomenon in Many Guises." *Review of General Psychology*, vol. 2, no. 2, 1 June 1998, pp. 175–220, journals.sagepub.com/doi/10.1037/1089-2680.2.2.175, https://doi.org/10.1037/1089-2680.2.2.175.

Noor, Norzalina, et al. "Bias, Halo Effect and Horn Effect: A Systematic Literature Review." *International Journal of Academic Research in Business and Social Sciences*, vol. 13, no. 3, 14 Mar. 2023, hrmars.com/papers_submitted/16733/bias-halo-effect-and-horn-effect-a-systematic-literature-review.pdf, https://doi.org/10.6007/ijarbss/v13-i3/16733.

O'Brien, Barbara. "Barbara O'Brien's Research Works | Michigan State University and Other Places." *ResearchGate*, 2015, www.researchgate.net/scientific-contributions/Barbara-OBrien-79529076. Accessed 4 Apr. 2025.

Office of Inspector General. *HEALTH CARE COMPLIANCE PROGRAM TIPS the Seven Fundamental Elements of an Effective Compliance Program*.

OIG. "OIG Reports $25.9 Billion in Savings and Expected Recoveries in FY 2010." *Office of Inspector General | Government Oversight | U.S. Department of Health and Human Services*, 15 Dec. 2010, oig.hhs.gov/newsroom/news-releases-articles/oig-reports-259-billion-savings-and-expected-recoveries-fy-2010/. Accessed 16 Apr. 2025.

Panian, David. "Dr. Lesly Pompy Acquitted of All Charges in Federal Drug and Health Care Fraud Case." *Monroe News*, The Daily Telegram, 10 Jan. 2023, eu.monroenews.com/story/news/crime/2023/01/10/dr-lesly-pompy-acquitted-all-charges-federal-drug-case/69790454007/. Accessed 23 May 2025.

Porter, Jonathan. "Federal Judge Acquits Physician Following Criminal E/M Fraud Conviction at Trial." *Healthcare Law Insights*, 28 Dec. 2023, www.healthcarelawinsights.com/2023/12/federal-judge-acquits-physician-following-criminal-e-m-fraud-conviction-at-trial/.

Quran.com. "Surah Ya-Sin - 9-39 - Quran.com." *Quran.com*, 2025, quran.com/pt/yasin/9-39. Accessed 8 Apr. 2025.

Rifai, Muhamad. "The Use of Artificial Intelligence in the Enforcement of Health Care Regulations." *KevinMD.com*, 24 Sept. 2024, kevinmd.com/2024/09/the-use-of-artificial-intelligence-in-the-enforcement-of-health-care-regulations.html. Accessed 8 Apr. 2025.

Roppolo, Lynn P., et al. "Improving the Management of Acutely Agitated Patients in the Emergency Department through Implementation of Project BETA (Best Practices in the Evaluation and Treatment of Agitation)." *Journal of the American College of Emergency Physicians Open*, vol. 1, no. 5, 3 July 2020, https://doi.org/10.1002/emp2.12138.

Ruan, Petitioners, and Shakeel Kahn. *SUPREME COURT of the UNITED STATES*. 2021.

Rush, Benjamin. "Evans Early American Imprint Collection." *Quod.lib.umich.edu*, 1798, quod.lib.umich.edu/cgi/t/text/text-idx?cc=evans.

Saini, RajivKumar, et al. "Transcranial Magnetic Stimulation: A Review of Its Evolution and Current Applications." *Industrial Psychiatry Journal*, vol. 27, no. 2, 2018, p. 172, www.ncbi.nlm.nih.

gov/pmc/articles/PMC6592198/, https://doi.org/10.4103/ipj.ipj_88_18.

Schafer, Alisa M. "Dr. Charles Szyman Trial: Jury Finds Ex-Manitowoc Doctor Not Guilty of Drug Trafficking." *Herald Times Reporter*, Manitowoc Herald Times Reporter, 17 Nov. 2017, eu.htrnews.com/story/news/2017/11/17/dr-charles-szyman-trial-jury-finds-ex-manitowoc-doctor-not-guilty-drug-trafficking-overdose-deaths/872710001/. Accessed 6 June 2025.

Schwartz, John. "As Jurors Turn to Web, Mistrials Are Popping Up." *The New York Times*, 17 Mar. 2009, www.nytimes.com/2009/03/18/us/18juries.html.

Specker, Lawrence. "Doctor Found Not Guilty in Overdose Death of Former 3 Doors down Guitarist." *Al*, 22 May 2018, www.al.com/news/2018/05/doctor_found_not_guilty_in_ove.html. Accessed 6 June 2025.

Stanford Law School. "DOJ Drops Charges against Former National Security Advisor Michael Flynn." *Stanford Law School*, 11 May 2020, law.stanford.edu/2020/05/11/doj-drops-charges-against-former-national-security-advisor-michael-flynn/.

Stansbury, A. J. "Founders Online: James Madison Speech in Virginia Convention, 2 December 1829." *Archives.gov*, 1829, founders.archives.gov/?q=The%20essence%20of%20Government%20is%20power%3B%20and%20power%2C%20lodged%20as%20it%20must%20be%20in%20human%20hands%2C%20will%20ever%20be%20liable%20to%20abuse.&s=1111311111&sa=&r=3&sr=. Accessed 19 Mar. 2025.

Sunnah.com. "Sunan Abi Dawud 3855 - Medicine (Kitab Al-Tibb) Sunnah.com - Sayings and Teachings of Prophet Muhammad (peace be upon him)" *Sunnah.com*, sunnah.com/abudawud:3855.

Swanner, J.K., et al. "Developing Diagnostic, Evidence-Based Approaches to Interrogation." *Journal of Applied Research in Memory and Cognition*, vol. 5, no. 3, Sept. 2016, pp. 295–301, https://doi.org/10.1016/j.jarmac.2016.07.001.

Tanenbaum, Michael. "Extortion Charges against Ex-Labor Union Leader John Dougherty Are Dismissed." *PhillyVoice*, 15 Aug. 2024, www.phillyvoice.com/john-dougherty-extortion-charges-dropped-mistrial/. Accessed 18 Apr. 2025.

The Associated Press. "Former Judges Who Sent Kids to Jail for Kickbacks Must Pay More than $200 Million." *NPR*, 18 Aug. 2022, www.npr.org/2022/08/18/1118108084/michael-conahan-mark-ciavarella-kids-for-cash.

The Charlotte Sun. "Ex-HMA Exec Acquitted at Federal Trial in Fort Myers." *The Star Banner*, 2025, eu.ocala.com/story/news/2014/11/13/ex-hma-exec-acquitted-at-federal-trial-in-fort-myers/31948553007/. Accessed 21 May 2025.

Toobin, Jeffrey. "Casualties of Justice." *The New Yorker*, 27 Dec. 2010, www.newyorker.com/magazine/2011/01/03/casualties-of-justice.

United States Code. "U.S.C. Title 42 - the PUBLIC HEALTH and WELFARE." *Www.govinfo.gov*, 2011, www.govinfo.gov/content/pkg/USCODE-2011-title42/html/USCODE-2011-title42-chap7-subchapXVIII.htm.

United States Courts. "Table D-3—U.S. District Courts–Criminal Statistical Tables for the Federal Judiciary (December 31, 2024)." *United States Courts*, 31 Dec. 2024, www.uscourts.gov/data-news/data-tables/2024/12/31/statistical-tables-federal-judiciary/d-3. Accessed 22 May 2025.

United States Courts 2. "Table D-4—U.S. District Courts–Criminal Statistical Tables for the Federal Judiciary (December 31, 2024)." *United States Courts*, 31 Dec. 2024, www.uscourts.gov/data-news/data-tables/2024/12/31/statistical-tables-federal-judiciary/d-4. Accessed 22 May 2025.

United States Senate. "U.S. Senate: Impeachment Trial of Judge Harry E. Claiborne, 1986." *Www.senate.gov*, 1986, www.senate. gov/about/powers-procedures/impeachment/impeachment-claiborne.htm.

University of Rochester Medical Centre. *Https://Www.urmc. rochester.edu/MediaLibraries/URMCMedia/Ctsi/Clinical-Research/ Documents/10-Domains-of-De-Escalation.pdf.*

UTHSC. *In Memory of the Late Dr. Lester VanMiddlesworth.* 2016, www. uthsc.edu/endocrinology/news/documents/van-middlesworth-memorial.pdf.

---. "Profile." *UTHSC*, 2022, www.uthsc.edu/faculty/ profile/?netid=kmalik. Accessed 8 Apr. 2025.

VanHofwegen, Rose. "Peña-Rodriguez v. Colorado." *Quimbee*, 28 July 2020, www.quimbee.com/cases/pena-rodriguez-v-colorado. Accessed 22 May 2025.

Vella, Vinny. "A Man Accused of Killing an Upper Darby Infant in 2013 Is Incompetent to Stand Trial, a Judge Has Ruled." *Inquirer. com*, The Philadelphia Inquirer, 4 May 2021, www.inquirer.com/ news/ummad-rushdi-delaware-county-baby-abducted-20210504. html. Accessed 5 June 2025.

Vera Institute of Justice. "In the Shadows." *Vera Institute of Justice*, 2020, www.vera.org/publications/in-the-shadows-plea-bargaining.

Vogue, Ariane de, and Tierney Sneed. "Supreme Court Revives Case Brought by Postal Worker Seeking Religious Accommodations." *CNN*, 29 June 2023, edition.cnn.com/2023/06/29/politics/ supreme-court-groff-dejoy-postal-worker/index.html. Accessed 18 Apr. 2025.

Walter, Michael. "Fraud Charges against Cardiologist Dismissed after 8-Year Legal Battle." *Cardiovascular Business*, 5 Jan. 2024, cardiovascularbusiness.com/topics/clinical/interventional-cardiology/fraud-charges-against-cardiologist-dismissed-after-8-year-legal-battle. Accessed 5 June 2025.

Weaver, Jay. "Judge Throws out Pandemic-Era Fraud Charges against South Florida Doctor for Second Time." *Miami Herald*, 14 Dec. 2023, www.miamiherald.com/news/local/article283022593.html. Accessed 21 May 2025.

Weiss, Sean. "Justice Served… Again!" *DoctorsManagement*, DoctorsManagement, LLC, 12 Oct. 2022, www. doctorsmanagement.com/blog/justice-served-again/. Accessed 5 June 2025.

Whittaker, Zack. "How the Ransomware Attack at Change Healthcare Went Down: A Timeline | TechCrunch." *TechCrunch*, 27 Jan. 2025, techcrunch.com/2025/01/27/how-the-ransomware-attack-at-change-healthcare-went-down-a-timeline/.

Yin, Tung. "Martha Stewart Is Convicted in Insider-Trading Scandal | EBSCO." *EBSCO Information Services, Inc. | Www.ebsco.com*, 2022, www.ebsco.com/research-starters/law/martha-stewart-convicted-insider-trading-scandal.

Zachary A, Woodward, et al. "DOJ Indicts Hospital for Healthcare Fraud: A Rare Occurrence | Enforcement Edge | Blogs | Arnold & Porter." *Arnold & Porter*, 2025, www.arnoldporter.com/en/perspectives/blogs/enforcement-edge/2025/01/doj-indicts-hospital-for-healthcare-fraud. Accessed 5 June 2025.

www.ingramcontent.com/pod-product-compliance
Lightning Source LLC
Chambersburg PA
CBHW071535200326
41519CB00021BB/6493